Praise for *A New Position on Sex*

"Dr. Juliana Hauser guides us back to our bodies, our boundaries, and the deep truth of what we really want in sex and love. *A New Position on Sex* is a must-read for anyone longing to bring more truth, vitality, and presence into their erotic life."
JILLIAN TURECKI, New York Times–bestselling author of *It Begins With You*

"A holistic, empowering framework that centers sexual agency as not just a right, but as a powerful path to deeper self-knowledge, relational integrity, and embodied confidence. This book is a compassionate, intelligent guide for anyone ready to step into their most embodied, powerful season."
LILY WOMBLE, founder of Date Brazen, author of *Thank You, More Please*

"*A New Position on Sex* tackles the topic of sex with deeply felt empathy and scientific clarity. Dr. Juliana Hauser's book is a mental, physical, and philosophical road map to greater sexual agency—and better health in general."
SEAN HOESS, CEO of Eudēmonia Summit

"This is the perspective we've needed for so long: a holistic vision that weaves together nine essential pillars, demonstrating how sexuality is inextricably linked to our overall well-being. I can't recommend this book more highly!"
KARINA MACKENZIE, head of programming at Eudēmonia Summit

"*A New Position on Sex* is the first book to teach us how to know ourselves as sexual beings, and to have agency over the part of ourselves that can amplify the joy in our lives."
DR. SUZANNE STEINBAUM, CEO and founder of Adesso by Heart-Tech Health

"Dr. Juliana Hauser shows us that when you understand who you are sexually and step into agency, you can show up more fully in every part of your relationship. *A New Position on Sex* is authentic, empowering, and exactly what we all need to feel more connected to ourselves and our partners."
COLETTE JANE FEHR, couples therapist, author of *The Cost of Quiet*

"Dr. Juliana Hauser walks us through how to reveal our true essence by unpacking social and cultural expectations, and tapping into desire, pleasure, and connection. It is a holistic approach to sexuality, which for many is the final frontier to unlocking true health and wellness."
DR. STEPHANIE ESTIMA, women's wellness health expert, author of *The Betty Body*

"This remarkable book not only reminds us that sexual health evolves as we do, but supports our creativity, self-expression, and overall health."
DR. SUZANNE GILBERG-LENZ, author of *Menopause Bootcamp*, chief clinical officer of Monarch MD

"*A New Position on Sex* reminds you that sexual confidence, pleasure, and sensuality are your right and are in your control. Dr. Juliana Hauser gives you the tools to blissfully make sexual agency a part of your midlife and beyond."
KATIE FOGARTY, founder and CEO of The Reboot Group

"Dr. Juliana Hauser's approach is not confined by ideology or limited by gendered expectations. Empowerment stands as a core pillar of her work, opening the door to agency, pleasure, and true embodiment."
AYDIAN DOWLING, entrepreneur, activist, co-founder of Point of Pride

"*A New Position on Sex* offers a liberating and evidence-informed path forward. An essential read for anyone who wants to move beyond outdated beliefs and into authentic, confident intimacy."
DR. KELLY CASPERSON, author of *You Are Not Broken*

DR. JULIANA HAUSER

A Guide to Greater Sexual Confidence, Pleasure, and Authenticity

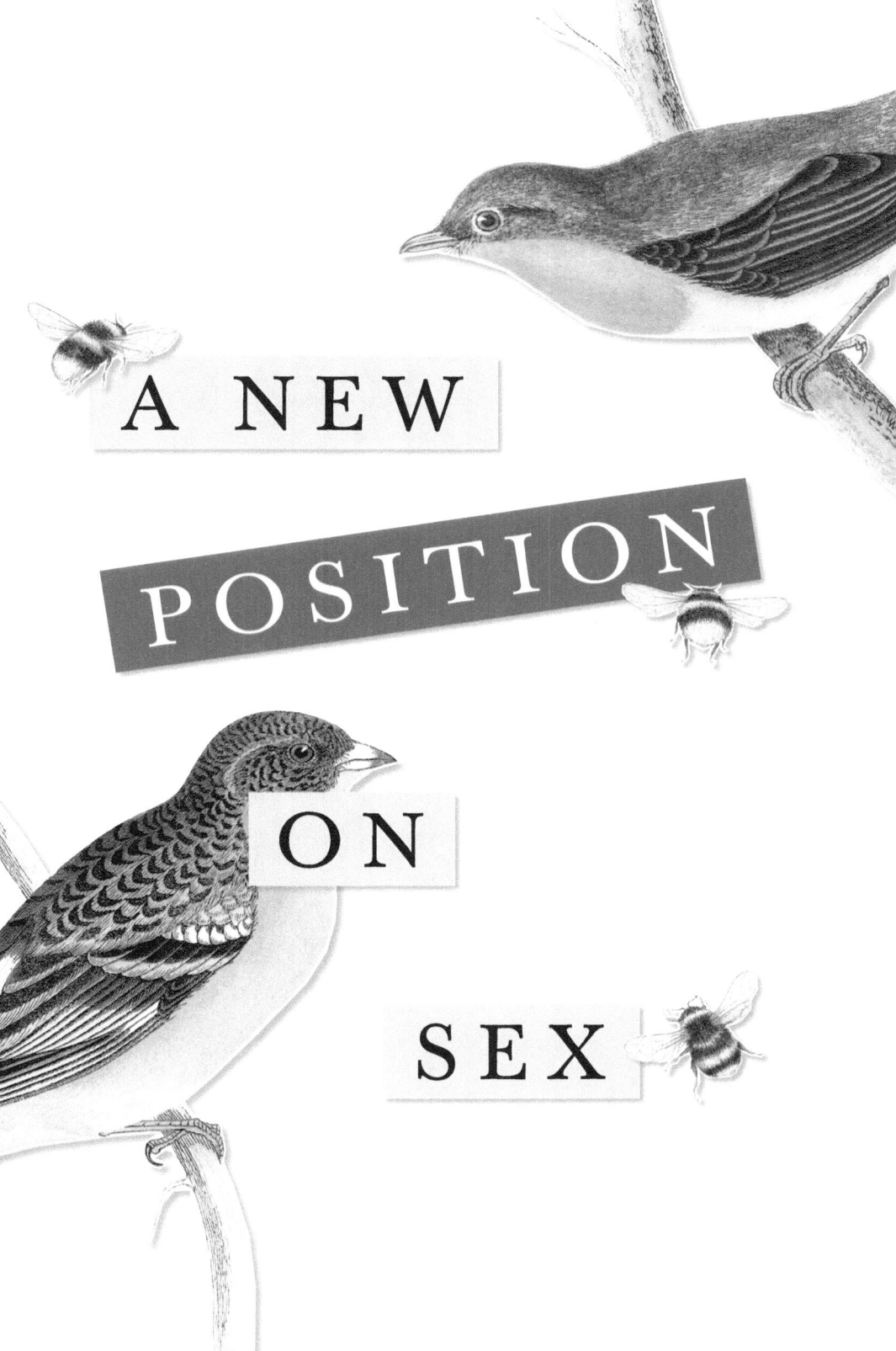

Copyright © 2025 by Dr. Juliana Hauser

All rights reserved. No part of this book may be reproduced, stored in a retrieval system or transmitted, in any form or by any means, without the prior written consent of the publisher, except in the case of brief quotations, embodied in reviews and articles.

Some names and identifying details have been changed to protect the privacy of individuals.

This book is not intended as a substitute for the medical advice of physicians. The reader should regularly consult a physician in matters relating to their health and particularly with respect to any symptoms that may require diagnosis or medical attention.

Betty Dodson® and Bodysex® are registered trademarks of the Betty Dodson Foundation.

The Revealed® course, community, and movement are a registered trademark of Dr. Juliana Hauser. Graphics on pages 41, 54, 58, and 160 are © Dr. Juliana Hauser.

Cataloguing in publication information is available from Library and Archives Canada.
ISBN 978-1-77458-450-7 (paperback)
ISBN 978-1-77458-451-4 (ebook)

Page Two
pagetwo.com

Page Two™ is a trademark owned by Page Two Strategies Inc., and is used under license by authorized licensees

Cover, interior design, and illustrations by Taysia Louie

dr-juliana.com

For everyone who was punished, shamed, or rejected for showing up in the truth of who they are as a sexual being.

For the ones waiting for their time to blossom.

For the ones who are brave and courageous, wanting to evolve as sexual beings.

For everyone who hasn't yet had access to learning about who they are as sexual beings.

For all the people who love sex, have had amazing sex, and want more of it.

For all the people who haven't felt seen, wanted, or valued as sexual beings.

For all the people who don't want to feel pressured to engage in sexual connection.

For all the people who have harmed others because they are threatened by sex and sexuality.

For all those who fight tirelessly for holistic sexuality and social justice.

For all the sex educators, sex therapists, sex counselors, sex workers, and sex advocates.

For the medical and mental health community leaders and wellness providers who understand the importance of sexuality.

To those who have walked alongside me on my own journey.

To those who know my stories in these pages and who know the stories I have left unwritten.

To the readers who find a piece of themselves within these chapters.

To every one of you who has known the feeling of wanting to experience sexuality in a healthy, normalized way.

To the stories that have shaped us... individually and collectively.

To you.

CONTENTS

What Is Revealed? *1*
So Much More Than Sex *3*

PART 1 SEXUALITY: THE FINAL FRONTIER OF SELF-DEVELOPMENT

Sex Expired: Why Take a New Position on Sex *15*
Holistic Sexuality: Stepping Into Your Essence *29*
Agency: Doing It on Your Own Terms *43*

PART 2 NINE PILLARS OF HOLISTIC SEXUALITY: WHERE AGENCY COMES ALIVE

Pillar 1 **Sensuality** *69*
Pillar 2 **Wellness and Fertility** *83*
Pillar 3 **Pleasure** *113*
Pillar 4 **Desire** *131*
Pillar 5 **Acts and Interests** *149*
Pillar 6 **Intersecting Identities** *165*
Pillar 7 **Power and Trauma** *187*
Pillar 8 **Relationship** *213*
Pillar 9 **Connection** *239*

Tuned In and Turned On: You on Agency *263*

Your People Await You *273*
Thank You *277*
Notes *290*
Resources *294*
Discussion Questions *296*

WHAT IS REVEALED?

WHEN WE OPEN UP to our sexual truths, we are *revealed*. Revealed is a course I developed, a growing community, and a movement that aims to change the conversation about sex—it is the backdrop for this book in many ways.

Revealed is an individual journey experienced collectively. A place to celebrate, to heal, to discover, to learn.

Revealed is not handed to you, but it is there for you. It is the work that happens not only in the brain, not only in the heart, not only through words, but in the connections, the combinations, the quiet moments—the in-betweens. In a heartbeat. In the blink of an eye.

Revealed is the full breath you finally remembered to take.

Revealed is in the contemplative moment and in the screaming rage. Revealed is a fight for your very essence—a fight for who you are.

Revealed is when you cry out loud and someone hears you, really hears you. It happens when you witness someone else. It happens when you hear another's story, truth, or insight, and it feels like your own.

Revealed is a sacred journey. It is the groundwork for everything else.

Revealed exists because... it is time to shed shame and guilt and to celebrate your beautiful, powerful sexual stories.

Because it is exactly what you need to become who you are.

Because you are ready to say yes to knowing who you are at your core.

Because telling your stories will change the world.

Because knowing how your stories inform, impact, and influence your journey will change your world.

I am revealed. You are revealed. We are revealed.

—Compiled by Kelly Bremner, PhD, from Revealed participants' reflections

SO MUCH MORE THAN SEX

SEXUALITY IS intrinsic to who we are as human beings, and yet we spend a lot of time and money avoiding it, controlling it, and focusing on all the wrong things in all the wrong ways. We tell each other, "You are wrong," rather than asking ourselves, "What is right for me?" Mainstream society sends us messages that we should be having hot sex everywhere, all the time. And if we aren't, we are less than, maybe even broken or undesirable—and definitely not fun. The effect of this is that most of us do not feel free or empowered in our sexual lives.

Sexuality is a fascinating study of contradictions. Fluid and ever-changing, sexuality is something we all have in common and experience wildly differently. Even what once fit for you may change over time. Sexuality is so powerful it creates life, makes people lose track of time and space, and unites people forever. But it can also topple your personal health, relationships, even cultures and nations.

The topic of sexuality makes people protest and threaten others, divides families and communities. It is messy and beautiful, obvious and subtle. It can make you feel both grounded and otherworldly. It can bring unimaginable pain and indescribable joy. It is gross, funny, and absurd. It is sacred and exquisite, innocent and naughty. It is private and public, desired and feared. It is no one's business and everyone's business. It is right and wrong.

Many of us have a hard time talking about our own sexuality, and current societal approaches to sex and sexuality contribute to that challenge. But at what price?

Maybe you are in a relationship that is struggling because of mismatched desire, and you don't know how to talk about it. Perhaps you have hidden an aspect of your sexual self because of shame or fear of judgment. Or maybe you have been beating yourself up because you don't have the kind of deep connection with your body that you hear someone else talking about with such promise. Perhaps you have never experienced an orgasm or aren't sure if you have. Or maybe you have an interest in learning more but don't know how to go about it. Perhaps you've experienced sexual trauma or a physical change that has affected your sex life. Or you could be longing to know what it takes to be someone who is genuinely comfortable in their own skin. The possibilities are, quite literally, endless.

Whatever limitation you are facing in your sexual life, you can address it. We all have that capacity within us. Without exception. And if you can't name any limitations in this moment and are ready to embark on a journey of self-discovery, we all have that capacity within us too. This book is valuable for us all.

When we normalize, talk about, and explore the world of sexuality, an enormous freedom is unleashed. I have seen this in my own life and in the lives of countless clients I have worked with as a couples and family therapist, individual counselor, sex educator, and (s)expert. And I want you to see this change, too, for your relationships and for our society. Your life will change for the better when the sexuality you uniquely experience is better for you, is fulfilling, and makes you feel complete. This deeply personal work is the heart of holistic sexuality. And let me tell you, it is powerful stuff. It changes you. And it has the potential to shift the world around you.

When I first started talking about holistic sexuality as a game-changing concept back in the early 2000s, people resisted the notion. Mainly because they interpreted what I said as "If you have great sex, your life will be better, and to have a great life, you must be having great sex." I do believe that having great sex makes a very positive impact on your life emotionally, psychologically, physically, and relationally. Great sex feels good. Great sex sparks your vibrancy and gives you physical benefits. It can help you feel better about yourself and your relationship and, if it is really great, help you feel better about the world. I'm a fan. Trust me.

I also believe that having a rich and vibrant sex life bleeds over into other areas of your life, compounding its positive effect. Our sexual life isn't experienced in a bubble even if it is kept private. It relates to all parts of us and to our relationships; it is a crucial element of who we are as humans and who we are as a community and society.

Of course, great sex is wonderful... but that isn't what I focus on currently or what I meant in my early days. Today, I have realized that having a great sex life (however you define that) is a part of being a holistic sexual being *and* that sex acts shouldn't be the first thing we examine, the sole focus of our sexual selves, the highlight, or the hot-button issue in sex education. I've learned that if you want to have great sex and a profoundly rich sexual life across your lifespan, you need to understand sex holistically on a societal scale and in your individual life.

The work of holistic sexuality is so much more than sex. It is intellectual, emotional, and self-reflective, and it has the potential to save your life. That may sound overblown because none of us has been given much of a sex education, and what sex education we do receive in school or elsewhere is rarely, if ever, holistic. Fear-based sex education, which falls short in depth, accuracy, and inclusivity, is the norm in North America and many places globally, and it is no way to tackle the divisive and emotional topic of sexuality. Gaining more accurate and extensive information, building more inclusivity and diversity into sex education, and exploring more kinds of sexual expression would normalize sex and sexuality in all its many permutations. Not just for individuals but for society more broadly.

Part of my goal with this book is to help you find *your* path. Your sexual journey. On your terms. I want everyone to have the kind of sexual life they have decided, through purposeful and intentional exploration, is right for them. I want everyone to be their authentic sexual self, whether that means having transcendent sex, scheduled sex, fun-as-fuck sex, same-as-always sex, deeply loving sex, or wild-as-hell sex. Or if you genuinely don't want sexual connection with others, I want you to live that truth with joy and acceptance. If in your social circles or in greater society, you feel as if you are forgotten, oppressed, unwelcome, or unsafe, I want you to find the people and communities where you are safe—as a sexual being and beyond. And I want you to feel particularly safe and welcomed within these pages. I also want to help create an evolved sexual culture worldwide for everyone. Whoever you are, I want you to know more about your particular brand of sexuality as well as hone the skill of supporting others to learn their unique sexualities. Seeking a deeper understanding of your sexuality isn't a luxury—it's a necessity, and it's for everyone.

The Nine Pillars of Holistic Sexuality

Although I have a master's degree in counseling from Auburn University and a PhD in counseling education from the College of William & Mary, along with two professional licenses, the bulk of my work in holistic sexuality, which I've been doing for more than two decades now, has been on the ground, with everyday people seeking deeper connection and agency in their sexual lives. I have gathered thousands of stories, conducted informal and formal research, written and facilitated numerous courses, led countless discussions with thought leaders and those in the work of holistic sexuality, run a plethora of retreats and workshops, and conducted a staggering number of therapy and coaching appointments. I can't tally up the hours I've devoted to this topic alongside other experts and everyday people working through their sexual journeys, education, and relationships.

It might surprise you to learn that my undergraduate degree from Centre College was in elementary education. Yep, a kindergarten teacher turned sex expert, but after your eyebrow raise, let me assure you there are commonalities between the two. The most relevant being that we are required to take complex thoughts and skills and shape them into accessible frameworks. My experiences have sharpened my focus on holistic sexuality as I've developed theories, explanations, exercises, and practices—all of which I have tested over time. I looked for correlations among people who described themselves as sexually fulfilled. I listened and questioned, composed and recomposed my ideas until the picture of holistic sexuality and its connection with self-development was crystal clear to me.

Here's an excerpt from my dissertation that highlights the complexities and never-ending nature of this work:

> Sexuality is not static, and it has the potential to change through the lifespan. It is not a problem to be controlled but a force to be utilized. Sexuality is a potentiality and not only an inherent force (Tiefer, 1995) and is constructed from many parts but is more than the sum of its parts. Further, its components help define the larger construct but also are influenced by the perception of the individual and context of culture, class, race, religion, and sexual orientation. It is fluid, reactive, self-defining, and impressionable.

I share this with you as the backbone of this book, the framework that guides me in all my teaching, and simplify it here by using the metaphor of pillars to describe the overarching and beautifully fluid components of holistic sexuality.

Pillar 1: Sensuality

Pillar 2: Wellness and fertility

Pillar 3: Pleasure

Pillar 4: Desire

Pillar 5: Acts and interests

Pillar 6: Intersecting identities

Pillar 7: Power and trauma

Pillar 8: Relationship

Pillar 9: Connection

Underpinning these nine pillars is the concept of agency—the energy source and guiding principle of my view on and concept of holistic sexuality.

In this book, I use a two-dimensional image to represent the pillars, but a three-dimensional model would more accurately reflect how these components of holistic sexuality are dynamic within our lifespan. You see this added dimension in the lifespan and soul lines within the graphic. Sexuality is fluid. Movable. Interactive. Ever-changing. Contextual. Intersectional. Each individual's sexuality intersects with the collective and global sexual climate and culture as well as with the details of their lives and relationships.

Think of your journey as a house being built. The foundation is agency, your relationship to yourself. Build your foundation with audacity and courage. Let the structure of the holistic sexuality pillars you'll explore create the framework, framing, and drywall of your sexual self, of your essence. The sex information and education we have access to currently is akin to an attic. Sex tips are often fun and informative, but starting there when examining your sexual life and deepening your self-understanding is like trying to build the attic before the cement of the foundation is set. It's important but incomplete and frankly dangerous on its own. Not devoting time to inclusive, holistic content and over-devoting time to fear-based education add to the dangerousness of most of the sexual education available to us.

My model of holistic sexuality is based on my course Revealed, which people of all genders and sexual orientations, racial and cultural backgrounds, socioeconomic statuses, nationalities, religions, and political views have gone through. As of this writing, the course is facilitated in eight countries and taught in five different languages through our Revealed facilitator program. The Revealed course, community, and movement are growing all the time.

My hope is that by reading this book, you will learn how to see yourself as a holistic sexual being, to unapologetically define your terms, and to find communities and relationships that support your sexual self-actualization. Everyone comes to this work for different reasons. For some, it is to heal from a wound or to mend a relationship. Others want to expand in self-knowledge. Some want general education, and some enjoy the topic. In doing this work, many people are surprised to discover the reasons they are drawn to explore holistic sexuality morph as they go. I hope you stay open to the lighthouses (guiding moments of insight), to the stories in your journey that raise their hands to you, and to the parts of you that will be revealed to you about your way in the world, your sexual history and future, and sexuality globally.

We'll start in part 1 by exploring my belief that sexuality is the final frontier of self-development. We will explore traditional sex education, holistic sexuality, and the concept of agency from a thirty-thousand-foot view. It may feel more philosophical and academic than the section on the pillars themselves. It is meant to validate your experience in our current sexual culture as well as provide a foundation for the individual work ahead. It concludes with a focus on the crux of my work—sexual agency.

In part 2, we get personal. We will go deep into each of the nine pillars, and finally, we'll revisit agency from this new perspective, with a broadened knowledge of who you are as a sexual being. In each of the pillar chapters, you will glean insights about yourself through the holistic sexuality framework. You will read some of my personal and client stories as well as receive questions for reflection, which help illustrate each pillar in your own life. I encourage you to use a journal to record your responses and to complete the "sexercises" sprinkled throughout the book. You are meant to read it from front cover to back cover, but you can move back and forth between the two parts as well. The magic happens when we learn and observe from both thirty thousand feet and under the microscope.

Is this book about sex? Yes. And I want to be clear: This book is *not* about the science of arousal or the journey of an egg from the ovary. It does not offer sex tricks to spice up your sex life, but it *does* offer you something so much more than that. It is a blueprint for self-reflection and self-discovery through the lens of holistic sexuality, the final frontier of self-development. This is the sex education

I want you to have before you go to sex tips, before your build your attic. This is the foundational work to do in order to learn who you are as a sexual being. That knowledge will guide you to further resources, support, and education. This philosophical shift into holistic sexuality will help heal past wounds as well as help protect you from future ones. This book is about the mental and emotional components and self-illuminating aspects of sexuality; it's about gaining lifelong tools for the times when things go right and when they don't.

In the pages ahead, I include selected personal stories to give you a glimpse of my journey and to join you in risk-taking—this is vulnerable work, and I honor you for doing it. Of note, I am in a different place today than I was at the time of many of the stories I share, because like you, I am evolving all the time. As you read this book, I encourage you to share your stories with others. Recall them and write them down. They will add depth in a multitude of ways to your growth and self-development. Write and say what you need to say.

Also, I want to acknowledge that I am writing from a North American perspective through the lens of a white middle-class cisgender woman. ("Cisgender" means someone whose internal sense of gender corresponds with the gender they were assigned at birth. I was identified as female at birth and identify as a woman.) I work with people from many cultural backgrounds who approach these topics differently. If some of what you read is new to you, get curious about it! If it doesn't fit with your experience or if it feels like I'm off base, I always welcome feedback about ways to expand my perspectives. You're invited to the conversation in the Revealed community. I am also a Southern-raised woman in her fifties, conventionally attractive, Episcopal Church–going, highly educated, conventionally physically abled, youngest daughter of two children to a Canadian mother who was a nurse and a Detroit-raised father who was a physician. I am a mother of two kiddos—a young adult son and a young daughter. I cuss a lot, laugh even more, and love my work, Pilates, rock-climbing, and all things music.

I sought permission to include the stories from and inspired by clients here. All the names and details have been changed to protect the identities of these precious souls whose stories are here for you to learn from and to explore. I tried to be inclusive and diverse in the demographics, details, and intent of the stories chosen, and I hope they help you feel the collective experience of holistic sexuality. A gentle urging: Find gems in the stories that you can apply to your life. The story doesn't have to have your exact details in order for you to relate to it and learn from it. I also want to offer a soft warning that some stories describe various levels of trauma. Take care of yourself when reading and skip ahead if something does less than inform, inspire, or enlighten you.

Finally, I hope this book influences how you see yourself within sexual connections and outside them and that you adopt a new, more compassionate lens on your life. I wish for you to feel ignited to keep learning about who you are and showing up authentically in the world. I want this book to encourage you to shed what no longer works for you and to inspire you to find out what does in the truth of who you are right now and where you want to be heading.

Let's start with the imperfect and inadequate introductions to sex through formal education that most of us received.

PART ONE

SEXUALITY

The Final Frontier of Self-Development

SEX EXPIRED
Why Take a New Position on Sex?

IF YOU WERE to ask me when my career started, I would say, "In seventh grade."

I was a naturally curious twelve-year-old, and I did not yet know that sex was something forbidden to discuss. Instead, I was the girl looking forward to our one and only day of sex ed class. This was before the internet, when encyclopedias were our search engines, and the bulk of a child's "sex ed" usually came from stolen soft porn magazines stashed in the woods or under a bathroom sink.

I was thrilled when my class was assigned to Miss Sara. She was a young and hot track coach. No doubt about it: My young self was sure she possessed the knowledge and was going to give me all the answers.

The day of that fateful class, Miss Sara was wearing short shorts, her poufy bleached-blonde hair in a ponytail, with the gym whistle hanging around her neck. She quieted the giggling group of girls with a clear, no-nonsense "All right, ladies. Today is sex ed day." To my ears, she might as well have said, "Ladies, start your engines!" I sat at attention on the edge of my seat. No giggling. No chatting. No passing notes. I was there to *take notes*.

At the beginning of class, Miss Sara passed out little pieces of paper and instructed us to write down questions. If we didn't have any, we were to simply write "no question" on the paper, so that

We're done with the way it's always been done.

no one would become gossip fodder. My heart soared when I heard her say, "No question is a dumb question. This is your chance to ask me anything."

Anything?

Anything.

Yes. At last. So many questions rushed through my mind: Does it hurt to have sex? Why does a penis go in the vagina? When would I start my period? What does it feel like to have your boobs touched? Why do guys like blow jobs? Does pubic hair fall out? I wanted to know it *all*. But after much thought and reflection, I landed on "the one," and I wrote my question out carefully in my most mature cursive, using my favorite No. 2 pencil that had a strawberry-scented ornament hanging from the eraser. What was my sacred, well-considered, this-will-change-everything, I-really-need-to-know question?

"What is the deal with vaginal discharge?"

Perfection. I folded my piece of paper with precision: double folded with a corner discreetly torn away so I would know when it was coming. I didn't want my face to turn red when Miss Sara was reading my brilliant question.

At last Miss Sara grasped my paper. The time had come. She opened fold after fold and read it to herself as I waited with bated breath for her answer. After an eternal pause, she said, "Oh. Wow. Inappropriate," folded the paper back up, and went on to the next question.

I died a small death. My face turned red, and tears welled in my eyes. I felt judged and ashamed, seen in all the wrong ways. Because she didn't read my question out loud, no one knew what was inappropriate so most shrugged it off. I rolled my eyes and shrugged for anyone who was watching, trying to play it off, but inwardly I felt exposed. I had taken a risk and trusted that no question was dumb, that my question would be answered. Now I knew there were limits to questions and their answers even when I was told it was safe; I knew there were intense judgments tied to sex and sexuality. And shit, how was I ever going to learn the deal with discharge?

I'll never know why Miss Sara thought a question about discharge was inappropriate or even why she voiced that out loud. I am certain she didn't know the impact it would have on one freckly faced, gap-toothed twelve-year-old. But it did have an impact. Even then, I knew I didn't want anyone else to feel like that: shamed about their body and particularly about sexual health and sexuality. This moment would grow into my passion to make sure that no one feels ashamed of any question related to sex and sexuality. My preteen shame transformed into a professional mission based on the understanding that we can't normalize sex, sexual desires, and challenges within our sexual life if our leaders, our teachers, our partners, and our guides aren't comfortable with the topic in general or with basic bodily processes that are not only normal but healthy and necessary.

You Are Owed an Apology

You weren't properly sex educated. And this matters. This point matters because our society talks a lot about the importance of long-term relationships, uses sex to promote and sell just about anything, and imbues a lot of conflicting rules into our sexual culture, yet it doesn't educate us remotely adequately to navigate our sexual world and the larger sexual culture. This discrepancy creates tension, division, and confusion on the best days and trauma and soul-changing shame on the worst.

You weren't taught what you need to know in a positive, inclusive, pleasure-focused, agency-driven context. I'm guessing if you had a sex ed class when you were in school, it was likely a stand-alone sort of thing folded into a health class and taught by a gym teacher or coach, like mine. Or you were handed a book. Or told the basics by a parent in an awkward tone. For decades, sex education has been damaging, filled with misinformation, or not even close to good enough—filled with fear and the idea of "wrongness." These are the clear errors in typical sex education: a lack of helpful and inclusive facts about health and reproduction, partial anatomy lessons, abstinence-only messaging partnered with scary and trauma-inducing photos of sexually transmitted infections (STIs) and videos of abortions. Even today, sex education is full of bias and usually heteronormative, relationship focused, youth or young adult oriented, and limited to a gender binary. Pleasure-focused education is absent. More egregious are the subtle but powerful errors of omission: not teaching the value of sexuality and that it is a powerful and positive force for each person to discover on their own terms.

We have not been supported to learn about sexuality in a sex-positive way. Not by our school systems, families, peers, media, culture, or spiritual communities; not individually, not collectively. Some of this has been purposeful, systematic, and politicized, powered by people and groups with agendas. Some of this has been through inheritance: generations of poor sex education and a perceived need for sexual control, the boomerang effect of sexual liberation and sexual conservatism.

We all deserve more accurate, inclusive, and comprehensive sex ed than any of us received. The first step in the journey of holistic sexuality is understanding that you likely have a lot to relearn, unlearn, heal from, and grow into. A sex education with a solid foundation includes self-reflection and agency.

The Miracle of Sexual Fulfillment Happening at All

When I work with couples struggling with sexual connection, I often start with a chippy comment: "You know it's a miracle any of us have any sort of sexual fulfillment on our own, let alone in a relationship." My reasoning? Because we aren't properly sex educated, we all have our own sexual journeys full of time bombs, wounds, shame, and secrets; we have great lover experiences, terrible sex stories, rejections, heartaches, and everything in between. We aren't taught how to debrief and integrate them. Then add the fact that we live in an era that punishes sexual liberation and sees sexual pleasure as verboten and finds sexual expression audacious. My normalizing callout to the couples usually makes them chuckle, nod their heads, and exhale deeply. Yeah. We are fucked. Pun intended.

Let's be truthful. Society puts so much pressure on "getting sex right" without teaching a tenth of the skills required, without providing the support that you need throughout your lifespan, and without teaching *why* sexuality—beyond fleeting, fun experiences and orgasms—matters. You are just supposed to get it right, except there is no "right." And you aren't supposed to know or acknowledge that fact either.

A sexual journey is first and foremost experienced individually. It starts with you, solo, in your body, in your thoughts, in the questions you hold, in the experiences you make meaning from. For me, this meant that I often thought I was wrong, too much, or not enough. And definitely not ever right. Because my curiosity for information was insatiable in all areas, including sex and sexuality, I desired to understand what the big deal was about this thing I wasn't supposed to talk about, know about, or be doing—sex. But no one, apart from my childhood bestie, felt safe to ask. She had a little more access to information through an older brother who was for sure having lots of sex. She had access to porn magazines and videos through babysitting jobs. But we were children. We saw things, did not understand them, and certainly did not know how to incorporate anything we observed into our understanding of sex and sexuality.

Later, I didn't know how to make sense of boys wanting other girls but not me. Or how to make sense of the dissonance between being curious about sex but knowing I wasn't ready to do any of it. There were so many complexities to navigate. Positive and negative. My sex education didn't prepare me to understand and integrate any of the real-life parts of sexuality.

I didn't know how to handle someone close to me getting an STI after a sexual assault and her parents freaking out, how to respond when my mom walked in on me masturbating in the Jacuzzi, or what to do when a new pediatrician, whom I didn't get a good feeling from, sent my parent out of the exam room and said he needed to look at my pubic hair... which seemed bizarre because I was in for a sore throat. I didn't know what to do with the bliss I felt when the cool guy called me "dreamy" as he handed me his necklace to wear that week.

In college, I didn't know how to navigate a sexual assault or how to handle a close friend not believing me about it or my boyfriend threatening the guy who did it. Or how to talk about how amazing it was when I listened to my friends and then encouraged my boyfriend to go down on me for the first time. In my thirties, I didn't know how to make self-supportive decisions when a physician shockingly denied me birth control because, and I quote, "You are single and thusly shouldn't be having sex." I struggled to verbalize my complete and utter support for a friend with an unwanted pregnancy within a marriage, even though I supported her entirely. I couldn't make sense of my sexual fantasies that didn't fit with what I thought I wanted in life. I didn't know with whom to celebrate having the most amazing sex with a partner I was deeply in love with. In my forties, I didn't even know how to intuit what I wanted when a kind and supportive lover asked me to take the lead in our sexual life. As I walk into my fifties, I see how underprepared both the medical world and I are for the second puberty—perimenopause and menopause. As my personal life and professional worlds collided, I realized I wasn't prepared for either the hard or the beautiful aspects of my sexual journey.

I'm guessing you aren't either.

Learning in sex ed that I had a vaginal opening and what a herpes outbreak looked like was valuable information, but it did not help with any of the above. Need to know? Yes. Good to know? Yes. Even close to enough to know? No. We need facts, but we also need skills, resources, frameworks, and guidance that we can draw on as we expand our experiences and relationships within a changing world that has so much power over our sexual lives.

You have your own unique experiences. Perhaps you are ashamed of your body and don't feel comfortable having a partner see you naked. Or you don't know how to handle not having sex when you crave it. Maybe you are embarking on a transgender journey without emotional or financial support. Maybe you've had a string of emotionally healthy partners, but no connection lasts after you have sex. Maybe you've experienced erectile dysfunction. Perhaps you have experienced pain during sex for the first time or a relationship with mismatched desire or an act of sexual violence you enacted on another or experienced yourself. Maybe you had an emergency hysterectomy and weren't prepared for surgical menopause. Maybe you want to be sexually active but have no takers. Maybe you are in your seventies and feel like your sexuality is forgotten by society, but you haven't forgotten it. Perhaps your child is expressing a different interest in sexuality than you expected, and you have no idea how to navigate it. Maybe you need to know how to tell a new partner you have an STI or that you don't like how they initiate sexual connection with you. Maybe your body isn't traditionally presenting and you do not know how to bring it up to new partners. Perhaps you need to tell your partner that you no longer feel aligned with your assigned gender and need to embark on a gender journey, or maybe you are navigating racial stereotyping within your relationship, which is greatly affecting your sexual relationship. The issues are vast in range, but I am certain you have experienced a lack of sexual education that leaves you feeling like you would benefit from knowing more. If you can relate to one of the above situations or can think of one of your own, you are reading the right book.

We need to evolve our sex education individually, in our relationships, and in our communities because a sexual journey begins individually but rarely stays in that bubble. You will interact with others in some form. Even though it is well understood that we are ill-equipped, society expects us to have profound sexual lives with others who are also improperly sex educated. It's a tall order without a framework, without a new position on sex.

A Society of Sexual Beings

I recall hearing Esther Perel share a powerful statement in an interview. I regret not capturing it word for word, but the essence of it was if you want to truly understand a country and culture, examine how they treat, control, and frame sexuality. I agree and add: If sexuality is viewed holistically, then that tells you even more. Cue me stepping onto my soapbox.

Sex is divisive. Period.

Sex is used as a weapon by religion, for political gain, between partners, within schools, among groups of people, and in communities. Society has been segregated into two camps: "They are right" and "You are wrong." Anyone who says they know what the "right" sex is usually thinks they are the authority on the "wrong" sex; in my experience, this false authority is often rooted in secrets, wounds, manipulative motives, and fears, and they will defend the righteousness of their stance and try to deny others the right to a different one. This bifurcation is hypocritical, harmful, and tries to and often succeeds at depriving people of their agency. Deprivation of agency is the root of an unhealthy sexual culture.

That last paragraph is not talking about stereotypically liberal beliefs versus stereotypically conservative beliefs. Evolved sexual education isn't about encouraging everyone to have free-for-all sex all the time. It is about providing accurate information and a safe environment for you to reflect about who you are and what you need and want as a sexual being, alongside other sexual beings doing the same. Weaponizing and politicizing sex, sexuality, and sex education are the antithesis of evolved sexual education and the direct result of poor sex education. A healthy sexual culture is relevant to our individual sexual journeys. The hard truth is this: When societies deny their citizens evolved and holistic sexual education, there is a rise in unwanted pregnancies, unfulfilling sexual lives and relationships, untreated STIs, divorce rates, low self-worth, deaths by suicide, political divisiveness, and a proliferation of sexual violence.

We all know there is an innate power dynamic in the topic of sex, and political parties and governments have harnessed this power as a tool. Shame and removal of sexual agency are dangerous weapons that can hit many targets at once and can fly under the radar like the best stealth missiles. In my opinion, evolved and responsible sex ed, which includes deep, emotional, pleasure- and essence-based principles, does not just improve your life, sexually and otherwise; it can have far-reaching positive impacts globally.

When a society holds an archaic view of sexuality, we surround a natural part of ourselves—sexuality—in shame, and we trample our birthright to pleasure, create unsafe environments for whole communities, and cause other detrimental outcomes, which we'll explore further in this book.

Sex and sexuality are not benign, nor is holistic sexuality. This is powerful stuff. And the quality of our sex education determines how this power is wielded and how it manifests individually, in relationships, and in our societies. Getting an evolved sexual grounding is critical. The sooner the better, and it is never too late.

The Experts Are Not Sexperts

Did you know that in the United States, most mental health professionals, such as couples and family therapists, counselors, psychotherapists, and social workers, do not need to take a single class on sex and sexuality to graduate or obtain a license? Did you know that most professionals in the medical and medical-adjacent fields don't either? That even applies to urologists and gynecologists. Most professionals you entrust with your sexual health and wellness or your sexual and relationship psychology are not adequately educated, at least not formally, when it comes to sex and sexuality. It's no fault of their own; it's just not offered or valued by the governing and credentialing bodies.

As you shake your head in disbelief, let me honor and celebrate the many professionals who are properly educated, such as sex therapists, sex counselors, sex coaches, and sex educators. I also profoundly appreciate the health professionals we rely on for our sexual health who do educate themselves about sex and sexuality. Many do, but they must do so on their own time and with their own initiative and money. I have my PhD in counseling education and, in all my years of graduate work, had the option to take *one* elective course directly related to sexuality. Everything I have learned has been through my personal efforts to broaden my education and understanding. It required a lot of time, effort, and money.

So, let's be clear on the state of things: We aren't given evolved formal sex education growing up; we are at the mercy of our informal sex education; and then we must rely on mental health and medical professionals—who are unlikely to be properly sex educated—to help us if we want to have healthy sexual lives and perhaps fulfilling sexual relationships and experiences with others who have had the same dismal sexual education... Sigh.

A client of mine, Carl, is a good example of how righting our societal wrongs can make a difference. Carl started working with me during his senior year of high school because he was experiencing erectile dysfunction (ED). As is often the case, the presenting issue did not remain the focus of our work for long.

Carl's formal sexual education was pretty evolved for the United States. His progressive parents believed in communication, education, and therapy, and they were a tight-knit family. They talked about sex with him throughout his childhood and adolescence. Carl lived in a progressive state that offered sex education in public school multiple times yearly for the span of his education. His sex education was positive and much more inclusive than the norm.

But still, with all of that going for him, it wasn't enough to equip him for the complexities of a real sexual existence alongside others. Carl didn't know where to seek help to navigate the intersection of his sexual and mental health needs. He wasn't given the tools to respond to the mother of a friend who repeatedly complimented his looks and positioned herself beside him at gatherings and school outings. His sex education didn't prepare him for the hit to his self-confidence when two attempts at sexual penetration turned into awkward retreat because "it just wouldn't work." Once people in his social circle found out, they started gossiping.

Under such pressure, Carl's drug and alcohol use skyrocketed, and his depression and anxiety rose to life-threatening levels. His parents sacrificed financially to get him medical and psychological help in multiple settings—and luckily, they had the means to do so. These advantages I recognize are also not the norm.

With the incredible amount of support Carl received and his determination to show up in his life and world differently, his situation took a drastic turn. He entered two consecutive relationships that weren't perfect but were maturely advanced. He experienced sexual connections that were fun, communicative, and meaningful. He learned how to work with ED so it did not interfere with his sexual confidence and connection. His drug use decreased, and his GPA soared. He spoke differently. He showed up for his familial relationships differently. His confidence grew. He showed up for himself authentically. That is what evolved and holistic sexual education offers.

EVEN THOUGH many of us have more access to information and more support in regards to our sexual health than ever before, we aren't given many safe places in which to ask questions, integrate it for ourselves, and apply it to our own life. The time you spend in this book is going to change this for you.

The saying "Be the change you wish to see in the world" reminds us to bounce back from a global focus to an individual concentration.

The Final Frontier

Sexuality is the final frontier of self-development.

That's a bold statement, I know. But I believe it deeply. Sexuality is a worthy and crucial use of your time. Why? Because more than likely you are in a version of one of these five mindsets right now.

1. You've already experienced a crisis or awakening that demands you take a deeper look inside yourself. That crisis might be an affair, a health issue, a disastrous relationship, a deep-seated wound or trauma within your sexual journey, or a career crisis.

2. You have a feeling deep down inside that there is something more, a better way of living in the world and a deeper way to connect with others. But life is busy and finances are tight, and you just aren't sure sex and sexuality are worth your time and expense. But still this feeling of something missing sears the edges of you.

3. You already know that sexuality is an important part of your life and that attending to this need would benefit you, but you just don't know where to look for help or how to make it happen.

4. You want to be properly sex educated, and you're seeking out resources. You may want this knowledge for yourself or to teach your children or others. It is time for a sexual audit.

5. You know our current sexual culture is garbage at best—it's toxic, harmful, and bullshit. You've felt hopeless when seeing legislation or policies that reflect the opposite of what you believe is culturally supportive and important. You've seen that doing personal work on sexuality may be a powerful antidote to our cultural and political issues. As the saying goes, the personal is political. (With thanks to activist Carol Hanisch.)

Our culture encourages us to spend more time looking away from ourselves and each other than looking into ourselves and each other. We live with voids, and so we try to fill them, avoid them, or overindulge them. But how do we truly feel fulfilled? We don't know where to get help or how to fill the gaps, so when an immediate crisis or emotion dissipates, we carry on as usual, until the next time.

Over the decades of my professional and personal life, I have learned that people are hungry to be asked about their lives and are desperate for a safe and helpful space in which to explore their stories—a place for them to connect, a place for them to fill their voids. But it can be a hard sell: "Explore your history, your stories, and you will forever be fulfilled, sexually and beyond!" It's a big step, a big promise, and while promising to improve your sex life with fun sex tips would be a lot easier, holistic sexuality is the final frontier of self-development because it's not easy. It is the part of us we have the least amount of ease in accessing or support to spend time on. Thus, diving into the fascinating, complicated, and meaningful world of your sexuality, in the holistic sense, will be a game changer.

Along this valiant and courageous journey, you will embark on self-reflection through a broad, holistic understanding of sexuality. Next, you'll narrow your focus to education and resources (like sex tips) that aid and support you along the way. If you do the work of self-development first, you'll know exactly where you need to go next: what sex tips you want to learn more about, how to feel more pleasure, and where and with whom you'd like to share these learnings. Your sexual confidence will grow exponentially. Sex tips are the decorations; holistic sexuality is groundbreaking, structure-building, and life-changing.

HOLISTIC SEXUALITY
Stepping Into Your Essence

IN BETWEEN getting my master's degree in counseling at Auburn and my PhD at William & Mary, I got divorced and, for a short stint, lived in LA where I pursued acting professionally. Plot twist, I know! My acting agent, Kristi, became my manager and ran a weekly coaching group for "her people." We knew each other well and had a high level of trust in each other and in her.

Kristi was a straight shooter, a no-nonsense sort of person. She wanted us to succeed for our well-being and dreams—and for hers. We trusted her observations and advice. One night, we met up in my tiny apartment in the infamous Oaks Apartments complex overlooking Warner Bros. Studios. Kristi started the session with a question: "What scene would be the biggest challenge for you?" She pointed at me first. So, I did what I was trained to do: answer without thinking.

"Having to seduce someone," I said. The words were out before I knew it.

I turned to the next person, thinking, "Right! Let's move on."

To my surprise, the guy next to me looked at me sidewise and said, "Um, raping a child."

The next person said, "Murdering a child."

"Killing myself."

Holistic sexuality
is the pathway
to your deepest self.

"Shaking a baby."

As everyone gave their answers, they seemed also to be saying, "What a weird answer, Juliana."

A group chuckle of sorts bubbled up as each answer grew more dire; these horrible crimes had not even crossed my mind, but seduction did. I was an outlier.

Oh, shit. I knew what that meant.

After everyone answered, Kristi looked at me with the knowing of a teacher in a teachable moment. "Juliana, go seduce Travis."

Oh, God. Why hadn't I said "killing someone"?

Without guidance, a script, a warm-up, alcohol, or music, I sauntered over to Travis, trying not to trip. I swayed awkwardly, mumbled a few words, made strange eyes at him. But I couldn't keep eye contact. I straddled him and moved this way and that.

"And scene!" Kristi finally called out. To me, her words sounded like "Make it stop."

Thank goodness. I slinked back to my seat, hoping nobody noticed. Oh, but they did. I was surrounded by deafening silence and feeling-sorry-for-me faces. I think it looked like I *was* trying to kill someone.

I kept my gaze toward the floor, but I knew a lot of people in that room were grateful they hadn't bombed as badly as that. The humiliation continued.

"Travis, were you seduced?" Kristi asked.

"No, ma'am."

"Did you feel anything?"

"Not one thing. Well, maybe embarrassment for Juliana."

Kristi nodded and then said, "Kimberly, go seduce Travis."

As Kimberly stood up and went to Travis, she exuded such sexiness that we were all turned on just watching. It was as though she knew exactly who she was, what she wanted, and had zero shame. She was dripping in sexual confidence. He couldn't keep his eyes off her.

"And scene!" Kristi chirped. "Did you feel anything, Travis?"

"Um, I can't form words, ma'am."

Kristi looked at me and said, simply and powerfully, "Fix that shit."

Here is the moral of the story for you: Integration of knowing who you are, the truth of who you are, and accessing *that* as your connection point is sexy. Pretending, performing, or inauthentically connecting do not lead to fulfilling moments or relationships. This example is a tad extreme for the point, but I want you to understand the power of it, as well as give you this as a powerful turning point for me.

It was when my personal and professional life collided for the first time.

I was youngish and attractive. I had been married, had a child already. I was getting lots of auditions for sexy roles, but I was landing exactly zero of them. In a later conversation, Kristi pointed out that I had a block regarding sex and all things sexy. She suggested I integrate my private sexual persona into my acting roles. I needed to own my sexuality.

She was right, but in response, I had a blaring internal question: "Okay, but how?"

Before I was married, in my marriage, and even after that acting class disaster, I had no idea who I was sexually. I defined myself through others' expectations of me—those of my parents, my peers, my childhood best friend, my husband. I saw sex and sexiness through the lens of sex acts, and I was more used to "performing" sexy than embodying an authentic sexuality.

I understood that I didn't understand who I was sexually. "Fixing it" wasn't about copying Kimberly or even turning on Travis; it was about finding out who I was. A 360-degree examination. Which included who I was as a sexual being.

I spent a lot of time wondering how to fix this problem. I had no idea who to ask or what professionals could support me, and Dr. Google didn't exist at that time. I looked for role models, but no advice helped me.

I discovered one layer of this lesson while still living in LA. I never booked the "sexy role," but I did end up starring in a series of thirteen commercials. I was a wife and mom in an ad series promoting Disney's Saturday morning lineup. Turns out authenticity was the key and also the start. I was a mom and had been a wife, and tuning into this truth landed me the role. I knew there was more. Much more.

Then I met Chris. He had a long list of sexual experiences, and after he and I forged a soul-filled relationship, his encouragement helped me to be real about myself and my sexuality, and I "fixed that shit" to an even deeper layer. With Chris, the light of my sexuality went from a flicker to a flame, and my essence burned bright.

Sexuality Is the Essence of You

Sexuality is at the core of who you are. It is a pathway to and the expression of your essence.

Your essence houses your motivating values, the critical aspects of what guides your choices. Your essence is your inner wisdom, your wisest, most-feeling self. It determines what you think of yourself and gives you the room to claim what you want and do not want for your life. It defines how you show up in the world and how you connect with others. It is the great creative life force, one of the most powerful renewable energy sources available to you. Your essence is your vitality and your lifeline, deserving of your full attention.

When you have a deep understanding of your holistic sexuality and the skills to communicate this understanding to others, you have the keys to achieving your needs and desires. As you examine, reflect upon, and strengthen your connection to your essence, you can express a deeper level of authenticity in who you are. When you know your essence, you can show up for others as your true self too. When you connect soul to soul with another, whether this connection is simple and swift or deep and long-lasting, a strong sense of your essence reminds you that you matter. You know how to give yourself the gift of being seen, heard, wanted, understood, and loved for who you really are. And because you show up authentically, you can accept being seen, heard, wanted, understood, and loved at ever-expanding levels. Due to the complicated, interwoven, and interactive nature of human sexuality, finding your essence here beams it out into the rest of your life. The ripple effects are enormous.

Talking about sex and sexuality brings up a myriad of reactions for people: humor, embarrassment, discomfort, excitement, interest, fear, offense. But underneath the layers of emotions and history, sexuality is common among all humans. If you are breathing, you have sexuality. If you live more than one day, your sexuality changes and grows. As you expand and interact with others, your sexual decisions—of which there are many—influence your view of yourself, impact your relationships, and shape your journey. If you do not consistently make sexual decisions that are aligned with your essence, you pay a price for it.

Perhaps in relationships, you speak about your sex life in funny vignettes to get to know your partners. You exchange your "number" or "body count," or you bond over horrifying catastrophes that explain a particular neurosis. But do you talk about larger issues related to sexuality, about the matters that you keep close to your mind and heart? Do you tell her "I like this but not that"? Do you talk about your need for emotional intimacy and safety? Do you describe to them the details of your fantasies that concern you? Or do you do a sexual debriefing that celebrates the amazingness of the connection? After years of sidestepping conversations about sexuality, you grow into a habit of not talking about the good or challenging aspects, not exploring, examining, or reflecting on them—and often this includes the people you have sex with. Or if you try to have conversations with sexual partner(s), you may lack the skills for communicating about emotionally and erotically vulnerable things with them. These attempts often don't go well, and this letdown makes you reluctant to dive into those waters again. Other taboos present themselves when you are partnered: talking about what is not working sexually with your partner or sharing the positive sexual experiences you have had with previous partners.

We are sexually mute in many ways, and in most cases, this silence affects us holistically and dulls our essence over time.

We've all heard it's important to have different kinds of friends: the friend you can go out and light up the town with, the friend who will tell you how it is, the friend you can call crying at three in the morning, and the friend who will bail you out of jail and take a selfie with you in the precinct... How many of us have a friend or partner with whom we can share the deepest parts of our sexuality or our sexual needs? The friend you can tell about the mind-blowing sex you had with your spouse last night. The friend who knows you have been watching hours of porn to fill a void in your intimate life. The friend you feel safe enough with to share that you have lost sexual desire, that your penis doesn't work, that your temptation to cheat is overpowering, that you feel ugly or old or sexually undesirable.

Do any of us have the safety we need to normalize such sexual discussions?

Are you having these conversations with others? And more importantly, are you asking yourself these questions privately and then reflecting inwardly on your sexuality? I can tell you that very few of us are, and most likely that's because we have been told that anything related to sex is dirty, bad, wrong, private, only for partners, not to be discussed or thought about. This is catastrophic messaging because sex and sexuality are intrinsic to who we are as humans. Sexuality is a necessity, not a luxury.

When you learn to talk about all aspects of your sexual self—the fun and braggy stuff, the misfires, the fears, and the questions—you kick off a domino effect. Other vulnerable, human, and important topics like mental health concerns, religious questions, parental insecurities, and career crises open up to you. By starting in the most challenging and most stigmatized places, you gift yourself the opportunity to have honest and authentic revelations. A dramatic shift takes place inside people when they are able to bare their secrets, fears, questions, and shame—light and transparency are on the other side. A bright and shining essence is waiting.

A client, Brianna, once started a session with this powerful phrase: "This weekend I didn't put on a performance while we were having sex. My mind is blown." As we explored this shift, she described telling her lover Kate what she wanted, needed, and how she wanted Kate to experience her. Brianna didn't want to *act* wild and bold. She wanted to *feel* uninhibited and to be matched by Kate in this space, and so she invited her lover in. Brianna's simple, profound realization was that by infusing her sexual connection with purpose and intention and by sharing from her essence, she could step into a deeper connection with Kate, and she never wanted anything less than that again. It clicked for Brianna that this one step during sex, which had great results, could be translated into the rest of her life. What she'd been withholding from her boss, from her parents, from her friends was now more accessible to share, and not only that, it was necessary to share. That is where honoring your essence and diving into holistic sexuality can take you, because if you can discover authenticity and agency in such a complicated aspect of yourself, you can build that skill in other areas as well.

Sexuality or Holistic Sexuality?

Words matter. In education, when conceptualizing a hard topic, and when communicating in general. I was taught this early in my career as a therapist and reminded again later just how ever-changing and provocative the topic of sex is for most people—even professionals in the sex and sexuality world. I attended a panel discussion with the American Association of Sexuality Educators, Counselors, and Therapists. The panel title was something to the effect of "Sex or Sexuality?" I didn't know what that meant exactly, and I was certainly not prepared for the heated discussion I witnessed. Therapy conferences are generally supportive events, and sex conferences are that plus a load more fun. But this panel discussion was more of an angry discourse—fingers were wagged, voices were raised, and people walked out.

The debate centered on terminology. Do we say "sex education" or "sexuality education"? Sex ed was backed with the belief in "meeting people where they are," and sexuality education was seen as better suited because it offers more dimension and accuracy. The argument grew from reactions to the statement "Sex is a part of sexuality, not synonymous with it." It was heated and clearly had been visited repeatedly by the leaders in my new career. The discussion ended with the decision to keep "sex ed" so as not to add another hurdle to the access point of the work, with the understanding that "sexuality education" was the preferred term. Habit dominated.

But... changing the term from "sex" to "sexuality" isn't really taxing and is a mere mindset and habit shift. I want to be clear: I prefer "sexuality," even though I use "sex" and "sexuality" in some places interchangeably in this book to honor where we all have begun. But I also encourage you to break the habit and keep pushing the boundaries of your thinking, starting with terminology and expanding from that point. Just because this is how it has always been doesn't mean it needs to stay that way. This book asks you to continuously stay curious about everything, especially things that feel like habit.

Let's progress our thinking about "sex" and "sexuality" to consider "holistic sexuality" as a mainstream concept. Allow me to explain. I encountered holistic sexuality at this same conference through the foundational work of Dr. Dennis Dailey, among many others. In 1981, Dailey published a graphic representing what is titled the circles of sexuality: sensuality, intimacy, sexual identity, sexual health and reproduction, and sexualization. In the middle of the cluster was values. These circles were meant to express the growing awareness that sexuality was more than just sex acts and to introduce various ways in which sexuality influences all aspects of our being.

In my beginning years, I referred to Dailey's circles in my practice and teachings to show clients and students the all-encompassing nature of sexuality in our lives. Then I began to see that the circles did not reflect everything I had learned and experienced, nor all that I had witnessed in my practice and personal life. By considering the themes in people's sexual stories, paying attention to people who identified as sexually fulfilled, noticing the pain points for my clients and students within their sexual worlds, observing communities that were doing a good job of advancing sexuality education, and testing and retesting my theories qualitatively, I identified nine pillars of holistic sexuality, which represent the various aspects of our being, as well as a foundational quality to all the pillars—agency. We'll dive into the foundation throughout, but first, here are my nine pillars of holistic sexuality.

Pillar 1: Sensuality. This pillar represents your experience and expression of, comfort with, and access to five senses: sight, taste, hearing, touch, and smell. Sensuality is how you actively experience the connection between sexuality and embodiment through your senses and how you activate senses individually and within sexual experiences with others.

Pillar 2: Wellness and fertility. Wellness focuses on mental, physical, and sexual contexts. This pillar focuses on your attitudes and behaviors related to fertility, the wellness of the sexual and reproductive systems, and the health consequences of sexual behavior. Your experience with informal and formal sexual education is infused throughout wellness and fertility. This pillar also includes your understanding of sexual anatomy and its connection to pleasure and an exploration of your relationship to your physical body.

Pillar 3: Pleasure. Pleasure is the active experience of fulfillment and enjoyment. It is the "yum" compared to its opposite, "yuck." Pleasure is your birthright and responsibility, and it requires you to be in the moment and to use your senses to fully experience your surroundings through body, mind, and soul. Pleasure is a vast continuum that includes self-pleasure and orgasm. Holistic sexuality does not make value judgments about what brings you pleasure.

Pillar 4: Desire. This includes sexual desire, arousal, and libido that you experience internally and express externally. Desire is the amount of interest you have in sexual connection with yourself and others and includes your concept of sexy, for yourself and others.

It also involves your relationship with your desire, the spark inside you, your overall vibrancy, what and who turns you on, who you are attracted to, and what and who sets off sparks within you.

Pillar 5: Acts and interests. This pillar is about the sex acts you do with your body solo and/or with others. It involves your yucks and yums, communication, skill level, knowledge base, choices, fantasy, kinks, taboo tolerance, and more. This pillar is about finding your edges, playing with them, exploring, and reinventing. It is finding the importance of authentic yeses and nos, rooting exploration in consensual and safe curiosity and seeing the value both bring us in collecting data about what we want and do not want.

Pillar 6: Intersecting identities. This pillar represents the context in which you experience your life and your personal identity, such as your racial or cultural background, gender, socioeconomic status, education, physical ableness, religion/spirituality, family of origin, and generation/age. It seeks understanding of the context of the life you were born into as well as your current life, which may express different access to choice and agency. It asks you to explore privilege, oppression, and marginalization, as well as the many factors that inform and impact the totality of holistic sexuality. It is a pillar that stands alone and is also infused throughout each of the other pillars and the hub of agency.

Pillar 7: Power and trauma. This pillar is about the inherent existence of power within sexuality. It examines the relationship between power and sex and the use of sexuality to influence, control, or manipulate others. This includes sexual currency, flirting and seduction, and the wide continuum of sexual violence such as harassment, rape, and molestation. It also explores negative life events, such as divorce, losing a job, major illness, death, or mental illness, which affect how you express and experience your essence and how that impacts your worldview.

Pillar 8: Relationship. Relationships are vital: They're how we learn, grow, and evolve, and they have a major impact on your present, past, and future. This pillar represents your ability to experience emotional closeness with another person and to safely accept this closeness with vulnerability. Your relationships are where you can expand your understanding of your core needs. Intimacy is a critical aspect of relationships.

Pillar 9: Connection. This pillar represents the deep need within human beings to be seen, wanted, and valued. There are many types of important connections, and each offers a different experience of being wanted, seen, and valued, with love being one of them.

Although these pillars are ordered and offered with purpose and intention, you won't necessarily live them linearly. Order is useful for learning and memory—but your experience will likely meander between the pillars of holistic sexuality as you live a multidimensional life. I took inspiration and began from Dailey's work for my pillars, but there are pivotal differences beyond the pillar topic changes. First, each pillar stands alone and also works in a stacking effect with each other. They are interrelated. You will also see two lines on the diagram that follows: soul and lifespan. These lines represent the fluid, ever-changing, and contextually reliant aspect of holistic sexuality. The soul line represents your connection to self, your essence, and how you see the core of you in context to the outer world. The lifespan line represents your age, life stage, and life details at all points of your journey simultaneously and within the context of each story and pillar. Where they intersect is your mindful, present moment. Intersecting identities is a pillar that must be examined within each other pillar, so it is represented as a circle around the other pillars. And finally, rather than resting on Dailey's hub of *values*, my pillars are imbued with and rely on *sexual agency*. Sexual agency is a guiding force that provides a foundation for your life both inside and outside sexuality. Sexual agency is about learning your terms and then learning to live them out—internally, within relationships, and throughout your lifetime.

In this book, I use a two-dimensional image to represent the pillars, but a three-dimensional model would more accurately reflect how these components of holistic sexuality are dynamic within our lifespan. You see this added dimension in the lifespan and soul lines within the graphic. Sexuality is fluid. Movable. Interactive. Ever-changing. Contextual. Intersectional. Each individual's sexuality intersects with the collective and global sexual climate and culture as well as with the details of their lives and relationships.

Nine Pillars of Holistic Sexuality

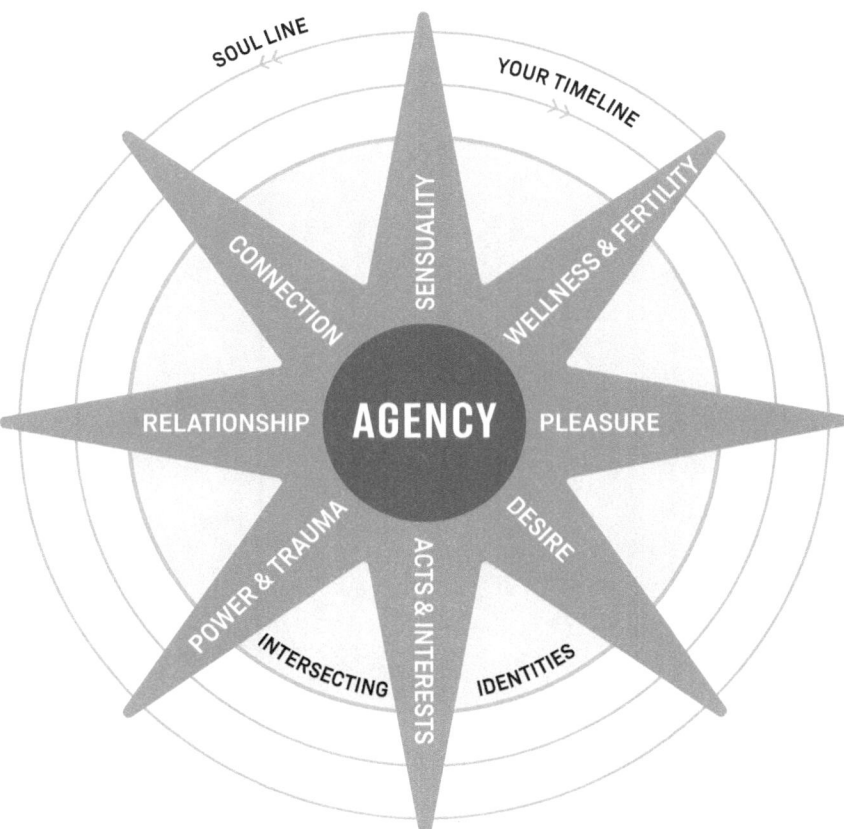

Sexual agency gets the spotlight in a minute, and it is layered throughout every aspect of the book. Take a few moments to review the holistic sexuality diagram; see what comes forward to you and what questions you may have. We'll unpack it throughout the rest of this book, and it is meant to have layered meaning and unique contexts for everyone individually.

AGENCY
Doing It on Your Own Terms

Years ago, I had gone on several dates with Shane. One night, we planned to go to a concert out of town and get a hotel room together. This was likely going to be the night we had sex, and I was excited. Or rather curious. We met at the hotel and got ready for the evening. Then as we were walking to the car, he casually mentioned that his brother and sister-in-law, plus his ex-wife, were joining us. Record scratch. His ex-wife was coming on our date with us? Not just to meet the group there but to ride in the car with us, eat dinner with us, and sit at the concert with us?

I did not say much in response. I am not at my best when I am surprised. My emotions were swirling, and I needed to get them in check and gather my thoughts. I wasn't sure if I should stay or go. Should I ask him to rescind the invite? Embrace her as a friend? He made the choice without consulting me, and I was taken off guard. I couldn't tell what I wanted. I was mixing up my reaction to the lack of agency he afforded me with how I actually felt about her being there. In principle, I was entirely positive about someone who was on such good terms with his ex that she would be included in a night out. I liked that notion and had that in my own life with my ex. What I didn't like was not being included in the decision or given

Agency is the foundation of holistic sexuality.

much heads up. I felt reactive instead of grounded. So, I focused on myself and how I felt and waited to see how things played out.

Turns out the whole night was a mess. She vacillated from being overly nice to me to shooting daggers. He would disappear and then she would disappear. They seemed to be together, then he would be overly affectionate with me, which I thought was to make her jealous—yuck. I went into survival mode and froze. Miserable and paralyzed in emotion and action.

As the night concluded and the ex awkwardly took another car home, I started feeling like I had abandoned all sense of myself. Shane and I went back to the room, and clearly he thought we were going to have sex. At last, I felt emotionally regulated and grounded in the consequences of my actions.

I said to him, "I'm not sure what is happening between you and her, but it seems unresolved. It hasn't felt right all night, and I didn't know what to say or what I wanted until now. I want you all to have space to figure out what you both want, and I need to take myself out of the mix between you two. I'm not staying tonight. I do not know what contact we will have moving forward, but I think it is best for me to leave."

He acknowledged he had kept things from me and that he was sorry for not being more up front about the evening and their relationship. He didn't know what he wanted next.

I paid for an exorbitant hour-long taxi ride home and went to bed. Although I was annoyed that it had taken me all evening to figure things out for myself, I felt satisfied that I had eventually made the decision that was right for me, activated my agency, kept grounded, and left knowing what I wanted and didn't want. Mainly, I was glad I finally showed up for myself. That felt good. Having not shown up for myself in other situations, I love the difference.

The road to activating your agency may not be perfect, quick, or like another's journey, but it is profoundly transformative.

AGENCY IS the foundation of holistic sexuality, of my work as a therapist, educator, and sexpert. I have seen the most staunch, defensive, and entitled people melt into the most beautiful, life-altered humans when they embrace the concept of agency, when they understand that agency offers tools to move through disagreements and challenges, and it doesn't take away one's rights. Agency doesn't take away another's rights. Agency makes room for everyone and does *not* allow room for marginalization, discrimination, or oppression in any form; those are behaviors and mindsets that harm people and community—the opposite of agency. Agency is about upholding your own needs and boundaries and respecting those of others. It should be the cornerstone of all education—a life skill taught and infused throughout our lives. Our kids should learn it as a baseline for personal development, relationships, education, politics, conflict resolution, and, well, everything.

The Noun That Is a Verb

I consider agency a noun and a verb, a concept and a skill—which helps explain why this term is so hard to grasp. In the context of my work, agency is a life skill and human need, birthright and responsibility.

Your understanding of agency may begin with words and phrases like "autonomy," "sovereignty," "self-determination," "finding your voice," and "being captain of your own ship." To grasp the depth of agency, you must dive further. According to the *Merriam-Webster Dictionary*, "agency," the noun, is "the capacity, condition, or state of… exerting power." It also refers to a person, the instrumentality, "through which power is exerted." That sounds like pretentious nonsense. But it helps us to understand that agency is who we are when we are acting within it and that we are also the vehicle for it. When I say "agency" is a verb, as in exercising agency, I mean activating your individual choice, your decision-making responsibility, whatever privilege and learning you have, and your terms for living.

Simply put, agency is learning what your terms are and then living them. Through agency, you can find a way to heal past experiences, shame, and judgments, and you can set up your future self for a life of fulfillment and resilience. It's a superpower.

Agency is rooted in finding out what you want and need, and the opposite. Agency sustains what is aligned with your purpose. Agency listens to your essence. It speaks to your essence. It prompts you to act in service of your future self.

I see agency more as a concept than as a strict definition. Like the idea of love or the Supreme Court's definition of pornography, encapsulating the idea of agency and feeling fully satisfied with the description are a bit of a riddle. The definition of pornography that Supreme Court Justice Potter Stewart landed on in 1964 was "I know it when I see it." What a profoundly elusive but obvious conclusion.

In the context of consensual sexual connections, sexual agency is making purposeful and intentional decisions in all areas of your sexuality, which connect to the truth of who you are, and having the skills to act and react in healthy ways to the consequences of your decisions, whether intended or unintended. Sexual agency is knowing what you want and don't want sexually. When you voice consent, you do it truthfully, fully, with confidence, and in partnership when applicable. And when you do not consent, you are clear, you show up for yourself, and you are grounded in the power of the no. Though activating your agency sexually or otherwise isn't always easy, and it doesn't always make other people happy, it's *always* authentic to you—and that's what matters most. Getting in tune with your sexuality holistically allows you to build confidence in your authenticity and gives power to the voice of your agency. More holistic sexuality means more authenticity, which in turn means more agency. Sexual agency is a cornerstone for fulfilling sexual relationships, positive sexual experiences, and grounded sexual self-awareness. As you read this book, look for how sexual agency shows up in your life, or where it does not, and consider how you want it to from this moment on. Observing where agency shows up or is lacking in your life, where it intersects with your deepest soul purpose and intentions, is a gift to your essence and bolsters the truth of who you are—inside and outside sexual connection.

Adrienne, who identified as a cisgender white woman from a middle-class background, took my course Revealed. She told the following story, starting by saying, "In high school in the 1970s, I had no idea how to show up for myself or that something like agency existed, let alone that it could protect me."

Her first love was a high school senior and football player, Jeff. The popular jock you see depicted in movies. Every girl wanted him, and every guy wanted to be like him. And she got him. "Little ol' her," as she put it. He was her first sexual partner. She thought he was a master at sex and taught her everything he knew. It felt like a lot to her, and a tad confusing, but what did she know? None of her friends had talked to her in detail about the sex they were having, and she didn't learn anything useful at home or in school. Jeff seemed so sure that how he "did" sex was the best kind of sex, so she believed him.

As prom season approached, tension grew in their relationship. He seemed to be losing interest. She started to worry and even felt dread as he threatened that they may not go to prom together if things didn't improve. But she didn't know what would make it better. Only he knew. As with most things in their relationship, he was in control.

One Saturday Jeff suggested she come over to his house because his parents would be gone for the day. This was her chance, she thought. A fun-filled day together to remind him of how great she was.

When she walked in, she was stunned to see Brett, a friend of Jeff's, sitting in the family room with him. Disappointed, Adrienne adjusted to the development. They ate a bit and watched some TV. Then Jeff casually said, "I think you and Brett should have sex." She giggled. Brett didn't. He didn't even act surprised. Was Jeff serious? Had he and Brett talked about this? Jeff's calmness and steady stare told her he was and they had. Shit.

In a flash, she decided she had to do it. She couldn't risk losing him, and this was her last chance with Jeff. So she said yes. She started to walk Brett into Jeff's bedroom, and Jeff stopped her. "No, here. I want to watch."

Adrienne and Brett quietly undressed themselves and started having sex on the couch in front of Jeff. She didn't remember there being any of the usual making out or even kissing. They went straight to penetration. No condom. It didn't feel good, but she moved and groaned as though it did. She couldn't bear to look at either boy's face. She looked up at the ceiling and acted out what she thought a woman enjoying sex would look like, so Jeff would think she was sexy and sophisticated. When Brett was about to cum, she felt relieved. It hadn't taken too long, which also surprised her because she thought Brett would have a hard time doing this in front of his friend. Guess he didn't. Brett came pretty loudly, but over the sounds of his orgasm, she heard something disturbing and looked to the source. With both arms raised straight over his head, Jeff yelled, "Touchdown!"

Decades later, the Revealed group listened in reverence to this courageous woman as she told this story and as she processed her thoughts about the experience. Adrienne talked about the compassion she had for the young woman she had been years prior. She grieved. Sobbing, she said, "Where *was I*? Where *was I* in that moment?" Then a powerful knowing emerged. "I would have done anything for his attention and what I thought was love."

Group members nodded, each carrying their own stories of similar self-abandonment with different details. Adrienne said, "That was not the last time I did not show up for myself. Many times after that, my body did something my soul objected to."

Adrienne's processing ended with a commitment to reclaim her body and her pleasure. She later told us a hilarious and poignant twist. Years after this, while having sex with a lover while the TV was on and enjoying many orgasms, she heard a football announcer yell, "Touchdown!" She glanced at the screen, disconnecting with her lover for the briefest of moments, to hear the word, to smile, and to know she could love football again. "Touchdown" was hers once again. The Revealed group clapped like she had just made a winning two-point conversion.

The Five Steps of Agency

Once you've been introduced to the *concept* of agency, whenever it happens (hint: now, for you), you'll begin to start practicing the *skill* of agency. To have agency, you need to practice it, so that you can live it. Simply put, yet complex to understand, when reviewing past stories of your sexual journey, the amount of agency activated depends on 1) how much choice you think you had in the moment and 2) if you believed yourself to be acting on your own terms, not pressured by anyone or anything else. Regardless of how much agency you can or cannot find in your past, it's never too late to start practicing these five steps in your present.

1. **Recognize that there is a decision to be made.** You consciously recognize there is a decision to address rather than "just letting it sort itself out" or avoiding it. If you need to make multiple decisions, you discern which is the first priority and address them in order.

2. **Determine an intentional action aligned with your purpose.** This is where the support of a therapist, friend, partner, journal, or other resource may be helpful, especially in the beginning. As you practice determining your actions, you gain confidence in your decision-making ability and begin to trust that you are the right person to make decisions for yourself at the time that is right for you.

3. **Act on your decision.** Having decided the action that will best serve your purpose in step 2, you now act on your decision. You do the thing!

4. **Live with the intended and unintended consequences of your decision.** Whether they are positive or negative, instant or long-lasting, you face the results of your decision. Oftentimes, you go back to step 2, relying on the confidence and trust you've built in yourself and your decisions.

5 **Make meaning of steps 1 through 4.** Either alone or with someone supportive, you reflect on how the first four steps played out, felt, went well, or could have gone better, and you make meaning of the whole process to fuel steps 1 through 4 again in the future.

Let me show you an example outside of overt sexual connection. One of my clients, Ling, was in his mid-twenties and identified as a straight American cis man. His uncle had written a group text to him and his girlfriend that was sexually suggestive and inappropriate. Ling reacted and immediately sent a text to his uncle telling him that wasn't okay, to never write a text like that again to them, and to delete the group text. Ling's text was full of language such as "Who do you think you are?" and "You aren't going to do that to me." His uncle wrote back an equally reactive message, defending himself by minimizing the intent of his words and blaming Ling for being overly sensitive and damaged. The situation quickly escalated into a major battle. Culturally it was not the norm for Ling to stand up to an elder like this, especially with an admonishing tone.

In a private session focused on agency, Ling and I walked through how to handle the situation by activating his agency rather than falling back on his old reactive patterns.

First, he considered the decision he needed to make: how to address his uncle having written a sexually inappropriate text and how to handle the situation with his girlfriend as well in a way that aligned with his purpose. He wanted to treat both people with respect while also respecting his need to set a boundary with his uncle. He knew he wanted to preserve his relationship with his uncle. But he also knew he needed to point out to him that their relationship had changed now that Ling was an adult. He would no longer allow lines to be crossed. Once he had some space from his reaction and recognized this purpose, Ling felt more grounded and confident.

He decided to contact his uncle again but from this place of agency. First, he consulted with his girlfriend to see what she needed and asked for her input on how to respond to his uncle. She appreciated him including her in the decision, and she didn't need anything beyond that.

So, Ling wrote his uncle an email that started with how much their relationship had meant to him over the years, especially when his father was absent. Ling acknowledged that his uncle had always had an edgy sense of humor and that he had never voiced concern about it previously. Ling also stated clearly that he remained concerned with the original group text message and reiterated that this kind of communication with him or his girlfriend was no longer something Ling wanted in their relationship. He requested that that sort of joking stop. He concluded his email to his uncle saying that he hoped they could repair things after this conflict and get back on track with clearer parameters around the relationship, now that he was a grown man and not just the younger nephew.

Ling was prepared for any outcome, prepared to live with the consequences of his decision. He accepted that his uncle had the right to respond however he wanted, whenever he wanted.

After seeing the email, his uncle picked up the phone and called Ling. He reciprocated by saying how much the relationship meant to him, owning up to the inappropriateness of the joke, and expressing some embarrassment about it all. He told Ling things felt better than ever, that he appreciated the open space to share how they felt and what they needed, and that he wouldn't repeat the mistake now that he understood Ling's needs. Ling knew that the call was good for both of them—agency is contagious; it opens doors.

Reflecting on the interaction, Ling still felt some discomfort in their relationship, but he felt at peace within himself because he knew he had acted in his integrity, and that's what mattered most. It built Ling's confidence in himself to work through steps 1 to 4, and the process allowed him a space to find his own terms and live them.

Ling accepted the consequences and trusted himself to deal with the ambiguity. Standing up to his uncle could have become a severing point for the relationship, or it could have been a blip on the radar. We all walk into every interaction with a load of baggage, varying needs and wants, lots of meaning-making, some personal agendas, and a whole universe of personality differences. Sometimes that all plays out in a millisecond. Other times the consequences of our actions are like a wildfire that starts in the underbrush, sweeps along slowly, and then suddenly bursts into raging flames. Even your own reactions can be hard to predict, especially when you are stressed. These five steps of agency give you the framework and space to take intentional action and foster a deeper responsibility for yourself.

A note: You may be feeling surprise or curiosity that some stories do not contain overt sexual acts and feel confused about why they are included. If so, remember this is due to our lack of education about the entirety of sexuality from a holistic lens. This is also because it is sometimes easier to understand a concept "outside of the bedroom" than in the heat of the moment. The wide range of stories that fall under holistic sexuality will get clearer and clearer to you as you progress through the pillars.

Empowerment Is Individual; Agency Is Relational

As I mentioned above, agency is contagious, and it's expansive. It usually begins with knowing you have a voice, a say in your life. When your voice conflicts with others', you develop the skill of navigating boundaries—your own and other people's. Working with the boundaries of others, you will grow in your ability to create your own boundaries. But both skills—navigating and creating boundaries—are complicated and take time to develop and become habitual. Boundaries are a baseline, a starting point. Not the end goal.

Eventually the skills of setting boundaries—with others and for yourself—and navigating them lead to two possible behaviors: *entitlement* or *empowerment*. Entitlement might look like demanding your partner take care of all their own emotional needs, because you need and deserve your space above all else, and judging them as needy and too much. Empowerment might look like negotiating space in the house to be alone once a week to make sure you get the mental and physical space you need with clear boundaries that serve your exclusive needs. In a monogamous relationship, entitlement could look like pouting, shaming, or blaming because you aren't getting "enough" sex from a partner without considering their needs, your contribution, or a partner-focused solution. Empowerment may look like emailing your partner an article you found online about how bad it feels to always be denied and only communicating from your perspective without an invitation to learn your partner's needs, wants, and perspectives.

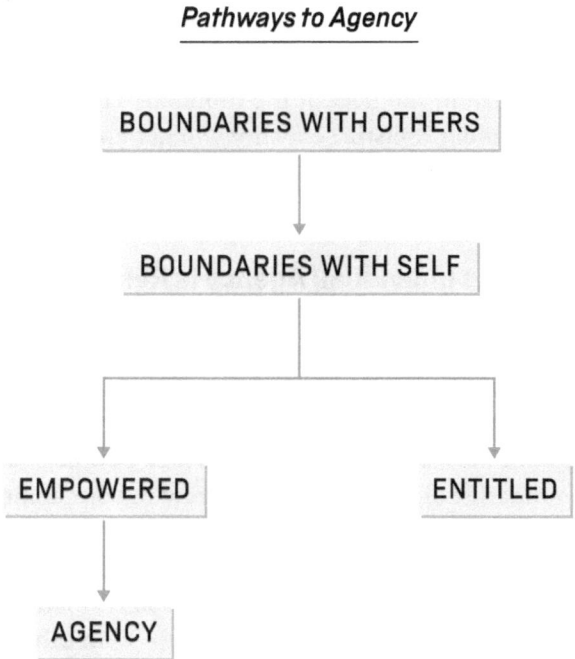

Pathways to Agency

You want to avoid entitlement. Entitlement is led by fear, anger, trauma, intolerance, and discomfort. All of us act entitled sometimes, and recognizing that in ourselves is harder than seeing it in others. Still, the goal when developing boundaries is to prevent yourself from getting entrenched in entitlement. Instead, see entitlement as a short detour toward or from empowerment, which is based in trust that you will stand up for and meet your needs. For many in the self-help sphere, empowerment is the critical goal. You find your voice, your needs, and your boundaries.

But my message to you is *don't rest in empowerment*. Don't bypass it, but do not accept it as the end goal. Because **empowerment is individual and agency is relational.** So, following on the example above, if empowerment looks like you negotiating space in your shared house, agency might look like you also agreeing that once a week, you'll make sacred time for a meaningful date that addresses your partner's need for devoted time together. Or going to your partner and asking to cocreate a sexual relationship that attempts to understand, honor, and meet both sets of needs. Agency understands that relationships are about recognizing our own needs and wants and the needs of the people we're in relationship with.

As I like to say to my clients: Boundaries are about *me*. Agency is about *we*. If your goal in life is to be relational (and this is the vast majority of us)—meaning we are connected with others—agency is the key. The most common pathway to agency starts with boundaries, especially as children. We know what we like, need, and don't like and need from others first. Then we learn how to hold boundaries with ourselves like, "I am not going to hug Aunt Maggie when I am told to in order to be polite, because she creeps me out." Next, we learn empowerment and/or entitlement, depending on our circumstances and experiences. The hope is that entitlement is a momentary lapse that we see as a reactive, problematic viewpoint rather than a long-term dominant decision-making philosophy. For some, though, entitlement is where the journey ends, and that's where we see the greatest degradation of connection. In the best case, one learns to be empowered instead, which then flows into agency. When you recognize that empowerment fails in conflict or when you're met with differing perspectives in a relationship, career, family, or community, either you activate agency or you can revert back to entitlement for a time. If you move through to agency, you come to understand that it affords you the opportunity to stay in connection with someone or to sever the connection if you deem it irrevocably harmful and unable to support agency. Agency considers the holistic perspective of the situation and equips you with the confidence to make the best decisions possible for you and the relationship. Agency requires boundaries with self and others, practices empowerment, and considers the complicated skill of being relational.

Keep the five steps of agency that I outlined above swirling inside your head and heart as you look at your own holistic sexual journey through the lens of sexual agency. Let this be the beginning of your lifelong journey with agency, as it has become mine.

The Feeling of Choice

When I was researching for my PhD beginning in 2004, I looked at ego and moral development, combined with sexual assertiveness, in college-aged women. My research uncovered that sexual agency, as I understand it and have shared with you, is not about the frequency of sex or the type of sex one has. Instead, it is about the feeling of choice.

That led me to examine the data with even greater scrutiny to determine in what ways I might help people feel more sexual agency, feel more in tune with their choices. I saw as a therapist that the touchpoints where choice was taken were the overarching places of unresolved conflict, pain, wounds, and traumas. When I asked people about their sexual decision-making, I quickly realized that although people think they know how to make decisions inside and outside the bedroom, in fact, they don't always. I discovered that if you want greater sexual fulfillment and well-being, you need to know how to make decisions.

Several important points related to sexual agency came out of my research.

- Many women feel sexuality "just happens to them" and is determined by external forces that society teaches us in a multifaceted way. Women are often seen as sexual gatekeepers and as people pleasers, and they frequently face sexual double standards. Women also understand that as a result they have been disempowered when defining their own sexual agency.

- In general, men are taught that they are in control of their sexuality and in charge of women's sexuality. Instinctively, however, this level of control doesn't feel right for most men—or for the women they are with when in heterosexual relationships.

- In their early years, people are not taught to explore, ascertain, or voice their sexual desires and needs. Rather than sex being something to enact, for many it simply happens. Instead of exploring their sexuality with other human beings, many adults feel they have been handed a sexual script that they passively repeat.

- Often people who identify as being from marginalized groups (for example, nonbinary, transgender, gay, lesbian, pansexual) are oversexualized, defined or viewed exclusively through a sexual lens, or they are left out of the sexual conversation entirely, with no sexual currency, relevancy, or rights.

The bottom line? Everyone has a birthright to agency, yet not everyone has the same entry point, ease in access, or room to activate it. Some can breeze through the entry point while others must squeeze their way into it. Once in agency, most describe the experience in similar terms. Peaceful. Grounded. A deep yes. Calm. Certain. Self-confidence and self-esteem correlate with your view of your choices in life. Sexuality isn't about sexual activity or experience or the lack of it; it is about your perception of your choices and your place in making decisions.

I've worked with individuals who have never had sexual penetration and were miserably unhappy with extremely low self-esteem. And I have worked with others who have never had sexual penetration and were profoundly happy and comfortable with themselves.

The difference? Choice and decision-making. Same goes for those with a vast history of sexual activity. Some were just fine with their number of partners and experiences, and others were ashamed and riddled with guilt. The difference was their perspective: Did they have decision-making power? Were they confident about their decisions, past and present? And were they comfortable with and able to foresee their access to choices in the future? Agency builds on itself. Self-knowledge (and authenticity) leads to choice and decision-making, which leads to self-confidence and trust in instinct, which leads to agency.

Agency Cycle

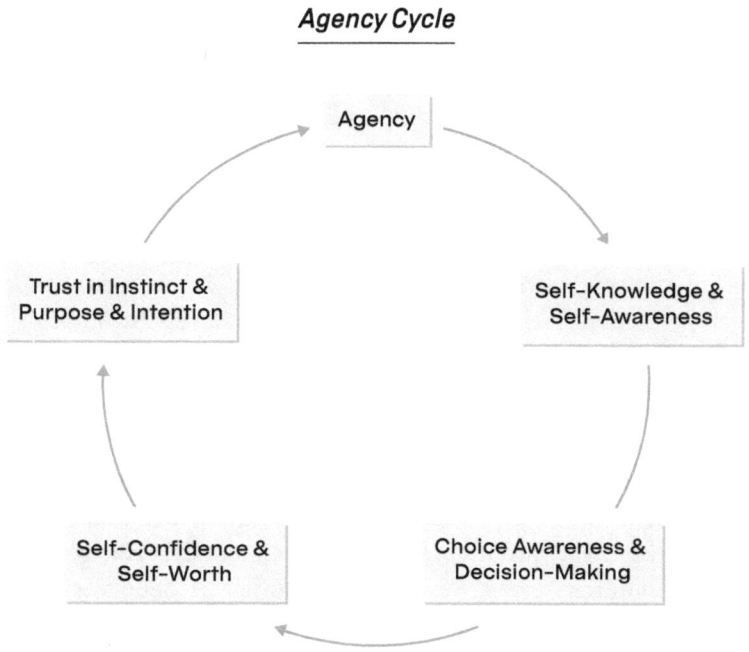

Juanita came to me to explore her confusion about her sexual orientation. She had had a few experiences with men, but none had felt natural or safe. She had had three committed sexual relationships with women. Intellectually, she thought she was likely a lesbian. But in her heart, she was uneasy. She grew up in a strict, religious family, and she knew they would not accept her as anything other than heterosexual. She had a lot of questions about her experiences, society, and what it all meant for her.

With these questions, we dove deep into agency because she wanted to know for herself who she was as a sexual being on her terms. Part of her work was to spend time expanding her self-pleasure practices, because we sensed it would lead to a release of deep shame that she carried about being sexual at all. She also left sticky notes offering agency-filled affirmations all over her kitchen cabinets. Releasing shame and embracing her own power of choice helped her be more accepting of her attraction to women. Her conclusion? She didn't need to know immediately who she was as a sexual being and didn't need to label herself. On each date, with each sexual possibility, she kept asking herself how she felt: Was it a yuck or a yum? Was it a yes or no? Was it a warm and safe feeling in her body or an abrupt, gut-clenching no? Having let go of her need for certainty, she embraced the fun of exploring. The more she stepped into her choice to explore, the more she deepened her self-knowledge.

Finding sexual agency is just one part of the journey of holistic sexuality, but it's a big step. Take me, for example: I once believed that when I reached the sexuality nirvana of agency, I would be so enlightened and evolved that bad things wouldn't happen anymore. That I would draw only healthy people toward me and I would have boundaries of steel. I thought this hard work would make my friendships perfect, my sex life boundless, and my marriage one that would inspire film scripts. While I do have some of those things, other aspects of that fantasy didn't happen.

My sexual agency didn't prevent me from having an important relationship with someone suffering from a debilitating porn addiction. But it did help me get back up again after being knocked down when a sex worker he hired contacted me because he had given her my website address. My self-agency didn't prevent a partner from breaking two of my ribs, but it did help me gather strength and resolve to get a restraining order and surround myself with people who would support me during our brutal breakup.

"Humaning is hard," as I often say to clients. Agency is not a seal of certain protection. It is not a guarantee that no harm will come to you. We have heard about how women in midlife must make an effort to protect their bones, to strengthen physically, and bolster their vitality—but even if you do so, it doesn't mean you won't end up with osteoporosis, a broken bone, or degeneration. You make those efforts for your present and future self. Further, what it *does* mean is that you've put in the time, effort, and work to ensure your foundation is sound, your ability to heal is supported, and your strength to endure is reinforced. The same is true with agency. It is a well of resiliency that allows you to carry through, that picks you up, that reminds you of who you are, and that gives you hope. Agency changes your experience of what is difficult and what is good. If I hadn't done this work, I wouldn't have made it through the hardest of times. And I say that boldly, with somberness and heft.

Sexual Healing

Saying that agency can help you to heal from past wounds is a strong assertion. What I have seen is that although you cannot change the past, with time, distance, and growth, you are afforded an opportunity to make a different meaning out of it and to create a new relationship with it. This is not about toxic positivity or asking you to find silver linings in the worst of situations. However, agency can help you heal places that are still tender and sore by giving you choice about what to do with the memories and how you interpret your actions. You can find a different angle on the experience and, most importantly, where you place it in the here and now. Agency, as a healer, gives you a safe harbor to do a 360-degree review of the pain point.

I also see agency as a protector. It gives out a "no more" energy. Agency can help you feel less vulnerable when you see your behavioral patterns illuminated, and it can buoy you when you move to change a pattern, behavior, or relationship that no longer serves you.

The power of agency within the context of sexuality explodes exponentially. The dynamic energy of sexuality and the vastness of expression and experiences make it the hardest place to enact agency—and the most important place to do so.

Li, a college student, came to me having experienced rape the previous year by someone she used to date. She was angry and defensive, and the trauma had coaxed her into a place of empowerment as a protective mechanism—she didn't want connection. Li had made up her mind that she was never going to be in a relationship again; she was going to be a political activist, use violence if necessary to protect herself; and she chose self-pleasure as her source of healing. I met her in this place, listened to her anger and grief, understood why she was using empowerment as a practice to disconnect, and slowly introduced the concept of agency as it relates to holistic sexuality in our work together. I presented it as a concept that could be both healing retroactively and protective in the future. I told her it was a way to regain control and well... agency in the past situation. She didn't like it at first. To her, it felt like she was doing all the work, not the offender, and that there wasn't any justice. It felt offensive to her, but she was open to the concept through the gateway of regaining control. She softened as she felt safe in a space to explore and activate her agency in ways big and small. She rediscovered pieces of herself that she had hidden for protection and abandoned in her grief and anger. Working with her agency, Li grew in confidence in both herself and the world, recognizing that connection is crucial to being human and that agency was the missing piece she needed to reframe her past, present, and future.

Samuel, a past Revealed course participant, was an unpartnered gay cisgender male. He had never been able to understand himself as a sensual being, but he hadn't been able to put words to it until Revealed identified it for him. In order to be a better partner to future lovers, he sought out workshops and retreats that would help him discover his yeses and nos within his senses. With his new learnings, he became empowered with his knowledge: He knew he wanted a change, he took charge and opened his perspectives, and he got a clear picture of his wants and needs. This allowed him to live more in the moment and feel less anxious about future relationships. As he remained single and experienced sexual connection with various partners, Samuel used what he had learned through his curiosity and exploration to inquire about his partner's sensuality—what they liked and needed—and practiced the skill of meeting in connection, both when needs and wants lined up and when they didn't. He didn't just succumb to the needs of his partners, and they didn't just succumb to his; together, they were able to develop thriving, fun, sexy, and agency-filled experiences that had a deep and lasting impact. Learning the skill in a sexual context allowed Samuel to begin to see how agency, once enacted sexually, can be much more easily applied to every aspect of life.

Sovereignty Is Powerful

Sexuality shouldn't "happen to you." I want you to feel you have a say in and be empowered by your own sexuality, to have agency in your sexual development. Once you own your sexuality, everything feels possible: You feel safer, a different confidence, and hopeful about your future. And then you can really start kicking ass because you are living your life on your terms. Sovereignty is powerful.

When you have fully actualized sexual agency, you make decisions from a centered place, a place of self-direction, and you are no longer swayed by outside forces, whether those forces are the media, family proclamations, religious tenets, propaganda, or fear of judgment, rejection, or loneliness. Agency-driven decisions are better decisions—better decisions that are essence-based, aligned with your purpose, and for your future self. When you begin accumulating experiences built on agency-driven decisions, you build confidence and feel safer in the world. Deepened safety helps you to access agency. Your sexual agency does not take power away from others. Instead, you define things for yourself. And almost magically, in that process of self-awareness, you support others so they can create agency for themselves.

You cannot force agency on others, but you can provide room and opportunity to others you engage with sexually to be their best sexual selves as well. This mutual or shared agency disrupts today's culture of hurting each other. Shared sexual agency provides a protective layer against the media's and politics' pernicious influence. Believe me, when an individual stands in their own authentic, honest, accountable certainty, the world changes. When someone feels safe because they feel connected with their agency and are operating in relationships and situations where agency is the baseline, the world transforms.

Because when you feel safe enough to be "me," you can expand to the safety of "we."

Further, a person living in sexual agency doesn't have the need or motive to judge others, and they understand that each of us has our own journey and path. They know they need to focus on their own healing, exploration, and expansion instead of trying to control or harm others through judgment, shame, and punishment. Oppression, hate, bigotry, and discrimination are not and never will be a part of agency—there's a zero tolerance policy here.

Now, shit happens. Life isn't easy. When you are dealing with humans, a measure of unpredictability plays into all your interactions. Sadly, the most fully actualized person can be raped or stay in a relationship that isn't good for them or experience other tragedies. Self-agency doesn't fully prevent the harm and consequences of not having a culture of agency, unfortunately. It does, however, change our healing journey and inner experience when you have well-developed and practiced agency. Bluntly, we don't live in an agency-filled world, and sometimes agency is not enough to protect you when you're faced with politically motivated oppression or individual aggression. However, you can have a sexual life led by a strong inner compass, knowing it was built and oiled by your own terms and values; you can be confident those values were not merely inherited but chosen with purpose and intent.

If I hadn't figured out who I am and grounded myself in sexual agency, I would not have been fortified to withstand the challenging times I've endured with grace and resiliency. Now, I'm not saying I didn't have moments on my knees or times that I doubted myself or interactions when I acted like a crazed asshole. I have made choices that didn't serve me. I still get triggered by entitlement. I'm human. We also have the choice *not* to activate our agency. I may not always act in agency, but I know how to move to it more quickly now. I know the warning signs when I am not in agency. I know agency requires continual work. Learning isn't a one time thing. It requires continual attention because of its interaction with all areas of our life and our sexuality. A constant engagement with agency has to be prioritized, and that doesn't scare me anymore because I know the benefits of it. There may be times when my access to agency requires more work than I would prefer, but on the whole, my relationship with agency excites me and allows me to grow.

And I want that for you.

Agency is the skill you access in self-reflection, in healing, and in planning and protecting your future. And because agency fuels, feeds, and flows through holistic sexuality, it shows up constantly throughout the nine pillars.

In part 2, we move from unpacking the problems with our sexuality education and culture and learning the fundamentals of agency toward the substance of holistic sexuality. We are moving from a global outlook to zoom into you and your journey behind you and ahead of you as well as the here and now of your life. The education I am offering to you is an education *on* you. This is the work I suggest you do *before* you get into the sex tips and concrete sex facts. This is independent soul work: introspective reflections on who you are, what you have experienced, and where you want to head in your sexual journey as a sexual being.

At the end of each pillar chapter, look for the self-reflection prompts, which can be used as a catalyst for introspection—either kept to your thoughts, discussed with others, or written in a journal. You will see "sexercises" offered to help put your thoughts into actions. You will also see QR codes, which will lead you to a multimedia collection of additional stories that exemplify the community and movement aspects of Revealed. Some pillars are longer, some are shorter; they vary in content and tone, and each has been crafted to ensure you connect deeply with the concepts—no two pillars are alike. As a reminder, all stories that involve others have had identifying details changed; they may contain information that is shocking in wording or detail and may trigger you. Take care of yourself as you progress through the pillars. Stories from your life will appear, align, bump up against, and be vocal as you read my own stories and my clients' stories. Stay curious, have fun, and laugh at the stories ahead too. We're moving from the thirty-thousand-foot view to the microscopic. Let's start with the pillar of sensuality, which is the first of my nine pillars of holistic sexuality.

PART TWO

NINE PILLARS OF HOLISTIC SEXUALITY

Where Agency Comes Alive

PILLAR 1
Sensuality

SENSUALITY IS the first pillar in holistic sexuality. Sensuality is all about pursuing, noticing, experiencing, and expressing the physicality of your body's senses. Sensuality means being aware of the embodiment of our senses. Your sensuality can be experienced as pleasure or at other times as unenjoyable. "Sensual" is often erroneously seen as synonymous with "sexual." Yes, the two are related, but they are not the same thing. You can be a sensual person and not sexual. You can be sexual and not sensual.

Sensuality connects your mind, body, and spirit, but it is different from your intellect and soul. It includes bodily or sensory pleasure, which is not necessarily sexual, even when viewed holistically, but it is crucial to your sexuality.

Your sensuality refers to the five senses—sight, taste, hearing, touch, and smell—and your access to, experience with, and expression of each of them. Sensuality also focuses on the ways in which each sense individually and collectively ties you to or removes you from the present moment. The five senses provide you with valuable information, and you need a keen sense of presence to be tuned into them. Sensuality is a key component of holistic sexuality because it is a gateway to mindfulness. And mindfulness is a pathway to accessing your essence. As you will discover, sensuality

Your senses
are a gateway to
pleasure.

is closely related to pleasure and can be a powerful connector to presence as well.

Your five senses awaken your body. So, examining what you like and don't like, what turns you on and what doesn't, is important. We all have sensual styles, just as we have personality types and learning styles. For example, one person may feel pleasure only with an intense, rough sexual partner, while another may be completely turned off by rough sex but get excited through a gentler, teasing approach or through humor. One sexual partner may love the taste of someone's genitals, but a subsequent lover may find the taste distracting. Sensuality can be the ultimate connection or a barrier to sexual compatibility, attraction, arousal, and desire.

I invite you to redefine your concept of and relationship with sensuality. Here, you are presented the opportunity to go all in on the concept of holistic sexuality. I hope this pillar inspires you to want to learn more about yourself and explore a bit about how it feels to have sexual agency, deciding and learning for yourself. Be open to the idea that your curiosity may become a craving. Sensuality is critical to core connection and is a powerful force to employ and explore when looking to reconnect to your own sexual energy or enhance it with a sexual partner.

Making Sense of Sensuality

Not everyone has access to all five senses or full access to all senses. If that is true for you, your sensual self is not diminished. These are simply details about who you are as a sensual being. All of us have a sensory style and formula. You will have senses that dominate and are comfortable to you, senses that seem foreign and blunted, senses that you've ignored, and senses that propel you into other orbits. This pillar asks you to open to a sense reformulation, an awakening of new parts of your senses, and a shift within your understanding of what it means for you to be a sensual person.

When I first considered my sensual life and my own relationship with my sensuality, I felt like I was on an awkward blind date. I could not have felt more out of touch with who I was as a sensual being. I also considered sensuality only within the context of sex with someone else. I didn't understand that sensuality was a lifestyle. It was everywhere in my life, an internal and external part of me.

I once met a woman in Bali who exuded what I thought was the only way to be sensual. Her flowing clothes, her wild hair, the way she walked, the soft tone of her voice—her sensuality was reflected in the air and lightness of her being, her yogic vibe, her floral-print caftan. I felt simultaneously in awe of and attracted to this woman's verve. But I didn't live in Bali nor did I have her vibe. My hair was naturally curly but blown out and coifed, and I typically dressed in jeans and collared shirts.

The punchline? "Sensual" was not me.

At that point, my sexuality was still largely performative (remember that cringey seduction scene from my acting class with Kristi?), and if I got wild and crazy in bed, it was often after drinking, so my inhibitions were lowered but my senses were dulled. I felt uncomfortable with eye contact and closed my eyes a lot when experiencing sexual pleasure. Essentially, I did not know how to stay in my senses consistently. I loved music, but I didn't understand my holistic body and soul response to it. I just knew that I responded well to it. I considered food to be for health and family-bonding time rather than for pleasure or enrichment. In my home growing up, we didn't hug much, and I was touch-starved until I was in college.

I wanted to change this lack of mind-body-soul connection, so I embarked on a journey to find out who I was as a sensual being. I didn't want to mimic the woman from Bali—I wanted to discover my own sensual self. My approach was to focus on one sense at a time and ask questions of myself: What do I like? What do I not like? What turns me on? What does not turn me on? When embarking on a journey like this, an experience where you can really immerse yourself can help. I chose to attend a retreat at the Chopra Center.

The retreat focused on Ayurvedic medicine and philosophy, connecting the mind, body, and spirit in teaching and experience. One of those experiences was silent lunch. I walked into that first silent lunch with a huge plate of salad. Let me tell you, that lettuce was the crispiest lettuce of my life! Never had I been so acutely aware of eating, of the taste of lettuce, the salad dressing, and the sunflower seeds. Before this silent lunch, I had never noticed the tang of a fork's metal or the deafening crunch of fresh lettuce. Wow. I wanted to apologize for the noise. With each bite, I felt I needed to atone for breaking the silence. But as I got used to the absence of speech, I started enjoying the taste of my food, and I found I absolutely loved the experience. I loved eating in silence and relishing each and every bite.

Once I was exposed to the concept of purposefully exploring all of the senses, my sexual experiences leveled up. I knew how to find pleasure through my senses, how to stay embodied and present-minded during sexual connection, and I learned the importance of knowing my yucks and yums, communicating them with my partner, and eliciting the same information from my partner.

What Is Your Sensuality Style?

Earlier I mentioned that each of us has a different style when it comes to sensuality. I naturally like touch. I am a hugger. I love holding hands with my kids and loved ones, I sit close to my dear friends, and I love massages—that is, when I am feeling connected and good. When I am angry, I typically do not want to be touched at all. And if I feel sad, sometimes I want to be held, and other times I just want someone close physically but not touching me. I've learned to explain this difference to intimate partners and those in my inner circle.

The skin is our largest sensory organ, and so touch is considered the first sense we acquire. Touch matters. So does a lack of touch. One aspect of touch is skin hunger, which is the longing, aching, or desire for physical contact with another person. My favorite way to satiate the sensation of skin hunger is having my hair brushed and played with. I love it. Well, I crave it. I've joked that I would pay to have someone brush my hair for fifteen minutes every night. I also playfully blame my mother for this, because she would play with my hair for the whole sermon every Sunday. It was heavenly. In my youth, I usually zoned out during the sermon, but I loved her playing with my hair as I nestled into her lap. That touch is associated with safety and nurturing. I love a firm bristle and a solid contact with my scalp. I love having my hair pulled into a loose ponytail and having the base of my neck brushed with even pressure. I've had partners brush my hair, and that experience often proved to be such peaceful times of safe connection for us. I also love having my hair played with and pulled during sexual connection. The sensation of excitement it brings me is instantaneous, if done correctly—a slow gathering of my hair together and a gentle and assertive pulling that slowly draws my head back. Yes, please. Yum.

The way I describe having my hair brushed may sound completely bizarre to you. Maybe you can't relate or you think I am a little too into it. That's okay. That doesn't yuck my yum. I know there is a sensation that is equally as satisfying and wonderful for you. Yucks are as valuable and wanted as yums. This may be a yuck for you, but you'll have *your* yum.

A partner of mine felt this way about back scratching. He loved it lightly on his back and would go into another realm when I did it. He loved to be scratched on his scalp so forcefully I feared I would draw blood as he directed me to go harder. It was perfect for him. He loved back scratching as a form of connection and fulfillment and at choice times during sexual connection. He loved a soft brushing over his thighs while making love and over the small of his back and top of his ass right after.

In a different way, I find pleasure in my touch sense with water. I love baths, specifically jetted baths and hot tubs, and I prefer the water pressure in my shower to be like a fire hose. I recently had my shower head changed to one with more pressure, and the quality of my life improved dramatically. Such a small thing, but it made my shower pleasure-filled and fully embodied.

Maybe your sensuality style is all about sight. I had a dear friend for whom time stood still when he saw a sunset. He would be mesmerized and stop talking. Sunsets got his sensuality juices flowing. When he described a sunset, he looked as if he was seeing the sunset at that moment. He even incorporated them into his glass art. Sight was the sense that he accessed most easily, even though his art required the finesse of physical touch.

But what happens when you are disconnected from your sensuality?

Malia was a cisgender woman who went through my Revealed program individually with me. A lovely, measured, and quiet person, Malia needed time to build trust in me before she felt comfortable sharing information about her concerns. She often tackled emotionally heavy matters with emotional detachment.

Malia had come to me for help in finding a way to enjoy sex with her long-term boyfriend. He enjoyed long-lasting, emotionally connected experiences. She preferred short, get-to-the-point sexual connection. After their sexual encounters, she was left feeling inadequate or as if there were something wrong with her. During the couples therapy that I'd done previously with Malia and her partner, it became clear that he believed a fairly pervasive myth in our contemporary culture: If you don't love foreplay or don't want sex to last for hours on end, it means you're not sensual; you must have a block or be closed down, and this needs to be "fixed." His attitude was that he was right and she was wrong. From my standpoint, that attitude is not okay. If we discover there is a block, then yes, we'll work on it. But I don't operate under the assumption that everyone's needs are the same or that there is a right or wrong.

What struck me about Malia's story was that although her partner saw her as fairly vanilla and even boring in the bedroom, she had tried almost everything I could think of. She was adventurous and assured me, "I'll try anything once." This suggested she wasn't blocked or inhibited; she had explored enough to know what she liked and didn't like. Her list of tried sex acts was anything but boring, and I've been exposed to a wide range of people's lists of sex acts.

Malia felt a particular resistance to the topic of sensuality. She rebuked the notion that she was a sensual woman. Intellectually, she understood she was sensual because she experienced the world through five senses, but she was adamant that as a detail-oriented, no-nonsense, emotionally reserved person, the word "sensual" was not on the list of adjectives to describe her. Still, she was up for exploring each of the senses, finding out what turned her on and off, what lit her up and what didn't. Gradually I saw brief glimpses of a softening in her stance. Malia gravitated to the sense of touch and so we began to explore various textures in pursuit of her yeses and nos, her yucks and yums.

The homework I gave her at the end of one session was to find five types of fabric or other surfaces to touch. Malia found that she had plenty of things that didn't work for her. For example, she hated velvet, a go-to for many people. Instead, she liked hemp and denim, and she giggled as she reported that sandpaper was surprisingly hot. But then she found a texture that "took her to another world." Sheepskin—that soft, plush natural fabric that she had in her closet (a vest) and on her floor (a rug) but had never paid much attention to before. She loved the feel on her bare skin. She couldn't get enough of it. She ended up getting sheepskin covers for her car seats. As she sat on them all the way to work, the sheepskin both soothed her and turned her on.

Not long after this discovery, she came to our session bubbly and talkative. She could not wait to share her new self-knowledge. Through her exploration of sensuality, Malia experienced a revelation: "There's nothing wrong with me. What pleases me is just different than what pleases my partner." The flint hit the rock. Spark.

Now Malia could tell herself, "I'm going to get pleasure in my life through my senses. But I'm going to get it on my own terms." As part of her exploration of holistic sexuality, we talked about the fact that her experience of sensuality need not happen only in the bedroom or in the context of sex. She could embody sensuality throughout her daily life, where she was free to explore and would always be fully in control of her yeses and nos.

She also began to remember that she'd had partners in the past who enjoyed the same style of sex that she did, with minimal foreplay and a let's-get-to-it approach. Malia had become so enmeshed in her current partner's needs that she had forgotten a time when she didn't feel wrong or broken during sex. She no longer felt like a lesser or not fully realized sexual being just because she didn't subscribe to the dominant view of what being a sensual woman means.

Sensuality proved to be Malia's gateway to agency. Ultimately, what she learned about herself gave her and her partner the courage to end their relationship so that they could both seek a more compatible one. Neither was wrong in their needs; they just weren't well matched. And so her journey continues—only now she's in the sheepskin-covered driver's seat.

Sensuality Is Mindfulness

Sensuality is one of two pillars of holistic sexuality that demand you stay in the present moment. The other is pleasure. Exploring who you are as a sensual being can happen as a solo experience or with other people, but it needs to be explored with purpose and mindfulness. You need to be fully present in your body to connect your mind, body, and soul. Here's how that can work.

I dated a man who was a wonderful sexual partner to explore sensuality with in creative and fun ways. We set a safe atmosphere for our sexual connection easily, and that made for consistency in our creativity. I wanted us to try some new tantra exercises I had learned. We had a long-distance relationship so there was often a lot of buildup between our visits. I wanted our next night together to be focused on our sensuality, particularly our sensual connection as a couple. I thought about what each of us liked and didn't like within our senses, as individuals and together. The night aligned with a sleepover for my daughter, so my home was a safe zone for us to focus on our pleasure and connection. I wanted to make this exploration a special experience for us as a couple, a way for us to learn more about each other, so we could pick and choose what we wanted more or less of.

On the night, I set the stage by dimming the lights all over the house and lighting unscented candles. I knew the outfits he liked to see me in and put my favorite one on. Music was an enormous connector for us, so I made a playlist of songs that would be pleasurable for us to listen to: songs we had sung together in the car, had fun dancing to in my kitchen, heard at a concert we bonded over, or songs we had listened to while making passionate love. I arranged the playlist to allow us time to talk and hug and reconnect after spending time apart. And I had a separate playlist to use as a backdrop for when the touch portion of our sensual connection heated up.

Next, I incorporated taste. We didn't find a lot of pleasure incorporating food into our sexual connections so I didn't plan for that. He loved bourbon so I left the door unlocked and poured a glass of prized bourbon over ice. I propped a note against the glass inviting him into the space upstairs where I was waiting to give him a feel for what was in store for us that evening. I don't love the taste of bourbon in his mouth, but he loves it so much I knew the pleasure it would bring him would be worth my lukewarm reaction to it. I poured a glass of wine I loved and took purposeful and mindful sips as I waited his arrival. I wore my favorite perfume to enliven my sense of smell. And I sprayed a scent he liked over the stairwell when I knew he was close to arriving.

The main focus of this evening was touch. I invited him to join me in getting comfortable in fewer clothes, and we sat knee to knee on my fluffy rug. I love this rug so much as it reminds me of a cherished trip I took to Morocco where I bought it. I was thinking about the trip while we were sitting together; I felt safe, deeply comfortable, and present.

We started eye-gazing, which took a little time for us to sink into. We laughed a little, got lost in it a little. We came out of it and got back into it. We would stop to take a sip. It felt powerful to have our knees touching but nothing else. At last, we sank into each other's eyes and held the gaze for quite some time. It was amazing to stare at each other's faces, to let other things go, to still my thoughts, to smile, to tear up, to feel deep love.

When we both felt the meditation time end, we simply held each other. It was quite beautiful. We moved to my bed. We sat knee to knee again and began exploring touch. I went first, massaging his hands and forearms. Then we switched roles, and he massaged my hands and forearms. As time passed, we found a wonderful rhythm of giving and receiving touch, moving from our arms to the crown of our heads.

I had him lay down and tried a new breathing exercise that involved me putting my hand on his chest and checked in with what resonated and what didn't. I appreciated how open he was to receiving, and I was intensely enjoying exploring this new exercise with him. I loved watching his face, seeing the flicker of the candle, tasting the faint hint of red wine on my tongue. I loved catching him stealing glimpses of my body as I moved over him. We switched positions, and he tried it on me. I have a history of struggling to accept the receiving end of experiences like this, but I was so in touch with my senses and in safety with him that I could get out of my head and into the moment. I stopped hearing the music and focused on his touch, the closeness of his face to mine, the way his weight shifted me toward him on the mattress.

I was blissfully present-minded and in soulful connection with him. Our connection when we experienced this sensual night together was extraordinary for us, because we were so completely and utterly present, soaking in our senses, reveling in our differences and commonalities, and the world melted away.

Minimal alcohol was involved and it was not used to escape, as I had done in my youth. If you had described this scene to me twenty years ago, no doubt I would have rolled my eyes and scoffed at wanting anything like it. I wouldn't have believed I could enjoy making my and my partner's sensual life a priority, sacred and fun, and not being afraid to try new things.

You don't need a whole night constructed with sensual purpose to experience the benefit of sensuality. Simply paying close attention to your breathing can improve your sensual connection. My colleague Barbara Carrellas wrote a groundbreaking book called *Urban Tantra* that brilliantly teaches breathing as a sensual and spiritual awakening. It can be experienced with a powerful playlist or lying on an intentionally chosen fabric, but ultimately it focuses on embodiment and energy as a conduit of senses. Check her work out.

SEXERCISE: Exploring Sensuality Through Touch

To develop more agency in this pillar, explore your sensuality through four types of touch. **Water** is a light to medium touch with movement to it, mimicking a babbling brook. **Air** is an extremely light touch that skims the surface of the skin with slow movement. The touch is so light that if their eyes are closed, the receiver may feel the energy of the other person but not necessarily the physical touch of skin to skin. **Earth** is a firm touch that indents the skin with smooth, consistent, deep pressure—similar to kneading out knots—or slow, deep strokes. **Fire** is rapid, unexpected touches to the skin like slapping, pinching, and tickling.

1. Start on your forearm. Try each type of touch on your skin between your hand and elbow if you have access to this body part. If not, try your head, back, leg, or foot. If you cannot do the touching yourself, ask a trusted person to try it on your body.

2. Ask yourself, How does my body react? What are my thoughts about and responses to each touch? Which touch do I prefer? What touch do I not enjoy?

3. Decide: What were yucks? What were yums?

4. Note your responses in a journal.

If you enjoy this exercise on your arm, move to other body parts, such as your head, legs, back, feet, hands, and genitals.

Your Sensual Awakening

Your sensual awakening will differ from everyone else's, and I promise you that this will be an exciting and fascinating exploration. You cannot, however, move into an expanded holistic sexuality without incorporating a heightened awareness of your senses into a daily practice inside and outside sexual connection.

There are so many things to discover about your sensual self. Many delightful surprises are waiting for you. Learn what you love. Allow your senses to keep you centered and connected within yourself and/or with a lover (or lovers). Communicate what you know about your senses and be open to learning more about each of them. And if you have a partner, find out the needs and loves and dislikes connected to your partner's senses.

Sensuality allows us to become more mindful gently and over time, which connects us to our essence and keeps us in our bodies. Each of these characteristics enhances our sexual fulfillment.

Having explored our bodies through the senses, we move to the next pillar, wellness and fertility, and we will examine our bodies from a different vantage point.

REVEAL YOURSELF TO YOURSELF

- What is your current relationship to sensuality, inside and outside sexual contact?
- Which dominant sense of yours might have clear yucks and yums?
- Identify someone you would describe as a sensual person. What is it about this person that makes you think of them as sensual?
- How might you incorporate sense more purposefully and intentionally in your daily life?
- Is there a particular sense you would like to explore further within sexual connection?
- Describe your unique brand of sensuality.
- What agency can you activate within sensuality?

PILLAR 2
Wellness and Fertility

MY MENTOR, Betty Dodson, profoundly impacted my life and continues to be in my ear even since her passing in 2021. She was brazen, cutting-edge, opinionated, colorful, and incredibly present for and tuned into me. She created a consciousness-raising workshop called Bodysex®; I attended several of them and eventually became a certified Bodysex facilitator. The premise of the Bodysex circle is to reduce shame, to promote self-awareness, and to educate vulva owners about pleasure and the importance of self-pleasure... and everyone in attendance is fully naked. While attending a naked workshop isn't a requirement to get an A+ in the wellness and fertility pillar, I *do* hope that my story will inspire your own growth and transformation within this topic.

The first time I attended a Bodysex circle in Betty's Madison Avenue apartment, I was nervous about being naked. One aspect of the workshop that was particularly profound the first time was the genital show-and-tell. Betty had a purposeful process with a mirror and a light. She presented us with her genitals as we sat around her in a semicircle. She showed us her labia and her urethral opening. She pointed out how her anatomy had aged and what she felt self-conscious about. For her, it was that her inner labia were asymmetrical (a common occurrence), and she felt embarrassed about

Sexual health is about so much more than *p*'s and *v*'s.

this because early in her childhood she erroneously convinced herself it was a defect caused by her self-pleasuring. After Betty had gone through the show-and-tell, each of us volunteered to sit in the light for our own genital show-and-tell.

When it came time for me to show and tell, I was shocked by how hard it was for me to open my legs. As I sat next to Betty, she was patient. She alternately asked me to name what was going on and made light of my resistance. I wanted to do it but was terrified to embrace the experience. My professional work within the sexuality space was through verbal teaching. We talked about it; we talked *through* it. We didn't *do* it; we didn't get *physically personal*. In fact, mental health professionals are taught that this is strictly harmful and unethical. The realization was dawning on me, though, that this kind of show-and-tell was such a missing piece and quite needed. I also realized I was bumping up against a foreign context of interacting with my genitals outside a sexual or medical context. I had no name for this context. Self-knowledge?

With hesitation and some fear, I finally opened my legs. I wanted to know. I wanted to nudge myself to take a risk, knowing Betty and this circle of amazing women were safe.

Even though I was in my forties, sexually active for many years, the mother of two kids, a well-known sex educator and therapist doing work in this space globally, and had had many medical professionals see my genitals during appointments, this moment felt wildly different. I was showing my vulva outside sexual connection, and Betty was walking me through my genitals like no medical provider had ever done. I was surprised I didn't know how some of my anatomy looked (what my urethral opening looked like) or how some parts were in proportion to one another (how far my clitoral glans was from my urethral opening). New fears emerged. I felt worried that my vulva wouldn't be pretty like some of the others. Were my inner lips too long? Maybe so after seeing the others. I wasn't sure the color of my genitals was right, because others had a more vibrant color palette and I liked their look better. These are thoughts I had *never* been conscious of before this experience.

With my legs apart, staring across the room at her mantlepiece lined with an array of dildos standing on end, Betty started complimenting me, which she did for each of us who shared. I was hyperfocused on the nuances of everyone's facial expressions as the group watched me. Basically, I was a mess and couldn't believe how hard it was for me to sit with my legs open, seeing others see me and seeing myself see me and taking it all in. Betty had a powerful way of guiding you to a place of safety and normalcy during this anything-but-normal experience. With her witty repartee and subtle tenderness, I relaxed, got curious, and became more comfortable so I could take advantage of the personalized anatomy lesson. Where else will a group of people applaud for your genitals and genuinely create an atmosphere of warmth and support when you are in such a vulnerable state? And of course, Betty was irreverent, whispering dirty jokes to me to get me out of my head. She gave me such a soulful hug and nod of approval for my bravery that I recalled the reason I flew to New York City in the first place.

Many Bodysex circles later, the genital show-and-tell is completely ease-filled for me—and the memory of that first time is still potent. I've also witnessed many other women process the experience in a wide variety of ways with one common thread—positive transformation. Outside the immense psychological benefits, I left that first workshop marveling with the change in my body awareness. I gained a thorough understanding of my vulva and inner reproductive and sexual system, as well as a passion to encourage others to learn this about themselves too. I also faced a realization that there is a limit to where talk therapy can reach in some topics and challenges. Understanding your anatomy in this way is not just a weird thing that only a sex educator should experience. What Betty gave me in her Bodysex circle is for all of us: self-knowledge. To learn about your anatomy, you can attend a Bodysex circle facilitated by a certified leader, do a self-exploration, or you can ask a trusted and sex-positive medical provider to review your anatomy in detail with you, regardless of what body parts you have. We all have a right, and frankly a responsibility, to understand our anatomy.

IN THIS PILLAR, we're going to explore your relationship to your physical body. The wellness and fertility pillar focuses on our attitudes and behaviors related to reproduction, the wellness of the sexual and reproductive systems, and the health consequences of sexual behavior.

The Secret Porn Shed and Other Forms of Sex Ed

All of us have had some sort of informal sex education. You may have learned things from your best friend down the street whose older sibling spilled the tea to you. You might have found articles on the internet. You may have walked in on your parents having sex or seen sex acts in a movie. Your education may be exclusively through pornography. Maybe you saw a pamphlet in a doctor's office, or a medical provider told you a few things when you asked a sexual wellness question. Or perhaps you heard something on the news about legislation that restricted or protected reproductive rights. Bottom line is that you've absorbed information about health and reproductive topics through multiple avenues.

The informal education we have access to varies as does our formalized sex education. As explored in part 1, the sex education system in the United States is broken. Depending on which state you live in, you may get a few hours of highly curated sex education that reflects a heteronormative, relationship-focused, one-kind-of-sex, fear-based, and abstinence-is-best curriculum. This curriculum too frequently omits so much that you need to know about your body, other bodies, and the differences between biology and gender. For clarity, biology refers to anatomy—the physical traits you were born with—such as a penis and testicles, a vulva and ovaries and a uterus, or a mix of these parts. Gender is a social construct spectrum of a person's internal identity and how they express it externally from a binary or nonbinary viewpoint. Most of the terminology in this pillar will be referring to biology rather than gender.

Most, but not all, public sex education globally falls in a similar place as the United States in terms of its inadequacy and focuses mainly on health and reproductive matters. The general line is that female bodies were made to make babies and awful things happen to their bodies if they do anything outside marriage and procreation. Discussions in class or with family tend to boil down to "This is good. This is bad. These are the rules. This is off-limits. This is shameful. This is what is right. This is what is wrong. These are the bad things that happen as a result of sex. Oh, and there is a penis and a vagina, and that's it."

I am tempted to tell you that having no education at all would be better. There would be so much less to unlearn: "Look at this terrible thing that will happen to your dick if you do this. And this dramatic, scary thing is going to happen to your body when you hit puberty. Sex will be painful; it is for reproduction only; self-pleasure is not a necessary part of your sexual self. Sex is bad before marriage and magically good after the ceremony."

By the end of it, you might feel shamed into a black hole because your body isn't the "right" sexual body, and what you are doing or thinking of doing with it isn't "right" either. Good luck feeling your sexuality is healthy after all that.

Study after study shows that fear-based education, whatever it's about, doesn't work. Yet society continues to think that if we give people condoms, they will have sex. And if we scare them, they will not want to have sex. Nope. It doesn't work like that for the vast majority. In fact, when kids and adults are fully educated and armed with information that is pleasure-focused, factual, and inclusive, they are more likely to make informed, agency-based decisions. A fear-based introduction to health and wellness is entirely and profoundly damaging. People are already often afraid of seeking medical help. Add a bunch of stigma around sex and sexual wellness into the mix, and the resistance to seeking support can increase exponentially. It begins with embarrassment and extends to avoidant fear.

If you feel under- or miseducated about sex, you are not alone. You are among many who weren't given correct health and reproductive education in school; with each changing political administration and from generation to generation, improperly educated people are raising more improperly educated people. This is a systematic, societal, intergenerational, and global problem.

We have already talked about how, currently in the medical community, even those who directly work in sexual health fields do not have to take one class on sexuality to graduate. In the mental health space, most programs and licenses do not require a sexuality class, and if they do, it is just one class that is not standardized. So, medical and mental health providers aren't educated properly, and those we trust to care for our sexual health and wellness are often not personally or professionally trained either, unless you know of and have access to a rare specialist in the sexuality field.

Instead, we have heaps of people walking around guessing shit, "shoulding" all over each other, and secretly consulting Dr. Google or Professor Instagram on most things. Now, I am happy that the internet, AI, and some social media offer access to a more robust, positive, and life-affirming sex education. But we don't all have the same access, and not all information online is accurate or without bias and censorship.

The health and wellness pillar holds an important place in holistic sexuality. Understanding the names and complexities of anatomy is crucial. Connecting the knowledge of those elements with pleasure is a game changer.

No matter how old you are, you can correct any misinformation you learned and expand your knowledge. Health and sex and reproductive education doesn't stop in eighth grade. You need to keep learning about health and reproduction topics throughout your lifespan, because sexual health is not static. For example, becoming a parent can profoundly affect sexuality. You might feel differently about your body and pleasure, and desire may be squelched because you are busy taking care of a baby. Mental health interacts with our sexuality. We are not taught how to navigate our sexuality when an SSRI is successful in making you less depressed but leaves you with an inability to ejaculate. Similarly, sexual health issues, such as STIs or reproductive cancers, can also change your sexuality.

Factual information is critical for prevention and treatment. Aging is a catalyst for change in sexual wellness and health. How you feel about and your access to sexual health care, your experiences during sexual health appointments and procedures, and your ability to seek treatment and advocate for sexual health all greatly affect your sexuality.

Wellness and fertility is about so much more than a penis and a vulva. Sure, it involves your sexual organs: naming the parts accurately, explaining how they function, and understanding how the anatomy works to create pleasure and sexual wellness in our bodies, whether that is for your body or another person's body. You need to understand hormones, nerves, muscles, tissues, complex interactions, and how things change as you age. Spoiler alert: Things *do* change.

Being informed about wellness and fertility encourages you to have as much agency as you can in your sexual health and reproductive journey. Seek a holistic understanding of wellness and fertility, if for no other reason than because if and when things change in your sexual wellness, you can act from an informed place instead of a shame-filled, dependent-on-the-expert one.

Unconventional Lessons in Anatomy

In one of my Revealed workshops, a course participant, Taylor, told a story of when, as a young girl, she told her mother that she had two heartbeats. She wondered if her mother did too. She said she had one in her chest and one down there. Her mother, a conservative woman from a rural town, was mortified, horrified, and walked away without saying one word in response. Taylor said she felt scared for years that something was wrong with her because of her mother's response.

Many of my clients tell me, with a tone of shame, about experiences they had with same-sex, consensual, and age-appropriate genital play and exploration. Yet this is normal and a healthy way to begin learning anatomy. When I was in middle school, my best friend and I would show each other our vulvas out of curiosity. We didn't have names for what we were looking at, but the comparison and normalizing of looking at ourselves felt healthy. I never saw it as shameful, but I realized, even at that age, that society would not sanction this behavior. I know now that holistic sexuality sees such explorations of anatomy as a healthy aspect of sexual development.

We need to rewrite the anatomy script and claim the information that we have not had access to. Evolved and holistic views of wellness and fertility demand that you know the biological components of sexuality, so that you can develop a personalized understanding of how anatomy informs and influences your pleasure. This kind of education includes things like

- learning names, functions, and optimal functioning of anatomical parts;
- normalizing the variance of genital expression;
- learning how reproductive organs function and change as you age;
- understanding the physical effects of various types of birth, how they impact sexual fulfillment, and how they can affect your partner(s);
- learning how pain and discomfort can occur in various parts of anatomy;
- learning warning signs of serious issues, such as injury or cancer;
- understanding the changes in anatomy in a transgender journey; and
- understanding the complexity of the difference of anatomical virginity, a social construct I like to call the "sexual debut."

As mentioned earlier, the scope of this book isn't to give specific facts but to help you discover where you need to go further to support your holistic sexual health. A sexual audit of sorts. I encourage you to seek out trustworthy sources for information you need, but I want to give you a head start within this pillar. Check out the resources section at the end of the book (on page 294) for some suggestions.

Supplementary sex education is vital when big changes are happening in your sexuality. Take, for example, a couple who contacted me for support in navigating one partner's transition from cisgender male to transgender woman. Beth was planning for top and bottom surgery (that is, breast augmentation and gender-affirming vaginoplasty, which is the surgical creation of a vagina, clitoris, and labia majora and minora from the penis and removing the testicles).

Beth and her partner Corry were handling the change of gender well emotionally and relationally, but they were struggling over the change of anatomy and curious about the sexual changes it would bring about in their relationship. Corry and Beth were grieving the loss of a penis and were uncertain what their options for sexual pleasure would be.

The first thing I did was connect them with a supportive community where each could talk to others who were going or had gone through similar transitions.

The couple wondered if it would be important to them to have a model of the penis that could be kept or used for sentimental or sex play options. They had different values and feelings about the penis pre-surgery. Beth wasn't sure she had a strong attachment to her penis and voiced she may never look at it again but thought it was possibly a novel experience to share together; Corry mourned the loss and felt nostalgic about it. After deliberation, they decided they wanted to have the option to have the penis model; we found a company that makes silicone replicas of penises before gender-affirming surgery, and they turned its creation into a fun experience together.

To educate themselves on postoperative pleasure possibilities, they asked me for clothed anatomy lessons on their current (preoperative) bodies, and they wanted to translate their knowledge to pleasure possibilities after Beth's surgery with verbal instruction and video recommendations. They requested multiple photos and diagrams of post-surgery anatomy and found several post-surgery trans women who were sharing details of their post-surgery bodies and sexual lives. This enabled Corry and Beth to learn more about how her new vulva might look and function.

This honoring of physical and gender changes by equipping themselves with facts about anatomy grounded the couple's decisions in real-world self-knowledge. After Beth's surgery, Corry and Beth worked through a lot of changes in their relationship, including Beth's physical and hormonal changes. After Beth's acute physical healing process, they got to a place where they could begin exploring sexual connection with a new level of knowledge about anatomy and pleasure.

More Than a Biological Clock

Another key component within this pillar relates to reproductive health and specifically fertility and changing hormones. From my vantage point, most formal sex education focuses on reproductive health but insufficiently; it mostly covers how bodies change during puberty and how "natural," or traditional conception, occurs—and possibly how to prevent it. This focus (often attached to religious and historical lineage obsessions) suggests that our sexuality is valuable only in regards to reproduction. By now you know, though, that the view is so much wider than that.

Reproductive education typically takes a narrow view, for example, teaching that conception occurs only through vaginal penetration by a penis. More children now in elementary school were conceived with IVF than of any previous generation and have parents of many variations. I have worked with several organizations that focus on reproductive health: I've consulted for Planned Parenthood on a state and a national level and for numerous gynecologists, midwives, doulas, and birth photographers, and I've worked with an IVF clinic. I have worked with people who have experienced unwanted pregnancies; ended pregnancies by choice; had miscarriages; gotten pregnant easily; made multiple IVF attempts; and experienced late-term fetal death, stillborn children, and infant health issues and death. Fertility is such an important topic for all genders, although there is an obvious focus on people with uteruses.

I experienced fertility issues myself at the age of thirty-seven. I found myself desiring to have another child, my second, with a partner I was in a relationship with. One doctor I consulted uttered those dreaded phrases: "advanced maternal age" and "the clock is ticking fast." I knew that in the fertility world, thirty-five was the magical shift to "advanced maternal age" and "geriatric" or "high risk" pregnancy, but it had not felt relevant to me. I felt so young.

The doctor recommended going to the IVF clinic in town for a full review of my fertility status. I was shocked. I wasn't prepared for the years that followed. I was book-educated yet entirely clueless emotionally and scientifically when I walked into the IVF journey. I went through four unsuccessful attempts at IVF, trying every procedure and trick recommended, none of which was covered by insurance.

Not long into the process, we decided to not share information about it with anyone else. Talking about what I was going through felt taboo, and it was a topic that people had a lot of opinions on, which we didn't want to have to navigate on top of everything else. I had been on the receiving end of so many hurtful opinions (no matter how well-intentioned) and insensitive questions. Enough was enough. But the decision was not easy. I felt isolated and confused. My body was suffering too. I had many injections, resulting in bruises all over my abdomen and ass, and intense discomfort with bloating. I spent many hours on the road to and from the clinic, spent many hours on the phone and in chat rooms, looking for information and tips, and the price tag was a staggering amount. I wanted to stop and restart the process many times. In hindsight,

I can see how useful it would have been to have support, a place to process all the feelings, experiences, and decisions.

During the journey, I saw many couples and individuals come and go, silent in the waiting room, crying after getting hard news, going in and out of the "donation" room with embarrassment. I saw the staff experience a range of emotions. They experienced the high of telling a beloved patient they were pregnant at last, as well as absorbing the anger from a frustrated and desperate couple experiencing yet another failed attempt, knowing they were running out of time and money.

My fifth and final attempt was positive, which was amazing and resulted in my darling and precious daughter. I am fortunate to have her in my arms, and I know many do not have such a happy result. The journey took a toll though. We spent hundreds of thousands of dollars and countless hours on it, and I experienced emotions ranging from great hope to great fear, without a lot of time or safe space to process. My sexual education had not prepared me one bit for any of the physical specifics or emotional complexities of the journey or the toll on my relationship.

You need to be equipped with sexual health and reproduction information in advance of any fertility journey. You need to take the space now to work through your pain points. You also need to learn the intersection of sexual health and mental health.

Finally, there is a lifespan and generational aspect of sexual education. Holistic sexuality supports a thorough understanding of our fertility and how it changes with age—both before the information is relevant and when it is pressing. Holistic sexuality demands proactive education that is flexible and relevant in timing to expose us to information we didn't know we needed with the guiding premise of "How do you know what you need to know if you don't know?"

Is It Me, or Is It Hot in Here?

Everyone experiences hormonal changes as they age. Puberty begins with a bang, and the changes keep going throughout a lifetime. The variety of powerful moments is vast: from the beautiful story of a young person supported through their first period to another person's embarrassing first wet dream; from the fifty-two-year-old executive experiencing breakthrough bleeding that pools blood in her seat while she leads a company-wide town hall meeting to the trans woman seeking hormone therapy in later years. Hormonal changes affect how we see and experience our sexuality.

As an example, currently I am a few months post–surgical menopause, and my sister and mother went through surgical menopause (in their early forties). In a few short months, I have experienced a dramatic decrease of energy, a surge of emotional changes, sleep disruptions, joint aches, itchy ears, and hair loss. I have worked with many people along their menopause journeys and with multiple companies that have products to support menopause. Still, I remain shocked by how unprepared I was for my unique journey. We are vastly undereducated before and during individual menopause journeys, and systemically we know precious little about menopause in general, let alone about the emotional, physical, and sexual needs during this time. A supportive and educational community for people going through perimenopause and menopause is growing, but more evolved education is required and should be available early and to all genders, not just women. As a society, we need to become familiar with menopause and the range of its symptoms. We need to understand what kind of support people going through menopause need—and we need to provide it. The cascading effect of the lack of research, information access, medical support, and societal interest has been catastrophic.

We also need to give people with penises more support in their aging and hormonal journeys. Although the vast majority of scientific research is male focused, there remains a dearth of practical information about aging male bodies going through hormonal changes, and there's even less emotional support. I have heard countless stories from men whose energy, sleep, and sexual habits are decreasing as their hormones change, but they are mortified to talk about it with friends, aren't even aware the changes have potential solutions, and are worried it sounds like they are less "manly." I have heard many men describe the disconcerting experience of muscles changing, bodies morphing into a new shape, hair loss, and not recognizing themselves in the mirror while being confounded by what's going on inside their own bodies. The studies about aging diminish even more remarkably for those who've experienced a transgender journey with medical intervention.

We need to prioritize understanding the context of our sexual wellness and health within and throughout our lifespan and particularly in and after our forties.

One of my best recommendations for people going through hormonal changes is to find an aging mentor. There is so much benefit to having someone in your life who is willing to freely give their perspective and wisdom about aging. We need informal and formal information about our sexual health as we age. Information that comes from people's experiences in real bodies, right now, makes such a difference. You don't need to "just endure" the side effects of hormonal change. Scientific research, medications (like hormone replacement therapy when indicated), weight training (specifically for midlife bodies), mental health support from menopause-trained therapists, treatments (like acupuncture or other health practices when recommended), and the wisdom of those who have gone before you may help you find ease through changes. Agency in aging is a real thing.

"Is There Anything You Need to Ask?"

When I was in my early twenties, I had a gynecologist with this great bedside manner and way of doing exams. You met him in his office, a small, intimate room filled with photographs of his travel adventures, and he would chat with you a bit. He always ended this part of the appointment by asking, "Juliana, is there anything you need to ask me or anything we should be talking about?" Every time, I had a list of questions, and every time in that room, I would say no. Then I'd go to the exam room and he would do the Pap test and breast exam, and when finished, he'd ask again, "Juliana, is there anything you need to ask me or anything we should be talking about?" He always phrased the question the same way.

In my crunchy blue-paper gown, I would repeat my answer, "No. Nothing to talk about. Think we've covered it." I had a list of topics to discuss, but I was too embarrassed to ask. I'd get dressed and return to his small office where he would be waiting for me with a smile. He'd go over anything relevant and give me best practices for my age group and then he'd ask, "Juliana, is there anything you need to ask me or anything we should be talking about?"

Finally, I would go through my list of questions that I had been too mortified to ask before, pretending I had just thought of them. And he would answer without hesitation or judgment. I was always amazed that he knew three times was the charm. I thought of all the patients he must have worked with who needed that kind of gentle prodding, that amount of asking, that calm patience. I think of patients of all genders who need a medical team that knows how to create a space of trust and safety because they need help in asking for what they need in their health and wellness experiences. We need a health care system that supports our medical team having the time to give us.

When that occurred to me, I was both impressed and angry—with our culture and with myself. I felt frustrated that I had such shame around my sexual health needs that I couldn't ask outright and needed him to prompt me three times. What would I do when I moved and didn't have a gynecologist with this process? So, I made a commitment to one day walk into an appointment with a written list of questions, to advocate for my needs, and to ask, even if embarrassed, for my concerns to be addressed. It was a game changer for me.

These days, I walk into my sexual health appointments and the first thing I ask is "How much do you care about my sexual health?" I am fortunate to have the ability to determine if I stay with a provider based on their reaction to my question. I don't expect a perfect response, but I gauge their comfort level with the topic. I've had some providers laugh, others not miss a beat and disclose a lot, others ask me to explain what I mean, and some have scoffed and ignored the question. What I've learned is this: I want a medical team that acknowledges, feels comfortable with, and cares about my sexual health. I want them to be competent on sexual health, and I want them to have a team approach to my health care and cocreate my medical care with me. This one question sets the tone for me to determine who is on my team.

Finding health care providers who match your values and needs is not easy, let alone ones that are covered by insurance or aren't cost-prohibitive and who are comfortable with and have a deep knowledge of sexual health needs within your gender, race, age, and cultural contexts. I get this. In many ways, we do not have a lot of options to meet the ideals, *but* they do exist and may be available to you. And if they are not, you can work to change this problem. Doing so is a crucial part of your sexual health. With the understanding that, unfortunately, not everyone has access to the options needed to enact the following, here is an ideal to-do list for you as you build a medical health team that supports your sexual health.

- Research the wide range of providers who can support your sexual health and wellness.

- Identify practitioners who resonate with you, your values, and your lifestyle. At first appointments, use the screening question I mentioned above or develop your own to ascertain whether they are the right fit for you.

- Develop a level of trust with providers and knowledge of your body so that you feel confident in knowing when things are functioning well or when you should be concerned.

- Ask for medical and mental health support when things are uncertain or not functioning as usual.

- Activate your agency during appointments to speak to what you want (see the sexercise at the end of this chapter) and to co-create your health care with your providers.

- Examine how the medical community, insurance providers, and governmental bodies have supported or not supported your sexual wellness journey.

- Understand how your culture, race, age, orientation, ability, and other factors of your identity intersect with your experience of wellness and fertility.

Health and wellness experiences vary greatly, depending on who you are and the political and social context you live in. Many years ago, I toured the United States filming individuals who identified as women to collect stories about their experiences as women. One interviewee, LaTosha, a Black woman in her early thirties, told me about a moment in her teenage life that had a profound impact on her. She said, "I know the exact moment I learned to lie down, be quiet, and do what a man told me to do, no matter how much it hurt and I didn't want to do it," she said. "I was thirteen, and it was my first gynecological exam."

LaTosha's mother had arranged the appointment because she figured LaTosha would be having sex soon, if she wasn't already, and she did not want her daughter to get pregnant. When the day of the appointment arrived, her mother didn't take LaTosha. Her big sister did. LaTosha remembered feeling scared and not knowing anything about what a gynecologist was or did, but she felt a gut-based fear that something not good was awaiting her. She pressed her sister for more details, and her sister only said, "You go in, you take off your clothes, and they stick something in you, and it's over. I'll be outside." That miniscule amount of knowledge, without any reassurance or support, created an intense amount of tension and anxiety in LaTosha.

She sat in the near-silent waiting room with washed-out framed prints on the walls and outdated magazines on the tables. When her name was called, she walked in and was told to undress and put on the paper gown. LaTosha did, and she waited. An older white man and a white woman walked in. They asked her when she had started her period and told her to lie down. Not another word was said to her. They didn't give guidance, reassurance, or instruction, nor did they check in with her. She explained she was used to not having Black providers, but this appointment in the sexual realm made her feel exponentially more vulnerable with the race difference. They ignored her tears, moved her legs into the cold stirrups, put the forceps inside her, and when she winced and cried out quietly in pain as an IUD was being inserted, she was met with indifference. The doctor removed the speculum, told her everything was fine, and gave her a piece of paper to give to her mom. The nurse told her to get dressed. And that was that.

LaTosha told me that appointment was when she started teaching her body to override discomfort, fear, and lack of consent. Especially when relating to men. She told multiple stories of how sexual partners had since held their own versions of this type of power over her. Not talking to her, not seeking consent, not seeking partnership or agency in the encounter, and exhibiting no concern for her pain or pleasure. She didn't matter to them, and she stated she did not matter to herself for many years.

This example shows why, more than ever, we need to teach people how to advocate for their sexual health and wellness, and we need to change systems, especially those that do not support marginalized communities. Everyone should receive equitable access to quality, compassionate care.

SEXERCISE: Advocating for Yourself

Review the following tips, and prep for the ones that are relevant to your ideal health appointment. Not every tip will apply to your situation.

- Hire a provider you can count on. Your criteria might include: convenient hours and location, good customer service, doesn't make you wait too long, doesn't make you feel rushed in your appointment.

- Within your comfort level, reveal personal information to the person making the appointment so they can schedule enough time for your concerns.

- Set clear goals for the appointment, and communicate them with your provider. Do not downplay your symptoms, try to be a hero, or start with self-doubt.

- Bring a written list of all your physical symptoms, changes, concerns, medical history, and relevant family history. Be specific and give details. You never know what will be a relevant piece to the puzzle. Sometimes sexual health is an art form. I keep a typed document of my family history that I bring to all appointments, just in case. When you're tired, feeling rushed, or surprised by information, you may forget things.

- Bring a written set of questions that you want answered. Prioritize the ones you need answers to before the end of the appointment. Be specific. This can help your provider understand your concerns and your symptoms. Ask things like "Could this be something else?" If given a treatment plan, ask questions about other options.

- If this isn't your first appointment about this topic, arm yourself with information and questions about treatment options. Ask about the provider's experience with this topic or treatment.

- Take notes. Ask for clarification. Ask for spelling of a diagnosis or medications. Do not be shy. Review the basics of what you heard to make sure you understood correctly. Make sure you know the next steps after that appointment.

- Don't believe everything you read on the internet. Limit your time on Dr. Google and WebMD, and stay far away from most medical image searches.

- Bring someone with you to appointments who can listen, ask questions, take notes, and otherwise support you.

- Be confident in what you know of yourself and your body. Be persistent in your pursuit of understanding and support. Respectfully pushing back when you experience concerns can be helpful. Grow comfortable with disagreeing if you feel like you aren't aligning with a treatment or diagnosis. Sometimes disagreeing can cue a provider to devise an alternative plan, explain their idea from a different perspective, or recommend a specific provider for a second opinion.

- Ask for what makes you feel more comfortable in your appointment. Ask for an extra gown. Ask for the resident to leave. Ask for another provider to join for an examination. Ask for more time with the practitioner. Ask for consent before touch. Ask for them to walk through an examination in detail before or while it is happening. If you have trauma, that would be helpful for the provider to know.

- Know you have a right to change providers. Work on building a positive relationship and rapport with your provider, but do not stay with a provider who isn't a fit. Hire slow and fire fast. Although insurance can complicate flexibility, you are typically not stuck with your provider. If something feels off, act on your intuition.

- Further, listen to yourself. Trust your instinct. In your body. In your feelings during an appointment. In your treatment options.

In your provider team. See people in your life, your health care team, and the internet as members of your advisory board rather than a team of presidents of the decision committee.

- Remain grounded in the belief that you have agency in your sexual health and wellness. Your health is worth the time, financial investment, and the pursuit of support, options, and answers.

Most health care providers have years of education and access to research and treatment options specific to their specialty that others don't. This is so valuable. Your knowledge of you is equally invaluable. You know the most about your body, symptoms, history, experiences, family history, context, and needs. So you are both valuable experts in your appointments with different areas of expertise and different vantage points. You and your provider need to make this the baseline understanding in your appointments. Putting your needs first is the foundation of self-advocacy and the cornerstone of cocreating a working relationship with a provider that will support your sexual health needs.

Mental Health

Mental health is a critical component of sexual health, and to fully understand your sexual health, you must examine mental health. Many things affect the relationship between mental health and sexual fulfillment, such as mental illnesses, psychotropic medications, self-esteem, relationship quality, substance abuse, sex addiction, and hormonal changes.

The quality and consistency of your mental health greatly affects sexual fulfillment, pleasure, and function. The level of impact ranges from an anxious day or a day of feeling depressed to major mental health concerns such as bipolar disorder, chronic anxiety or depression, mood disorders, and psychosis.

Ruminating or intrusive thoughts can make it difficult to stay in the moment with sexual pleasure or to remain connected with a partner. Feelings of hopelessness and low self-esteem can lower sex drive and desire or lead to isolation and avoidance of sexual connection with yourself or others. Anxiety can greatly affect erectile function and premature ejaculation while depression can contribute to anorgasmia (trouble experiencing an orgasm).

Depression, anxiety, and mood disorders can be linked to sexual dysfunction, and they can result in decreased interest in and frequency of sexual bonding and connection. Some mental health diagnoses, such as ADHD, borderline personality disorder, and mania, can lead to impulsive or higher levels of sexual activity.

Substance abuse and addiction can have a large impact on your sexual life. Substances can prevent sexual functioning, disable your ability to activate your agency, inhibit sexual pleasure, affect fertility, and diminish your ability to give or read consent. I once led a group of people through my Revealed course who were all in recovery, and their sexual lives were the last aspect of their healing they addressed. They each had a deep well of pain, trauma, and shame. It was powerful to see them release the stories, dispel shame, and claim sexual agency in their sobriety.

I have also seen the deep impact of a porn or sex addiction. One client, Larry, described years of battling an addiction to pornography that had morphed into a compulsion for hiring sex workers. His marriage had ended, his children weren't speaking to him, and he was full of self-loathing. When he made the hard decision to say out loud what he was battling and get help, he experienced a layer of shame and discrimination he hadn't anticipated. There was only one sex addicts anonymous meeting within a two-hour radius of his home, and participants had to be vetted through two phone interviews and had to show ID before being told where the meeting was held because the group had experienced hate and anger from community members who judged their addiction rather than supported their efforts at sobriety.

When someone isn't feeling good about themselves or is unwell mentally or physically, interest in sexual connection can be minute. If a relationship is having troubles, sexual connection is often greatly affected by the discord. I have seen antidepressants like SSRIs do wonders in alleviating depressive symptoms while impacting erections, the ability to ejaculate, or levels of sexual desire and interest in connection.

Our bodies experience hormonal changes throughout our lifespan but particularly in the bookends of puberty and menopause or "andropause." For bodies with uteruses, the cyclical hormonal fluctuations can impact mental health with emotional dips and highs as well as more debilitating conditions like premenstrual dysphoric disorder or polycystic ovary syndrome that directly affect mental health, sexual functioning, and pleasure. Menopause has a large impact on mental health, with a sharp increase in anxiety and depression. Studies show that cisgender women between the ages of forty-five and fifty-four are at a high risk for suicidal ideation and completed suicides due to the impact of menopause on mental health. Men experience the lowering of testosterone levels, which affects mental health and sexual health as well, but not enough studies have been conducted to know the depths of the link.

Sexual Functioning

There is some debate in the mental health, sex therapy, and psychiatric worlds on how to conceptualize, label, and treat challenges that arise in sexual functioning. I lean toward a model of competency and challenges rather than dysfunction and labeling, but I will not jump into the points of that debate in this book. I would be remiss, however, if I didn't mention the *Diagnostic and Statistical Manual of Mental Disorders (DSM-5-TR)* and the impact of this foundational text. It is the American Psychiatric Association's professional reference book on mental health and brain-related conditions. There are several sections related to sexuality in it. Examples include female sexual arousal/interest disorder, female orgasmic disorder, genito-pelvic pain/penetration disorder, male hypoactive sexual desire disorder, erectile disorder, premature (early) ejaculation, and delayed ejaculation. I have problems with how it addresses gender and transgender journeys, but again I will save that for another book. Although problematic in my opinion, the *DSM-5-TR* is relevant to holistic sexuality because it is used not only to guide therapeutic treatment but also for insurance coding. It is important to be educated on the biases within it, the limitations within it, and the power of labels; it also provides important research-based information on symptoms that can normalize challenges and guide treatment.

Body Compassion

One final key aspect to address within this pillar is the relationship you have with your body. Your relationship to your body is the hum in the background of every aspect of your sexuality. Sometimes the volume is turned up. Sometimes it is barely audible. But it is the background and wired in. An extraordinary leader in the body relationship space, Chrissy King wrote a powerful book that speaks to the need for our society and for each of us to change the script on how we relate to our bodies; *The Body Liberation Project* was incredibly well received because she put words to how so many of us feel. We must find a different way to experience and relate to our bodies because the consequences of not doing so have been so dire.

One of the presidents of the Society for the Scientific Study of Sexuality, Dr. Karen Beale, and I teach a course, Awaken, which is devoted solely to enriching your relationship with your body, because the body is such a powerful aspect of your sexuality. Terms like "body image" and "body positivity" are thrown about constantly these days. But the research shows that *body compassion* is one of the most powerful ways to build your relationship with your body into one that supports your growth, your insight, and your sexual journey. Many clients have told me they do not want their partner to see their body because of weight gain or aging, or they cannot embrace pleasure because they are hyperfixated on a body part they don't love. I have heard many stories from people feeling betrayed by their bodies because of a debilitating condition, terminal illness, or different access to abilities. Many trans individuals have a powerful journey with the intersection of their body and sexual health. In all these instances, embracing compassion for your body is vital.

I will never forget my friend Aisha recounting her efforts to prevent her teenage daughters from seeing her chest after her double mastectomy. She talked frequently about protecting them from "the horrors" of her body. She had decided not to have reconstructive surgery, resulting in visible scars and no areolas or nipples. One day, her daughters walked in unexpectedly as she was taking her shirt off. They gasped. She fell to the floor sobbing, covering herself and saying "I'm sorry" over and over again. Her darling daughters ran to her, hugged her, and said, "Sorry? There is *nothing* to be sorry for, Mom. Finally! Why have you hidden this from us?" As they wiped away her tears, the girls flooded Aisha with compassion and told her they saw her body as a novel of how hard she had fought to be alive. They were proud of her, not horrified by her body. They saw her scars as evidence of her fierce love for them. That shift was beyond powerful for all three of them. Their body compassion inspired her own body compassion.

Holistic sexuality understands that how you feel about your body, the vessel of your essence and sexual experiences, is critical to your development and fulfillment, and that ripples through generations.

One of my clients, Stacey, offers a beautiful example of how agency unfolds within this pillar. She experienced severe domestic violence with her spouse, who was struggling with mental illness. During this period, she gained weight. Sometimes the weight gain troubled her; sometimes it was the least of her worries as she sought safety and places of refuge. But as the years passed, her weight increased. With each pound, she didn't just see changes in her body and the fit of her clothes, she saw the result of abuse. She started associating her new body shape with trauma, with her spouse's illness, and with a lack of safety.

As we started our work together, I asked her, as I ask all my clients, "What is your relationship with your body?" Stacey was surprised by the question initially, and her answer was clipped. This was the starting point. We often are asked about our body image or how we feel about our body, but our relationship with it? Not as often.

Stacey and I revisited the question over the months and years. She took Awaken with Dr. Beale and me, and it wasn't easy for Stacey. She worried that the group would judge her if they knew about the spousal abuse, which was so deeply woven into her relationship with her body, and that she had chosen to stay with her spouse. She stayed with him while he was hospitalized and accurately diagnosed and medicated. At this point, he was on a different trajectory, one of healing, and was gaining insight and accountability.

Stacey's own healing journey was underway on her own terms. My groups always allow a wide berth for agency. Everyone has their terms, their path. Stacey had the right to her story and choices free of judgment. As she stepped into that freedom, lighthouse moments started shining through. (Recall from the introduction of this book that those are moments of insight that guide you on your way.)

Stacey realized that she actually didn't mind the weight or the change of her shape. In fact, she liked the new curves. She found them sexy and fun. She didn't like the meaning she had made of the journey to curves, so this is where we focused our work.

In a writing exercise, she wrote a letter reframing parts of her relationship to her body that no longer served her and another letter giving much appreciation and compassion for her body. She came to this gorgeous reframe of her weight and found compassion for her body through all those years of feeling unsafe. She saw that the weight had brought her safety. It had given her the heft to keep a door closed to protect herself when he was in a rage.

This story doesn't end with magical weight loss, because that was not the point of Stacey's journey nor should it be. Her goal was to trust her body and see the weight as strength and not as weakness. It was to see her weight as a companion of courage and steadfastness, not a symbol of abuse and sadness. That was the magical shift.

Stacey continued on her journey to grow in body compassion and trust in herself. She does the most amazing physical feats with her body. Her relationship with her body helped her seek medical support for a completely different issue because she saw that she and her body did not need to suffer and endure more pain. Her relationship with her body was one of beautiful reclamation.

HOLISTIC SEXUALITY sees all aspects of our sexual health and wellness as integral to being a fulfilled sexual being. This includes thorough information and ongoing education that teaches us what we need to know before we need it.

From here, we leave the nuts-and-bolts vibe of wellness and fertility and move into another pillar that requires and promotes mindful presence: pleasure.

REVEAL YOURSELF TO YOURSELF

- How comfortable do you feel advocating for your sexual health in medical appointments?

- Do you consistently take care of your reproductive health?

- Have you had any outlier experiences—positive or negative—with your medical providers and/or health care team?

- How well do you know your reproductive parts and how they work? Do you understand how they all work together to create orgasm and pleasure? Do you know how your body changes during your excitation cycle?

- Describe your fertility journey to date.

- If you are a parent (of any kind), how has being a parent affected your view of yourself? Your sexuality?

- What body parts do you love? What body parts do you not love? How comfortable are you in your own skin? How do you feel about being naked alone? In front of others?

- How has your mental health impacted your sexual life? Has a partner's mental health impacted your sexual life?

- What is one way you can activate agency in your fertility and wellness?

PILLAR 3
Pleasure

SOMETIMES PLEASURE doesn't arrive at convenient times or in conventional ways. One night, at the end of a long day of filming for a short documentary, I ended up sitting alone at a high-top bar table in a restaurant in Napa Valley. I decided to indulge in dessert and order exactly what I wanted: the most amazing cabernet and raspberry sorbet combination. That cab was decadent. Velvety and fruit forward. Pairing it with my favorite sorbet made little sense until I had them both in my mouth. Without thinking about it, I moaned. Audibly. Probably weirdly... It was definitely different from the rest of the conversation in that restaurant. I wanted to undress and roll around in the combination of the flavors, textures, and temperatures. My body buzzed with presence and pleasure, and I had a grin on my face I couldn't control. I had this innate need to share my pleasure with others, although there was no one near me volunteering to join in. My pleasure felt like it was and should be contagious. There was nothing overtly sexual about this pleasure and yet everything about it was sexual. It was sensual. I am certain the whole restaurant knew how much pleasure it brought me. I didn't care one bit.

PLEASURE IS a crucial part of life. Pleasure sustains us, enriches our experiences, and often grounds us in the moment. If you feel

Pleasure is your birthright. And it's good for everyone.

pleasure, you are present in your senses. Yet many of us rarely put intentional effort into infusing pleasure into our daily lives, our inner world, or our relationships.

Pleasure has immeasurable power and countless benefits, but too often it feels like a luxury. The potential power of pleasure has made society deem it dangerous and unwieldy. When culture sees something as uncontrollable, it often sets out to control it. The result is that we see pleasure as selfish, self-indulgent, entitled, weird, irresponsible. As children, we learn quickly that rules govern pleasure. As adults, especially in North America, pleasure is reserved for weekends, vacations, the occasional night out, or compressed into pockets of time that usually end up in a binge of something, whether that's food, spending, drinking, or partying. Pleasure is unfortunately seen as a gateway to even bigger "sins"—selfishness, self-indulgence, and lack of productivity.

Worse, the message that pleasure is impractical and even shameful makes you less likely to talk about it or to seek things you love to do. Loving time with your kids or finding joy in helping others, that's okay. But seeking joy and pleasure in other forms is audacious. Going away for a weekend to support your son's baseball team is sanctioned; going away on a self-help retreat is selfish and odd. Pleasure is permitted after you deprive yourself of it. Being "so busy" with long work hours and family obligations gives you license to overindulge with vacations, shopping, Netflix, or spa and golf days. Those things are not inherently bad in moderation, but if this is the only pleasure cycle that our society supports and we follow it, it is a problem.

Infusing our lives with pleasure is linked to happiness, and how deeply and fully you embrace the concept of pleasure correlates to your sense of fulfillment. Happiness is external and fleeting, so in a present-minded way, it is powerful to stack micro moments of bliss on top of pleasure-filled experiences in your day-to-day to create a pleasure-activated life. When you don't prioritize pleasure in daily life, you deprive yourself of the physical and mental health benefits and you disconnect from this important aspect of holistic sexuality.

I also acknowledge that there's an important difference between pleasurable activities that are supportive to a pleasure-activated life and activities that may provide fleeting doses of pleasure but end up stripping us of pleasure in the future due to their avoidant, numbing, or addictive qualities. Often labeled as "vices," sometimes these activities provide pleasure in the moment but don't contribute to a lifetime of pleasure. Unfortunately, many of us aren't taught the difference. We aren't given support to infuse pleasure in daily life, to speak and ask about pleasure in our lives or others. We ask "Was it fun?" or "Are you happy?" instead of "Did it bring you pleasure?" Why do we partition off pleasure instead of infusing every moment with it? Why don't we talk about pleasure daily? Cyndie Spiegel, a powerful joy advocate, wrote a book called *Microjoys* that speaks to the transformational power of these small moments of pleasure in our lives. She teaches us that while pursuing happiness is an external chasing, focusing on microjoys is a way of being that allows you to see the complexities and wonder in the midst of life's hardships and pain. Little things like wrapping the softest blanket around you and hitting all the green lights on a stretch of road are highly and synergistically important.

Pleasure, the Healer

Pleasure demands that you rest in the moment. If you've ever stood in a field of wildflowers and smelled the fragrance surrounding you, listened to the chirps of birds and the cacophony of insect and animal communications, you have experienced presence of mind, and there is healing in mindfulness. There is restorative work in being actively present. Healing and restoration are both pivotal to resilience, and resiliency is crucial in healthy, holistic sexuality. So, occasionally I talk to my clients about the need to frame trauma as healings. Allow me to explain.

We all have painful moments of hurt, anger, sadness, embarrassment, or shame that happen along our sexual journey. It's the guy who grimaced when he saw the sag of your post-baby stomach when you took off your shirt. It is the time your penis wouldn't get hard when you really wanted to bang that hot guy and you awkwardly made an excuse about why it happened and how it rarely happens, although you know it happens too frequently. It is the moment you got your period when you hoped you were pregnant. It is the aggressive comment a stranger yells: "You aren't fooling anyone, I know you are a dude wearing a skirt!"

Many people have more significant moments of harm and trauma. Like the time you met a guy at the college party who sexually assaulted you by sticking his fingers into you without your consent when you were drunk. Or perhaps there was a woman who told you that you were a terrible lover and laughed at the size of your dick, or the menopausal changes to your vaginal tissue that resulted in sex hurting so much it isn't worth trying. Maybe an uncle coerced you into touching his penis while he fondled your penis. Or maybe it was when you realized you would never have your own biological child because you'd decided to wait for the One and they didn't arrive.

The details are different for each of us, but these points of pain and shame create detours along and away from our desired path. Those detours expand our shame and cause us to withdraw from vulnerability. Shame and fear of vulnerability are the antithesis of authentic and holistic sexuality. No one is impervious to pain and places of healing. So, we must make purposeful decisions to infuse pleasure into our lives to build up and strengthen our reserves of resiliency. To be clear, a focus on pleasure doesn't erase or directly heal traumas and negative experiences, but it provides a pivotal balance.

We are wired to store negative and traumatic events easily. Remembering what could hurt or kill them helped our ancestors survive. Storing happy memories was a luxury, an afterthought. This wiring has stayed with us through evolution, which means you need to put effort in to remember pleasure, to store the good, to anchor the bliss. We must do this inside and outside sexual connection with purpose and intention. Pleasure creates a surge of dopamine in the body, and this has a positive impact on your physical and mental health. When you practice finding pleasure in your life, this strengthens and promotes those neural pathways in your brain. So, pleasure has a purpose beyond a dose of "This feels good." Dopamine is a feel-good neurotransmitter. When you get a dopamine surge, you feel good, you get a jolt of yum.

Dopamine also reinforces behavior. When you partner pleasure with behaviors that serve your purpose and intention, you reinforce your agency, you protect and enhance your pleasure, and you provide a natural reinforcement of positive behavior that helps you live the life you want.

Is pleasure as simple as a raspberry sorbet dessert? Yes. And as complicated as that as well. I could have told myself that I had already hit my budget for the meal. True. And there are times that sticking to that budget is the most important choice to make. I could have hindered my expression of pleasure, lessening my enjoyment and also lessening the spectacle of myself. Instead, I chose to find pleasure and express it. I could have dampened my pleasure, I could have heeded the glances I was getting, I could have gotten embarrassed and adjusted. I could have, but I didn't, and neither should you when it comes to authentic pleasure. Authentic, agency-driven pleasure requires you to know yourself and your likes, to communicate them, and to express them. You tap into your essence and let your vulnerability shine. It's pleasurable to seek pleasure, and don't just take my word for it.

ROOTED IN TRAUMA, Sarah was deeply resistant to the thought of pleasure in her life. Pleasurable activities felt scary to her. Joy felt like a risk, and feeling good didn't last long. For Sarah, the transition from joy to pain was too devastating to navigate. So, our first task together was for her to find pleasure outside sexual connection.

She decided she wanted to find bodily pleasure in physical movement while she spent time on a property she cherished greatly. She decided to cut a path from her pool to the bay behind her home. Sarah had no idea how she was going to cut the pathway, but she wanted the satisfaction of the movement and the knowledge that her body completed this task.

One afternoon, she got some gardening tools and hacked through the reeds to find a natural path to the bay's waterline. She thought the act would be the focus of the pleasure experience and experiment, and although she did enjoy it, she discovered something else. She found pleasure in doing something other people might not find pleasurable. When the path was complete, flush with pleasure, she decided to jump in the pool fully clothed, laughing at her audacity. She stood in the pool, her hair soaked, feeling exhausted and satisfied. Sarah stood still, listening to the sound of the wind and the birds. She soaked up the complete and utter innocent joy of so much simplicity filling her soul.

At first glance, this story seems to have nothing to do with sexuality. But it does, holistically speaking. In this moment, Sarah was present-minded. She sought joy and invited in pleasure. She allowed herself to feel the heat of the sun and her wet clothing. Her senses were activated. Sarah formed moments of healing with her present-focused experience by allowing herself to feel pleasure on her terms, in her own way, and in her own time. And she made all of it count by not throwing any of it away. That is a skill that also translates into sexual connection and sexual agency.

The Pleasure Imbalance

An unhealthy relationship with pleasure happens both outside and inside sexual connection. Inside the bedroom, this imbalance often shows up as no sex, checked-that-off-the-list sex, or scheduled sex only. Then deprivation gives way to indulgence: vacation sex, hours of porn, orgasms found only within solo sex, drunk sex, or cheating on a partner. Although those behaviors are not individually problematic or innately harmful, they don't foster balance. And you may not have the tools to know how to do it any differently.

Where sexual connection is concerned, there often isn't a lot of space to talk about the pleasure you might feel in solo sex or with others. If you do have space to share, usually that sharing shows up as questions like "Was it good?" or "Were they hot?" or "Did his dick work? Did he have a good dick?" How often do you hear someone say, "I had so much pleasure last night with my new sex toy" or "I had mind-blowing sex" or "My partner did this move last night that was so scrumptious." How often do you say something like that to another person?

We should be able to speak about our sexual connections and experiences with as much normalcy as other topics to people who are safe and consent to the topic. I am not saying that talking about our sexual connections at all times with everyone is a measure of an evolved sexual culture. But there should be much more ease and much less taboo and control around the topic, so that you feel free to talk about sexual pleasure with whomever you choose that consents to the conversation with you.

Within a sexual context, orgasm is erroneously seen as the crown jewel of pleasure, the only sexual pleasure that is valuable. It is the sought-after goal of sexual connection. Orgasm is associated with skill level and body superiority; it is seen as a signal to stop sexual connection. But this is just another kind of pleasure imbalance.

Don't get me wrong. I am a fan of orgasms, all kinds of intensities of them. Orgasms are a beautiful aspect of pleasure. Bring on all the orgasms, please. However, I am just as excited about many other types of sexual pleasure and do not see orgasms as the only kind of pleasure worth pursuing. We cannot overlook the pleasure found in an amazing kiss, or oral sex that made your legs quiver and took you to the edge but not over it, or the comfortable beauty of holding hands. Not orgasming often gets labeled as a failure, a problem, a malfunction, or a less-than experience.

Once, after I posted on social media about this, I received a message from someone who assumed that I had never experienced an orgasm because of my lack of emphasis on it as the end goal. He was certain I would change my mind if "he gave me an orgasm." Insert eye roll about the many ick factors here. I didn't respond to him, but I know it is a natural thought, even if he could've framed it more respectfully, so I'll address it.

I have experienced many orgasms, all kinds of them: Tension-releasing ones after a long day when my mind couldn't relax. Mind-blowing, lost-track-of-time orgasms because the sexual connection was transcendent and my partner was so tuned in to me. Orgasms that made me laugh because of the wild silliness that got us there. Get-'er-done orgasms so I can start my day. Others that made me cry from the beauty of the love felt within it. The kind that felt like, "Um, lost it right at the end." Ones I felt in my head, my clit, my ass, my vaginal canal. I've had orgasms where I was pretty sure a light emanated from my toes and head simultaneously. I've had orgasms in a car, in a movie theater, during one certain move lifting weights, in a Jacuzzi jet stream, with sex toys, with tongues, with fingers, with penetration, with porn, with fantasies, with dirty talk, within seconds, within hours, by myself, with the love of my life, and with a group of people.

And because I have experienced this type of pleasure many ways, I can say with confidence that orgasms are wonderful and pleasure-filled and oh so yummy. But they are not and should not be the Mount Everest of pleasure. Orgasms should be part of the sexual journey when possible but not the criteria for "good sex."

Sexual pleasure can be experienced and gathered in many types of experiences. There's the fun of exploring bodies and finding hidden gems of pleasure. Remember the yums you discovered in the sensuality pillar? Those yums are valuable. They are lighthouses of joy and the embers of your desire. They are meaningful, and they matter. Here is where pleasure and sensuality meet: within the present and with your mindful attention.

Pleasure matters. Value and embrace pleasure in micro and macro ways. Talk about pleasure and ask others about pleasure. Infuse your daily life with it, and give it to others. Find a pleasure partner and support the pursuit of pleasure in all forms inside and outside sexual connection.

Many aspects of pleasure are considered taboo, but none, perhaps, more than self-pleasure so let's demystify it and see why that should not be the case.

Do Pleasure for Yourself

I had the coolest anatomy teacher in high school. Dr. Carling always had a side ponytail and a ribbon that in some way misrepresented her intelligence and in other ways highlighted her fantastic uniqueness. She taught me more about self-pleasure than any sex ed class. She had funny songs for memorizing body parts, and she would leave us each Friday with memorable words of advice. One Friday, as she was saying something about choosing joy—perfectly nice, good advice—she interrupted herself by proclaiming, "No! Not that. Listen. This is the best advice I can give you all. Masturbate. Masturbate this weekend. See you on Monday." We all looked at each other in what might have been the loudest collective silence while inwardly there was an uproar of teenage delight. We couldn't believe she went there! To this day, I wonder how many students followed her directive that weekend and if she got in trouble for saying it to public school students.

I love her advice and applaud her bravery in a public setting. My only tweak to Dr. Carling's advice is that I prefer the term "self-pleasure" to the word "masturbate." Most of us have negative associations with the word "masturbation," because of all the shame and cultural baggage surrounding the act. Also, to me, the word "masturbation" falls into the same category that the word "moist" does for some. Just yuck. Self-pleasure? Yum. So self-pleasure it is.

For many people, self-pleasure represents the first introduction of shame into sexuality. There are many stories of young people getting caught humping stuffed animals or being told that "polite young boys don't put their hands in their pants." And then there are the tales of horrified gasps and quick door closes when a parent or sibling walked in on a self-pleasure session. In conversation with a man I admired, he shared how he supported his children's right to touch themselves. He sounded proud to recount how he told both kids (who identified as a boy and a girl) that it was normal and healthy to touch themselves and that it needed to be done privately in their rooms. I was about to give words of support when he quickly added, "And of course I made sure my daughter knows to wash her hands afterward." He had no awareness that the gendered difference in directing hygiene for his daughter and not his son was biased and might be shame-inducing. But it doesn't have to be this way—and it definitely shouldn't be.

Our bodies experience pleasure in a variety of ways: through eating, through exercise, through music, through touch, through touching ourselves. I don't remember the first time I realized my body could bring me pleasure. I do remember when I sought it for myself: fourth grade gym class. I weighed nothing and could do tons of pull-ups. (I was the pull-up champion of '79 with thirty-two pull-ups, thank you very much!) But I really loved climbing the big ropes that hung from the ceiling. Students would climb hand over hand with the rope grasped between their legs. The higher you climbed, the more your arms would shake from exertion and muscle fatigue. The rope, right up against my clit and groin, was vibrating. And well, that felt good. I didn't know why or what was actually happening, and I certainly didn't connect the shaking, the specific body parts, and my body feeling good. But I knew I liked it, and I felt like it was something not to say to anyone else. And a lot of little girls were up on those ropes with me smiling and giggling while the boys below yelled up at us to hurry. None of us were hurrying.

A year later, my best friend asked me if I did anything "like that," and I understood I might not be the only one who had found out my body could feel good. And I could make it feel good. Even then, I couldn't admit it until she admitted it to me. She did it completely differently from me, but there was an air of complicit acceptance in our conversation. It started to feel like self-pleasure could be okay, still secret and separate, but also a part of me and my life that was acceptable with certain people. It was the start of me claiming my own body, a process, as you know, that has been a journey. It was also the beginning of my understanding that agency could be found within self-pleasure as well; we could find it ourselves, and our bodies sought and experienced pleasure differently. How marvelous.

Holistic sexuality asks you to embrace your birthright of pleasure and to see solo sex as inherently sexual and beautifully yours.

I introduced you to Betty Dodson's genital show-and-tell exercise in the previous chapter. On the second day of the workshop, we did an equally powerful exercise called Erotic Recess. Participation was optional, though I've never seen anyone opt out.

As we sat in a circle, Betty walked us through different self-pleasure techniques with her favorite sex toys: the Hitachi Magic Wand and her personally designed steel barbell dildo. Sitting on our individual mats, we practiced with her in our circle of pleasure, and then she set us loose to continue self-pleasuring if we wanted to. To be in a room with multiple people self-pleasuring (but no cross-touching) is a powerful experience. Seeing how others touch themselves, being watched—it was both sensual and sexy and pleasure-filled.

In my first Erotic Recess, a woman in her early fifties who had never experienced an orgasm sat next to me. Nothing felt good, and she felt broken. Betty went over to her and helped her move the vibrator into different locations until they found *the* spot full of pleasure potential. With one slight move, the woman orgasmed within seconds. She cried, we all cheered and cried, and it felt like we all healed alongside her.

When I ask my clients about their self-pleasure habits, at first most are embarrassed. By the end of our work together, my clients tell me their practice without shame and without being prompted and often with the words "You'd be so proud of me." And I love it. Why do we make self-pleasure so embarrassing? Why is it so awkward? Different? Why does it feel so revealing, audacious, or gross? I think self-pleasure is just as interesting and normal and important as our taste in music or whether we prefer mountains or the seaside.

Sex educator Jennifer Rahner shared an affirming self-pleasure story with me. When she was a sixteen-year-old girl growing up in a middle-class household in the city, she said, her father approached her and told her in a matter-of-fact but gentle manner, "You should know what gives you pleasure so that you can feel confident to tell your partners about it," as he handed her a vibrator with a hint of humor in the vibrator choice. He concluded, "You should be the one who gives yourself pleasure before you find pleasure with someone else." He was straightforward and earnest in providing information. She explained his even-keeled demeanor put her at ease with self-pleasure, and he helped her feel like he was giving her permission or acknowledging that she was a sexual person, which was in sharp contrast with her friends' parents who were shaming their children in a purity culture and disallowing self-pleasure in their homes. He did, in fact, express concern that she was having sex with her boyfriend but not in a shaming tone. She sees this interaction as the foundation of her shift from shame to pleasure to agency.

I fervently advocate for teaching children about their body parts and pleasure. So of course, I taught my daughter the correct terminology for her genitals. Vulva, labia, clitoral hood and glans, vaginal opening. One day when getting out of the bath, she pointed to herself and said, "This is my clitoris, right?" I admit that it felt hard to hear her say the word "clitoris" in her sweet little angelic voice. It felt different from hearing her say "vulva" or "vagina." That's because the clitoris is associated with pleasure, and the association of a six-year-old and body pleasure was instinctively uncomfortable for me because of societal scripts. Knowing something intellectually is different from putting it into practice. Even those of us in the sexuality education space have years of negative messaging to overcome.

Of course, I have some level of decorum and consent-seeking in the context of bringing up self-pleasure, and I don't push if someone doesn't want to share, but I make an effort in my personal and professional lives to make it okay to talk about self-pleasure, to ask about it, and to engage in it. I hope to contribute to a culture where this frankness is the norm by inviting in the topic when it is often avoided.

Self-pleasure is a way to discover self-knowledge and to learn how to self-direct within sexual connection. It teaches you your anatomical yucks and yums in real time. Self-pleasure educates you about your own pleasure points and styles. It allows you to be self-focused, to lose yourself in pleasure solely for you. You can focus on your needs and wants without the complications that may arise when someone else is alongside you.

There are many additional ways to look at self-pleasure: as a way to keep the fire stoked, as a stress reliever, as a way to fall asleep, as a way to wake up, as a superpower. All these are valid, and in fact, there are endless benefits to self-pleasure including but not limited to developing and refining neural pathways and providing a release of endorphins. More specifically, self-pleasure can help you

- get comfortable with your sexual health and yucks and yums within sexual connection;
- create more refined knowledge of how your anatomy works to bring you pleasure so you can communicate this to a partner;
- reduce stress, relieve tension, and improve your ability to fall asleep and your quality of sleep;
- find energy, boost your mood, and lessen anxiety and depression;
- strengthen your pelvic floor muscles;
- help promote blood flow and reduce inflammation;
- reduce pain, including menstrual cramps;
- boost interest in sexual connection;
- lengthen a penis owner's time from arousal to ejaculation; and
- boost immunity.

Self-pleasure can also be seen as a workout, may improve cognitive functioning, is a safer sex practice that can be done alone or alongside a partner, and may even lengthen your lifespan.

I believe strongly that emotional safety is a pivotal foundation of fulfilling and pleasure-filled sexual connection, and I also know that clear, authentic communication directed by self-knowledge creates emotional safety. When you can trust your own yeses and nos because you know your body well enough, and you can communicate with others who know the same about themselves in partnered sex, all involved can move more freely into and around sexual connection.

BILL AND GINA were a cisgender couple with successful, high-profile careers who came to me with a mismatched desire and libido cycle. During our work together to uncover their individual relationships to desire and theirs as a couple, we spoke a great deal about their self-pleasure practices. We discussed frequency of masturbation, porn use, privacy needs, variety, interest in it, and shame associated with self-pleasure.

Gina described herself as having little interest in her own self-pleasure practice, but she had no problem with Bill having one. She shared that in her family, sex was never talked about and was seen as being for reproduction only. She said that her parents adored each other, but "we are not a sexual family."

As Bill began to describe his relationship to self-pleasure in detail, it was clear that he had a lot of shame associated with it because of his Catholic upbringing. He described feeling like a "dirty old man" when looking at porn to become aroused and complete self-pleasure. He was also resentful that he needed to self-pleasure more than he wanted to because his wife was not interested in as much sexual connection as he was.

As he recounted his practice of jerking off in the bathroom with his phone propped up in front of him, tears flowed. He didn't see self-pleasure as a healthy part of his sexuality; it felt secretive and dirty. He also saw it as second-rate sexual activity in comparison to sex with his wife; it was simply a means to relieve sexual tension. His resentment heightened as he described his awareness that he had a high-powered job and was considered a catch because of his looks, personality, family man status, and career, and yet he was "standing in his bathroom jerking off looking at porn" every week.

Bill's shame and desperation landed hard with Gina. They

had little history in talking about their views of and practice with self-pleasure. I guided them through a discussion about their needs in self-pleasure and their self-pleasure agreement as a couple and through multiple discussions about how they could both change their relationship with self-pleasure to expand their relationship to desire.

Gina slowly came to see how gaining knowledge about what her body liked through self-pleasure—her yums—could benefit her. It was pleasure without needing to attend to a partner; she was free to give and receive pleasure without performing. Bill and Gina began incorporating mutual masturbation into their sexual connection. Bill was able to release some of his shame and resentment about self-pleasure and see it as a healthy aspect of his sexuality rather than a consolation prize because he was being denied partnered sex, as well as a way to take charge of his sexual pleasure. This was a win for both of them.

The Most Enjoyable Activism

Here's an idea: Think of self-pleasure as your own personal activism.

I once met a couple who liked to dedicate their self-pleasure orgasms to parts of themselves or the world. I found that so moving and interesting, and it led me down the path of seeing self-pleasure as a profound act of agency.

American culture has no shortage of elements that can destroy a person's access to pleasure and make them feel despondent about sexual culture and the world at large: legislation that removes human rights, defunded sex education, violence targeted at marginalized communities, to name a few. I'm not saying that self-pleasure fixes these things. (I'm also not saying it can't.) I am not positing we can change a damn thing in the external world through one act of self-pleasure, but maybe it can stack together to impact sexual culture. I am saying don't underestimate the power of self-pleasure. I am saying that it can change your inner world. I can change my inner world. And you can too. And together, maybe that energy can be infused into more global changes.

You get to decide what brings you pleasure and how to give it to yourself. You get to decide what turns you on. You get to decide when you start and when to stop. You can decide to tune out all the bullshit placed upon your sexual self by others, by politics, by our era, by your family, by past partners, by media, by you. Self-pleasure is a place to be an activist for you.

Normalizing self-pleasure has an impact at any age. My mother, who fainted when she figured out I was having sex in college, can now say "self-pleasure" without much hesitation. She talks about it in generalized terms or when referring to something I taught or through a shy but funny story that her bridge group discussed. We do not talk about our own self-pleasure. And that is okay. Everyone has different levels of disclosure and comfort. She's moved the dial powerfully for herself and for her friends, and that is inspiring to me. She is finding the sweet spot between nudging and shoving herself toward a new edge with this topic, for herself and on her own terms.

As you enrich your self-pleasure practice, consider the ripple effects in your life when you experience a heightened level of comfort with pleasure in general. Think about the power of living in a place where holistic sexuality is normalized and self-pleasure is as acceptable a topic as your dedication to good wine or something else that brings you pleasure. The potential potency of this transformation to your relationship with pleasure gives me chills.

NOW THAT we have covered sensuality, the physical mechanics of your body, wellness and fertility, as well as the radical practice of pleasure, the time has come to talk about one of the topics I am asked about most: desire.

REVEAL YOURSELF TO YOURSELF

- What is your relationship to pleasure? (For example, are you somebody that seeks pleasure in your life easily, or are you resistant to it?)
- What messages have you received about pleasure *outside* sexual connection?
- What messages have you received about pleasure *inside* sexual connection?
- What are some of the most pleasurable things in your sexual life that you have experienced?
- What are your pleasure goals within sexual connection? (For example, do you want to feel comfortable touching yourself? Do you want to learn how to share pleasurable sexual experiences with maturity and ease? Do you want to be in a relationship with someone where you need not hide self-pleasure toys or time?
- What is your current self-pleasure practice?
- Find one way to activate your agency within pleasure.

PILLAR 4
Desire

DESIRE IS so much more than arousal; it is a lifestyle. I once attended a writing retreat in France with the intent to write my course on desire called The Wanting. I was staying in this gorgeous, swanky, and frankly out of my budget villa, but I needed a break from a shit show happening at home. This was my way to reconnect with myself after a difficult time. Things were horrible in my second marriage and falling apart fast. I needed time and reconnection to my soul so I could release the trappings of daily hardship, and for me, there is no better way to do this than to sit in community with others, have rich conversations, travel internationally, and get out of my typical environment.

The retreat consisted of an intimate group of six people and was led by the magical business coach and lawyer Rachel Rodgers, author of *We Should All Be Millionaires*. We laughed and wrote together; we walked and rode horses through the French countryside; we walked the grounds of the villa and ate dinners by candlelight as music filled the halls. Slowly but surely, I started to feel a spark ignite. Nothing about that week felt overtly sexual. Sexual connection with myself or with anyone else was the last thing on my mind. But through the shedding of the shit in my real life while I hid away in this retreat setting, a reconnection with me, my soul, and I blossomed.

Spark and vibrancy
are the contagions
to catch.

I had the first deep sleep I'd had in ages, and the next morning I woke rested, happy, lighter, and excited. We were going to visit Monet's garden, and I couldn't wait to see it. I was one of the first ones to hit breakfast, and I heard a cheery voice, singing down the stairs. Deneise waltzed over to me, sat down, and with the most joyful voice said, "Girl! I don't know what crazy sexual magic you were emanating from your room last night, but I think it left your room and entered right into mine. I had the best sex dreams last night, had the most glorious time with myself this morning, and I just *know* it was you and your sexual desire seeping into my room!" We both laughed. She was joking, of course, but she had a point. I envision desire as a spark, a vibrancy, a frequency, and I believe it is contagious—in both its presence and absence.

Yes, the day before I had been talking about the content on desire that I was writing, but what I think Deneise picked up on was that I had arrived with a struggling spark (it was barely hanging on), and with each passing day, the intensity was growing. Subconsciously, her desire met up with my energy, and it was infectious. Our sexual orientations didn't match up, so this wasn't about our connection moving to something physical, but our friendship was growing and my private desire, my spark, was strengthening and shining.

DURING MY SPEAKING EVENTS, desire is one of the topics I get asked about the most. Typically people worry about desire. No one comes to me and says, "I have the right amount and kind of desire." We have been taught to look at libido as high or low, right or wrong; you are either a prude or a slut. If you are described as having low libido, you risk losing your relationship because you are the problem; you don't want to have sex and are a drag. If you are seen as having high libido, you are dangerous or are likely to step outside a relationship to have your insatiable needs met. You either feel alive or out of control or dead inside, but regardless you're always getting it wrong. Our societal view of libido and desire leaves no room for unique expressions, normalized variance, and life experiences. There is no space to grow and nurture a relationship with arousal and desire. All of us are harmed by heteronormative, gendered, stereotypical, and archaic views of desire as it relates to gender, orientation, and race. Perpetuating harmful stereotypes and restricting personal freedom and authenticity inevitably dull the collective spark. Remember that agency has no room for that. Every individual has a unique relationship to desire, arousal, and sexual connection. Here's an example of one stereotype: There is a societal expectation that men always have a high sex drive and are ready for sexual activity at any time. For many, masculinity is tied to their sexual prowess and frequency of sexual activity. If a man's desire doesn't match this stereotype, he can experience internalized shame and guilt, relationship issues, depression, and anxiety.

Scientific and medical communities typically use the word "libido" to describe the urge to have sex or the energy of sexual drive. But I prefer the term "desire." My experience has shown me that many people have negative reactions to "libido," and I think it's out of date. "Desire" feels more expansive and more evolved, more holistic. It is approachable and less laden with negative connotations and gendered biases.

Desire is in the same arena as arousal but is different. Arousal is a state of feeling excited or alert, sexually or not, in a sexual context. But desire is rooted in deep wanting, not just for sex but for connection, pleasure, and soul fulfillment.

Desire is a powerful wanting—an energy exchange. An energy source. Like holistic sexuality, desire can be both an individual and a collective experience. I mentioned Chris early in this book. He was the person who so profoundly awakened my sexual self and was a consistently positive cis heterosexual man in my life journey. Chris was in a successful rock band, and when he and I were dating, I saw how women in particular, but men platonically, too, were drawn to him and his bandmates while they were playing. The fist pumping and bra throwing were more than just a connection to the music; it was an energy exchange and not just a sexual desire. Desire here was a wish and hope for the desire to be offered, met, and matched, an "I want *you* to *notice* me. I want you to connect with me. I want you to want me. I want to share with you this musical experience."

Desire is an innate and natural spark within all of us; it is complicated and simple and an embodiment of vibrancy. Simply put, I believe desire is about understanding, protecting, growing, tapping into, and allowing the innate and natural spark inside us to glow. It begins outside sexual connection and grows into sexual expression and experience. Desire has a synergistic quality—what it feeds, feeds it. In the context of holistic sexuality, we can think of desire as related to sensuality and pleasure. The metaphor of a bonfire is illustrative. To ignite a fire, you need three things: oxygen, heat, and fuel. Sensuality is the oxygen, pleasure the heat, and desire the fuel. Heat (pleasure) is needed to raise the temperature of the fuel (desire) to its ignition point, and oxygen (sensuality) is inherently present but can also help ignite the fire and increase it as it burns. Fuel (desire) is the material in the bonfire that combusts, releasing energy in the form of heat (pleasure). Pleasure, sensuality, and desire light a fire in many forms and combinations, and each relationship you enter may require a different formula.

After you build a bonfire, you must tend to it or it will extinguish—and this is the same with desire. It may feel like work to you initially, but there is an anticipation that accompanies the tending of desire. Sometimes it grows gently and over time, so desire is roaring steadily and giving off light and warmth. Other times desire takes quickly and unexpectedly and then cools. Every bonfire burns differently, and we don't see this variance as broken or unexpected—we see it as a natural cause and effect. And so it is with desire: In the context of holistic sexuality, expect work to be involved, and know that you are responsible for tending to it. Desire is important for your well-being whether you're currently experiencing sexual connection or not. It's as much for you as it is for anyone else.

Vibrancy and Spark

When you want to create a new relationship with desire, you must connect or reconnect with the spark in your life and whatever fosters your vibrancy. Creativity is often a powerful place to focus in this initial phase. Pay attention to when your body buzzes as you are creating something, whether that's a meal, DIY home renovations, a piece of art, a business idea, a lemonade stand for your child, a new song, or a note of gratitude for someone. Creation is a straight shot to your life source. This is the energy to pay attention to.

For others, the process begins with asking the question "What creates a spark within me?" It may be entering the doors of your spiritual community or spending time with your children. It may be a long bike ride or a dinner table full of like-minded friends immersed in fun conversation. Perhaps it is game night or a family barbecue. Maybe it is settling into a cozy reading nook with your favorite book with no human around for miles. Approach this question with an attitude of openness, truth, and curiosity, and do not edit your answers as they flow to you.

There is no right or wrong type of desire, inside or outside sexual connection. What juices you is what juices you. And that is the beauty of it. Your relationship with desire gets to be yours and no one else's. You get to experience desire, express desire, and feel desire on your terms, whether you are in a relationship or not. Take responsibility for getting to know the source of your spark and vibrancy. Remember it, protect it, update it.

Authentic conversations with friends are a life force for me. I know that I am and feel vibrant when I have friends in my home for a meal or game night or just a night of music and fun community. I also love making new friends at retreats and workshops. I find a spark when I travel, whether that is down a tree-lined road near my home or in a far-off country that took a day to fly to. I know that I am sparked when I am completely and utterly present with my children. I find vibrancy when I hear my family saying they love the meal I cooked.

When you are creating a lifestyle of desire for yourself and embarking on a purposeful and intentional relationship with desire, do not look at it as something partitioned in your life. Just as I advised you to infuse your life with pleasure, infuse your life with desire-based thoughts, activities, relationships, and interests. A desire-filled lifestyle isn't about only doing things that are pleasure-based; it isn't about avoiding responsibilities or ignoring the roller coaster of emotions that life can take you on. It is about creating a database of options for you to tap into. A lifestyle of desire is about creating a relationship to desire that flows back and forth, inside and outside sexual connection, with synergy and ease. Once you have a good feel for your desire outside sexual connection, turn your exploration toward sexual connection.

Finding Sexy

There isn't one pillar of holistic sexuality that's immune to judgment, and desire is no exception, especially when we're finding our own brand of sexy. We receive judgment from ourselves, others, friends, and society at large, especially with the explosion of social media. It's gotten harder and harder to find our sexy; instead, the judgments pile up to impede our desire because we are not the "right" kind of sexy.

Both in subtle and overt ways, we also judge others: "Well, she wasn't having sex with him, no wonder he cheated" or "The woman he slept with is a total slut" or "She's single and has to be having the hottest sex of her life." Jealousy, judgment, and a "mean girl" mentality are barriers to finding your sexy and can certainly be barriers to your desire at large—as we judge others, we judge ourselves. As an exercise, the next time you see something stereotypically "sexy" on social media, read the comments. What comes up for you as you read other people's comments? This exercise highlights the insidious impacts that judgments and societal influence can have on us all.

As an answer to this, I created a workshop called Finding Sexy that tackles the concept of what is sexy for *you*. When I first started running it, I struggled to recruit participants. The word "sexy" was either offensive or a turn-off (ironically). That reaction is exactly why I designed the workshop. Fuck that. We should all feel sexy. And we should all determine what is sexy to us. I want you to find your sexy and live it unapologetically. So let me give you some ways and means to do that here.

Two powerful tools to access are the pillars of sensuality and pleasure. Both can serve as incredible ways to inflame your desire within sexual connection. Use your yums as a foundation for your desire. When you are doused with sensual pleasure, desire will be inflamed. Reward your body with pleasurable sensations, experiences, and positive hormonal sparks.

You can also do this with sex acts (see pillar 5). Why would your body desire to partake in something that does not please your senses or feel good? The answer: It wouldn't. Connect your desire with techniques and sex acts that bring pleasure to your body and sensual experiences that kindle your present-mindedness within sexual connection. Seek a sexual partner or partners that you have sexual synergy with—that's a polite way of saying seek sexual partners who, in your opinion, are good in bed. As I talked about in the previous chapter, cultivate a self-pleasure practice that fuels you. Make it playful, varied, fun, sexy, exciting, and authentically enjoyable. Prioritize it, and you will feel the benefits.

Let fantasies be a private fuel for desire. Explore fantasies that you have fun thinking about but don't think you would actually do and fantasies that you would consider trying out in real life. Give your imagination room to explore and play. Let it lead you to new places, to new edges and interests within you. Make a physical list or mental one that you can pull from to keep you stoked. Make it about you, not about what others say is sexy or risky or edgy.

Finally, honestly and authentically audit the emotional safety you feel in your life and particularly if you have a partner. Emotional safety is the number one aphrodisiac. I will die on a hill asserting that. If you don't feel emotionally safe because of mental stress, insecurity, or distraction, it can be difficult to have full access to your desire pool. If you don't feel safe within a relationship because of discord, inattentiveness, disconnection, conflict, or physical abuse, you will not feel desire for connection in many contexts. Similarly, if the skill level is off, if emotional intimacy isn't present, desire will be elusive as well.

Your essence asks: Why would your soul want to connect with another if you don't feel safe? Why would your body want to sexually connect if the exchange or sex act doesn't feel good or the person(s) aren't sexually skilled in a way that brings you pleasure and stokes desire and arousal? The answer, again: It wouldn't. When you partner with someone, focus on maintaining your relationship with desire and not falling into a trap of comparison and judgment. Simultaneously, you must also consider your partner's relationship to their desire as well. Standing in your relationship to desire alongside someone else's can be complicated if your desires don't align. But it can be done. This is often when a couple will seek out the support of a professional for help navigating the situation.

Owning your relationship to desire also shields you from society's messaging about desire comparison, that erroneous description of low and high desire that I talked about at the beginning of this chapter. You will experience shifts in your desire. At times, it will feel ever-present and easy to tune into. Other times, it will feel muted or distant. Neither is right or wrong. They just are where you are. If you want to change your relationship or access to desire, focus on sensuality and pleasure, not judgment of yourself. Make the change only if you want to without bowing to pressure from partners or a magazine article or an advertisement for a sexual health product or whatever messages you've absorbed about what desire is supposed to feel like. Find the agency in your expression and experience of desire.

Mapping Your Desire

I believe that "desire" is another term within holistic sexuality that is a concept rather than something that can be defined in a few words. When creating a new relationship with this concept, using imagery can be a great way to begin. Getting out of your intellect and into your creative, intuitive self can make a big difference. Art, imagery, music, and physicality can be wonderful ways to explore and express concepts within sexuality, if words are elusive.

Start with this question: What imagery comes to mind when you think about your current relationship with desire? Don't edit, judge, or try to make the answer "right." Answer it authentically and go with the first image that calls to you. Here are some examples that might spark you.

- A swamp—my desire is murky and mysterious.
- A babbling brook—my desire is lovely, quaint, moving along, and perfectly content.
- A display of fireworks—my desire can create some chaos and fear but can also make people feel excited and alive.

People relate to their desire in many different ways. None are wrong. None are right. They are either authentic or inauthentic. Having an emotional reaction to your imagery is normal, and I want you to invite in any emotions to this endeavor. Feel them, write them out, just don't judge them. If you find yourself judging nonetheless, find a separate piece of paper and write out all the judgments. Get them all out and then chuck that piece of paper. You must not avoid emotionally intense reactions or they will block your insights, but setting up permanent camp with them will also curtail change in your relationship with desire. Becoming aware of strong emotions and working with them when they show up will keep you moving in the right direction.

My client Xavier, a gay Black cis man in his thirties, came to me because he had put his pursuit of a committed relationship and family on the back burner as he focused on his career. As we explored desire, we found some resistance. And where there is resistance, there is insight waiting. We began exploring his experience as a young Black man in the South who was figuring out that he was gay. He felt out of place in multiple ways. He felt unsafe on several levels. But his mother was entirely and deeply supportive, and he felt secure in his own home and in his own skin when in the private bubble with her. Thus, his self-pleasure was plentiful and boundless, because it had been rooted in acceptance and safety. However, connecting his desire to others did not feel safe and in some ways was nonexistent.

He had moved north for college and then planted himself in New York City for his career, and together we explored his progression to self-acceptance in sexual relationships. Xavier realized he often established himself as someone's friend, the supportive, kind, and giving one. He was best friends with women, and he collected them without meaning to. He was also known for his work ethic and talent. In his eyes, he was not known for being sexy, for being a sexual partner, for prioritizing his sexual life. However, he was sexually active and did have several long-term relationships. He described their outward vibe to be of dear friends who sometimes had sex rather than steeped in sexual chemistry and desire. But they had it. Each of his relationships. Privately. Almost secretly.

During one session, he told me he didn't think he had the "vibe of a sexual person." I asked what that meant, and he sat silent. He wasn't sure. He just knew that wasn't him. Xavier had all the outward appearances of a conventionally attractive man. He was beloved, emotionally mature, smart, funny, engaging, confident, talented, and successful. He dressed immaculately. But he didn't feel in touch with his desire for others and didn't think others felt desire for him.

When I asked him to put imagery to his desire, he answered more quickly than most. Within seconds, he described his relationship with desire as a black lacquered box put on the third shelf of a bookcase. He explained that not many people notice the presence of the box and only see the decor surrounding it. And even fewer try to open the box. For those who do open it, they find this beautiful gift: a gold interior, shining and opulent. The gift of his desire awaits those who don't overlook that part of him.

When I asked him to describe the gifts desire had for him, Xavier began crying. He said it felt like years of discrimination, fear, lack of safety, lack of welcoming, lack of wanting, and secrecy were melting off him. And as I witnessed his shedding of pain and prejudice, he ended with a simple statement: "I am taking this beautiful box of desire off the third shelf and placing it on the mantle of my fireplace. I want it seen. I want it accessible. I want others to celebrate it."

What Gets in the Way of Desire?

For one of my clients, the biggest impediment to her relationship with desire was the stress she felt from an unfulfilling career. By the end of our work together, she discovered that her most immediate impediment was that the door to the bedroom she and her husband shared did not close tightly enough, so when they wanted to connect sexually, she could rarely sink into the safety of privacy from their young child. They bought an electronic coded lock for their door, worked on cementing their son's bedtime routine earlier in the evening, and introduced the concept of "parent time" that their son could not interrupt. Her relationship with desire shifted dramatically with these changes. Often the formula to a shift in your relationship to desire includes several factors with one dominating feature that may not be obvious at first. It can feel frustrating to not have an obvious reason or quick fix, but the web of reasons can present itself if you remain curious to the discovery from many angles.

Emily Nagoski, author of *Come as You Are*, explains expertly how female sexual excitation and desire works. The book is wildly successful because in it she breaks down, in a very accessible way, the science and psychosocial impediments women have with desire.

She uses a brilliant analogy of a gas pedal and brake to talk about cisgender women's desire. The gas pedal (an accelerator) responds to all sexually relevant information in the environment, sending a "turned on" signal. And the break (a dampener), operating at the same time as the gas pedal, responds to all the reasons to not be turned on and sends a "turned off" signal. The details for both the gas pedal and brake differ for each person but include the range of things below in the three categories I name mind, body, and soul.

Encountering impediments to the relationship to desire you want is common. Sometimes there are a few, and other times the list is plentiful. There are expected ebbs and flows in life, within each person internally and, if relevant, in the life of a long-term relationship. Know that acute and specific impediments may become a persistent pattern in your life. Some impediments are obvious, such as a side effect of psychotropic medicine or a shitty relationship, while others are not as obvious to us, such as a slight shift in our hormones or feeling stressed at work. Impediments often fall into one of three internal categories.

- **Mind:** anxiety, relationship stress, mental illness, work stress, parenting stress, distraction, racing thoughts, messages about sexuality, and not feeling good about your body.

- **Body:** medication, chronic illness, physical pain, hormonal changes, terminal illness, injury, and disconnection with body.

- **Soul:** safety, deep depression, spiritual or worldview crisis, soulful disconnection, loneliness, political violence, isolation, crisis of faith, global fear, trauma triggers, grief, loss, vulnerability, and intimacy.

Other impediments include logistics, such as a lack of privacy or a bumpy transition from parent mode to sexual connection, and the caliber of your sexual connection: when you are not partnered with someone who you think is "good in bed"; when you do not experience pleasure consistently or at all; when you do not see the value of sexual connection; when your body or your partner's is not functioning as you would like. Trauma and violence in any form, but particularly sexual violence and trauma, will often be an impediment in all or any of those categories.

Take some time to explore each of these factors, and let ideas flow as they arise. Trust any thoughts that emerge, and add them to your list. As you grow your list, you will likely start seeing patterns form. Rarely is there just one impediment to desire. Some impediments can be grouped together, and others are stand-alone. As you do this desire audit, suspend judgment and let the answers just flow to you.

When you have explored many possible blocks to your desire, chart the impediments and note how they affect your desire; list ideas to lessen their influence, further research the support you need to problem-solve, and keep track of effective and ineffective interventions as you try different approaches to overcoming the impediment. Track the presence or absence of the impediment as you grow and change your relationship to desire.

Changing your relationship with desire is rarely quick or simple. A pill may help with an erection, but it won't fix a couple's painful history of frustration that gets in the way of desire blooming nor will it automatically cause desire or pleasure-filled sexual connection. There is a powerful difference between physical ability and arousal, desire and excitation (orgasm) cycles. For example, women using menopausal replacement therapy (MRT) may see a difference in menopausal symptoms such as an increase of energy level, reduction of brain fog, and an increase in interest in sexual connection, but MRT may not directly increase physical and mental arousal and does not address the relational issues experienced from a pattern of desire impediments in a relationship. Yet for some, it does begin the spark of desire that can create a new baseline for exploration and healing.

There are often several hurdles to jump when transforming your desire relationship from where it is to where you want it to be. Some hurdles are obvious and can be solved quickly, and others take time and patience to untangle. Lucia, a client, is a powerful example of the complexity and timeline of a substantive change in relationship to desire.

At the age of thirty-six, Lucia came to me describing herself as feeling dead inside. She had experienced a rape in college and contracted an STI. Her parents discovered the rape through insurance claims from medical tests following the assault. Their reaction was negative and focused on her STI and what that meant to her future rather than to her mental health and well-being. Their reaction made her feel dirty and undesirable. "Broken" and "damaged" were two words she used to describe herself. She decided to not report the crime to the police or the college, and she took a semester off school.

When she returned to school, she focused on her studies and survived running into her assaulter on the small campus. Upon graduation, she realized that she and an old friend had more feelings for each other than just friendship. After a few years of dating, they married. They had a happy marriage, but their sexual life wasn't a priority or a place of comfort or passion. In many ways, they were best friends who happened to have sex every once in a while and figured out how to run a house, a family, and a life together. Lucia wasn't interested in a sexual life and didn't see herself as a sexual being or as attractive. Her husband expressed interest in sex and distress at not having an active sex life with her. Yet he also traveled a lot and didn't have a lot of time or ability to help with child-rearing and household chores. Lucia was often exhausted or resentful when he was home from his weekly work travels.

Several years after they finished having children and he got a vasectomy, she told him that she would be happy never having sex again and jokingly gave him her blessing to have extramarital affairs as he traveled for work. They had a don't ask, don't tell policy, so she wasn't sure if he had taken her up on the offer. Lucia laughed ironically with friends about her lack of desire and near disdain for the thought of having sex again. She felt happy with her role as a mother and with her growing spiritual relationship within her church community.

One day, Lucia was using her husband's computer and discovered that he and his best friend shared a membership for a site for sex workers. When she researched his history, she realized he had been hiring sex workers for the majority of their marriage and well before she had given her blessing for him to have sex outside the marriage. She told him what she had learned, and he gave her more information that included visits to massage parlors and multiple sex worker and porn site memberships.

They stayed together, did not seek therapy, and attempted to continue a relationship with each other. Their poor communication was a major inhibitor to success, and a month after they moved to a new state for his job, he fell in love with another woman who would not continue the relationship if he remained married. So he ended the marriage with Lucia.

Lucia came to me devastated and lost. Over and over, she described herself as feeling dead inside and that she would never love again, let alone have anyone interested in her. She had lost weight and felt disconnected from her body. She didn't know how she would date if she never wanted to have sex again. She described her image of her relationship with desire as a plug-in heater that was broken, covered in dust, and sitting next to a chair. She could see it and also ignore it in the mess of everything. She used the words "useless, pointless, cluttered, and a source of aggravation" to describe her view of desire. She said sex was not in her future, and "sexy" was for other people and not her.

We worked on processing her multiple sexual trauma experiences. I helped her to create a new relationship with her body and focused on unpacking the many things that got in the way of her relationship with desire, the first being her concept of desire. As she moved through the processing of sexual trauma, she learned to define her sexuality on her own terms rather than those of her parents, her perpetrator, or her husband.

Throughout our work, Lucia kept reminding me that she was feeling better about herself but did not want to have sex again. I reminded her that having sex again wasn't the goal. The goal was her discovering her yeses and nos, her yums and yucks. We set out to discover everything that brought her spark outside sexual connection.

After about a year of work together, she said she was interested in getting on a few dating apps to meet new people. We prepped for the apps and planned for the experience. Lucia was reluctant to hope and nervous to jump into the dating pool. When I suggested we explore the sparks within sexual connection, she reminded me again that she was not interested in sex. What she wanted was tips on how to make this clear to any suitors. We discussed a few strategies to manage this, including a line on her profile and a verbal script she could use on a phone call or in-person date.

After a few months of talking to and texting with several guys, she decided she wanted to go out with one of them. She liked how he was treating her, she thought he looked cute, and he offered up a fun date idea. She felt nothing stirring inside her beyond friendship and curiosity. She felt like he was cuter than her, and she wasn't sure why he'd be interested in her so she concluded it must be that he wanted a friend. They went on a date, and Lucia called me for an emergency session the following day. I was concerned but then relieved when she said, "Dr. J., he was great. He was nice and fun and asked all about me. I had no idea what it was like for someone to ask about me and listen. He wasn't on his phone the whole time; he looked at me. And it was so hot! He walked me to my car and asked if he could hug me. I said yes and we hugged and well... OMG, something happened inside me. He asked if he could kiss me and the earth stopped turning. It was the hottest kiss I've ever had. I got so turned on that I wanted to have sex with him on the spot. We didn't, but I wanted to. I went into this date certain I would never want sex again. Now it is all I can think about. My desire is no longer a plug-in heater; it is an electric fireplace and someone just flipped the switch. I had no idea I could feel this alive. I thought that part of me was forever lost, and now the floodgates are open."

The journey to this point was long and convoluted, but when the spark of desire ignited within Lucia, it spread like wildfire. For some, the spark ignites outside of a sexual context, and for others, that is the place it begins.

Desire is a complex web of mind, body, and soul; internal and external elements that need to be tended consistently; and an energy source for sexuality and sexual connections.

WITH THE BONFIRE of sensuality, pleasure, and desire lit, and the grounded force of wellness and fertility alive in your mind, let's move into a deeper exploration of sex acts in the next pillar: acts and interests.

REVEAL YOURSELF TO YOURSELF

- What imagery represents your current desire?
- What relationship to desire do you want to have?
- What impediments have you felt or do you feel between the relationship to desire you have or had and want to have?
- What messages have you been given about your type of desire, historically and currently?
- What is sexy to you? What is sexy about you?
- Where do you feel the most vibrant in your life?
- Where has your agency been inhibited within desire?

PILLAR 5
Acts and Interests

WE WERE SITTING in the bathtub together, bubbles surrounding us, things heating up. Our hands were wandering. We were throwing "the look" back and forth to each other. The conversation began to include things we wanted to do to, with, and for each other. My lover knew that I was turned on by sounds of pleasure and by storytelling and fantasies. I felt like I was in a safe place to explore as we had done before, so I told him a fantasy that was newly brewing in my mind's eye, one that I was excited to share. "What the fuck, Juliana?" was his response. I was stunned, hurt, violated. I felt so out there in the open, vulnerable and exposed in more ways than one.

I had meant for my fantasy to come across as just that, a fantasy that turns me on, that I love to think about but don't want to *actually* do. My fantasy certainly hit a nerve, and he went straight to judgment. We hadn't talked about what would feel safe that evening, but after sharing our fantasies many times before, I thought we had that part covered. Apparently not. He felt tweaked and confused by my newly stated interest, and I felt judged and shamed. Sexy time turned into "What the fuck?" for both of us. He yucked my yum.

WHEN PEOPLE think about sexuality without a holistic lens, they usually conjure images and memories of sex acts of all types. That's

Your yucks and yums guide you.

what this pillar is all about. Mostly this is the fun stuff. All the good and pleasurable things we partake in with ourselves and others. But because this is holistic sexuality, we're going to dive deep into meaning.

The pillar of acts and interests focuses on what you want and don't want *to do*. "Doing" being key here. Simply, these are the things we do with our bodies solo and/or with other people in agency-driven decisions that are based on what your body tells you is a yes or no. You might have a yes to receiving oral sex but a no to giving it. You may be a yum to doggie style and a yuck to sex in public. The continuum ranges from hand-holding and kissing to sex positions such as reverse cowgirl and scissoring to pegging, prostate-milking, and cuckolding. All this is within the context of your values, interests, edges, exposure, and options. You make meaning of what sex acts you want to experience and which you don't. This meaning varies as do the feelings we assign to it. You also make meaning of what sex acts you have access to and which ones you don't. Others make meaning about you based on your sex experiences too. Finally, there are the details needed for a sex act to be a yum or yuck and who you would want to partake in these sex acts with.

We don't often take the time to think through what we want to do in detail or with forethought. You may think broad things like, "I want sex more often" or "I wish it was spicy!" But figuring out the details of sex acts with forethought and purpose is pretty uncommon. Most societies set the standards for what constitutes satisfying sex but do not prioritize putting time into sexual fulfillment.

As in other aspects of holistic sexuality, there is terminology I want to encourage you to use. You may have noticed already that I use "sexual connection" or "inside a sexual context" instead of "sex" most of the time. This is on purpose. When we use "sex" as a catchall, it is based on an assumption that we are talking about penetrative sex. Though there is a large range of sex acts, we are historically coming from a heteronormative bias that places penetrative sex as the only kind of sex that matters if we are speaking about... sex. This thinking is akin to the archaic way of looking at virginity as being only about when a penis is in a vagina for the first time. I much prefer "sexual debut" as the terminology over "losing your virginity." The list of first sexual acts and connections could be endless and therefore becomes meaningless in some ways and dilutes something meaningful in other ways. Using "sexual connection," instead of "sex," may feel cumbersome at first, but it is reflective of a holistic sexuality mindset.

There are many steps to achieving a fulfilling sex life. Identifying what you like and don't like is one of them. Communicating this to others is another.

Do Your Own Research

Part of the formal sex education most of us received contained some not-so-helpful messaging: We aren't going to say what the sex acts are because that is classless and improper—but we will detail how your body parts will fall off if you do these unmentionable acts.

In the United States, national sex education began in the 1920s—and a lot of the curriculum used today reads as if it hasn't been updated since then. Most sex education was and remains heteronormative, cisgender biased, and relationship focused. And of course, abstinence based. Talk about the perfect combination designed to instill deep-seated shame in you about sex acts and pleasure exploration.

As noted earlier, up until the last ten years or so, regular sex ed classes typically did not describe or teach about sex acts beyond the acts that could result in pregnancy or STIs. This has changed to be more inclusive to an extent, but we have seen some significant backslides as well. Luckily, we have vast access to a variety of sex acts through professionals (somatic therapists, sex coaches, sex workers, sexual surrogate partners, and intimacy coordinators, for example), internet searches, online sex education platforms and organizations, sex-act specific tutorials, chat rooms, as well as better access to ethical porn in general. There are so many resources out there to support a move beyond sex tips, to embrace the full continuum of sex acts and connection.

This pillar demands that we activate our agency within sexual connection, which will translate to contexts outside sexual connection. Through my work, I've discovered that many people find themselves in the midst of a sex act without having thought it through with intention. It is "just happening." A common scenario of this sort is starting by consenting to kiss and make out with clothes on to taking some clothing off to "How is his dick about to go inside me?"

I will talk about consent, coercion, and sexual violence in pillar 7, power and trauma. Here we focus more on the agency of choosing sex acts that you want to do and choosing not to partake in sex acts that you are not interested in, either within the context of solo sex or with partner(s) who are fully participating in mutual consent. I want you to move out of "This just happened, and I went with it" to "I want this. This is an enthusiastic yes for me." I want you to pursue it with intent and forethought. I want you to get deeply attuned to this mindset of asking yourself what you want and do not want. "Is this a yuck or yum for me?" should become a question you ask instinctively, a muscle memory.

All Tied Up by Choice

As soon as I learned of shibari, the Japanese art of tight binding with ropes or silks, I wanted to experience it. I had experienced violence in a relationship, so I wasn't sure how I would feel about the restraint, but my instinct was that with the right person and in the right context, I would like it, maybe love it. I knew it might beautifully strengthen the mind-body connection through sensuality, pleasure, and desire. Even with my fear, I had an enthusiastic yes swimming around and awaiting circumstances that made sense. That happened at a conference where an expert was teaching about impact play, shibari, and how consent is negotiated with submissive and dominant playmates. The expert spoke and then he brought in one of his long-term playmates to talk about her experience.

The presentation felt tame and basic to me, but when the expert and his partner moved into a demonstration, the shift was jarring. Even though we had listened to their consent process beforehand, I still wasn't prepared for what happened. When she was blindfolded and tied up, she looked to me like a kidnap victim. My fear, trauma, and judgment ran right into the experience with me. It progressed from feeling like a question to me to "ugh... and yuck."

He circled her and pounced—impact. He slapped the shibari rope behind her as a playful acknowledgment of where he was and what he was going to do, and then he quickly came upon her and tied another limb. It was fast and slow simultaneously. He would walk back, crouch down, and watch her. When she undulated and swayed, giving him approval for what he was doing, he would move into another tying sequence. They had a well-choreographed and experienced dance.

As it progressed and as I settled into a knowing that she was giving active consent throughout the scene, I grew in that safety. It surprised me. At times during this performance, I leaned in with an excited yes and other times I thought, "What the fuck?" The yum and yuck yo-yo effect was strong. Sometimes it felt like I hadn't given consent to see it. I noticed other participants leaving or hugging each other. Others looked horrified, and still others were mesmerized and clearly turned on. When the scene was over, the couple debriefed. The expert and his partner moved from an incredibly intense connection to a normal casualness that was stunning. After hearing her reaction to the scene and listening to her describe how turned on she was and why she is drawn to submissive-dominant (sub-dom) impact play and shibari, tension in my body eased more deeply. My instinct was confirmed in hearing her say she was not only okay, she was feeling blissful. I saw that my fear was a "me" thing and not a "her" thing at all. Another fascinating reminder of the beautiful array of sexual interests of humans.

After a break, the expert announced that we would be pairing up to try rope-tying on each other. Since I knew everyone in the group, I felt automatically safe. This was going to be fun. Then he said, "I need a volunteer," and my hand shot up. He picked me. My first time with shibari was going to be with an expert. Hot damn.

To my huge surprise, although this expert was not my preferred type and I felt zero attraction to him, I was instantly excited. My yes was becoming so very enthusiastic. He went through the consent process with me and gave me his plan in generalities. Then he asked specific questions: Did I want to keep my shirt on or take it off? Could he tie my arms, my neck? Could he place me in a sitting position? I confirmed my yeses and nos easily: yes to tying my arms, no to my neck, yes to sitting, no to lying me on my side. He seemed satisfied with the consent process and I felt comfortable moving forward, but I still didn't know exactly what to expect.

He moved me into a seated position, and he began tying my hands and arms. He had quick motions and slow ones as he'd had with his first partner. None of it hurt, some of it felt tense, but I never felt a no. The rope was coarse, and some strands were thick and others thin. Every few minutes, he checked in with me. I nodded yes to each inquiry—I wanted this. I became aware of others around us and looked around. He noticed and quickly came up behind me and whispered, "I want you to close your eyes and not open them once. I am going to walk in front of you and watch you. Your eyes. Do not open them. I have you. I've got you. You are safe with me. It is just us. Here. Juliana, you are mine."

If I read those words back to you now, I would probably roll my eyes. Ick. No. Not sexy. They would sound misogynistic and performative and expected. But in that moment, the way he said those words made me feel like putty. It was a clear yes for me. I liked that he said he had me. I liked that he told me where he would be. I liked that he was clear about what he wanted me to do. Yes. Yum. I could not have been more turned on. I felt lost in the connection and loved feeling myself trusting someone so fully. I was attracted to the dynamic, not to him, and that felt fun to play with.

But then he wrapped a rope around my big toe and moved my leg in a new direction so quickly, without talking about it, and I needed a minute to catch up. I didn't like that he did that and didn't like the feel of the new position, and I told him that. The spell was broken. He responded with respect and asked if I wanted to continue. I checked in with myself, and it was a no. Not a damaged no, but a no. He unwrapped more of me, and we sat and talked. Attraction gone. Some of that was because of the reaction to the toe move, but mainly it was because with my eyes open and the scene done, we moved into a different space quickly. I realized that it was one of the first times I had felt safe to say no to a man without fear of reprisal. He had no resistance to and all respect for my no. An hour later, I was surprised to feel pleasure at seeing the indentations of the rope on my toe and bicep. It was an incredibly positive and yum-filled experience.

The important takeaway here is that agency is twofold. You can tune into your yeses and nos—what you want or don't want and need or don't need—when you are confronted in the moment and also with purpose and intention ahead of time. Despite my experience with violence in the past, I felt safe to explore with the shibari expert because we had meaningful consent, and it felt right for me in the moment. At this point in my journey, I had developed a strong sense of agency. I had learned how to say no in the middle of sexual connection and to not override my no because I worried it might be awkward or would cause an emotional outburst from my partner.

In the context of holistic sexuality, after you've experienced or while you are experiencing a sex act, you can explore if it will continue to be a yes or no for you. For yourself and from others, a yes is not an authentic yes unless no is an equally acceptable answer. Your body does not lie to you about what it wants or does not want. This is why it is so important to work on the skill of reading your body signals through mindfulness. Dr. Jennifer Gunsaullus's book *From Madness to Mindfulness* makes a powerful case for mindfulness in sex with meditation and embodiment. You must be able to read your body's cues of yeses and nos in order to activate agency. You will know your strong and certain yeses or nos when you reflect on how your body and mind feel about any given action. In an otherwise consensual and safe dynamic, it is important to exercise agency within sex acts, rather than push your body through a no to a reluctant yes. If your body and soul communicate something is a no, follow through with that no. Sucking it up and pushing through are damaging to your mind-body-soul connection and to your trust. It's a form of self-abandonment. Know the difference between a nudge and a shove. A mantra I adopted in midlife was "I no longer want to be good at doing hard things." And this begins with not pushing through emotional, relationship, or sexual nos.

The Yum and Yuck Continuum

There are many ways to determine what sex acts you want and work for you, and what sex acts you do not want and don't work for you. Start with what you know about yourself, what you know about that sex act, and who you want it to involve. These are your yeses and nos, or your yucks and yums, as I like to call them. Whichever you use, these two powerful sets of terms address the range of your wants, needs, desire, and pleasure, as well as your edges, nudges, and shoves. This is the yum and yuck continuum.

Two of my favorite sounds have familiar homes in this pillar. The moans of pleasure and "Huh!"—the sound of curiosity, like, "Who knew?" That sound communicates an attitude of accepting ambiguity: "I don't know, and I am okay not knowing yet." It means "I feel safe even if I don't completely get this." This attitude creates room for you to be messy and take some safe risks. Standing next to this concept is the idea of "no thank you" bites.

Early on, I agreed with my daughter that when she is offered new food that looks weird to her, she will take at least one "no thank you" bite. She is willing to try because afterward she gets to decide if it's a no or yes for her going forward. There are some things she doesn't have to try, and she always has the option to say no; I trust her gut on this. I'm teaching her how to trust her instincts. There is no force in this agreement, but there is some nudging to take a "no thank you" bite.

You can do this in your sexual connections too. You can take a "no thank you" bite, have an "absolutely hell no," explore a "why not," or jump into a "hell yes!" You control this process. Just be intentional with your choices so you create safety for yourself, and your partner as appropriate, as you explore your yum and yuck continuum. Activate your agency fully and consistently, and allow others to do so as well.

When you think about it, some parts of sexual connection are truly absurd, full of unexpected moments and physical happenings—the fluids, the positions, the noises. Knowing your yeses and nos sometimes feels clear and other times murky and full of "maybe or not" and "I think perhaps." Some of this is because of the messiness of sexual connections. Discomfort with uncertainty affects your decision to do a particular sex act more than once, or to invite a new one into your sex menu. When you find yourself in the maybe places, take it seriously and review it lightly. Allow yourself some looseness, but find clarity for yourself.

Keep reviewing your yucks and yums as you explore the sex acts that you are curious about. Remember that knowing your nos requires that you know your yeses. Become a lifelong learner about what you want to say yes and no to, so you can push the edges of your yum and yuck continuum inside and outside sexual connection.

SEXERCISE: Four Quadrants

This is one of my favorite exercises to give to clients, and I hope you enjoy it and open up to the wonders and gems that await you as you do.

Have fun with it. Your answers do not need to be set in stone or diagnostic. This is information that you can remain curious about and have fun with. Do this exercise solo or with partner(s) or people you have non-sexual relationships in your life. Take it seriously and lightly simultaneously. Here's how you do it.

1 Make a list of at least forty sex acts—every kind of sexual behavior or practice that you can think of. An act could be anything from having your hand held, kissing, and cuddling to the kinkiest, wildest, "may need to look up what it means" sort of sex acts. Include solo sex acts. Ask others or search on the internet if you run out of ideas. Think of sex acts that are solo and those that are with others. Go big and wide with your ideas.

2 Once you have a list you feel good about, consider the sex acts one by one and place them in one of the four quadrants in the diagram. (You may want to redraw this, or you can download the worksheet from therevealedlife.com.) Place every item from your list on the diagram.

3 Release yourself from judgment and shame every time it arrives.

When you are done, take a moment to express gratitude that you prioritized your sexual life and health and were brave to ask yourself these questions, which we often don't take the time to explore. If you decide to share with anyone else, thank them for hearing your desires, your yeses, and your nos and for sharing a safe space with you. Revisit this exercise periodically. Add to your sex act list. Shuffle acts into different quadrants, and add acts to your four quadrants.

If you are single, this exercise can help you understand your yeses and nos before connecting with another, as well as help you know your solo sex interests and seek partners who want to partake in partnered sex acts of mutual interest and who respect that you don't want to do certain acts. It allows you to bring a clear path to new partners. It can take out the guesswork ahead of time.

Acts and Interests

I HAVE DONE THESE THINGS	
I would do these things again	I have done these things and would not do them again

I WOULD DO THESE THINGS	I WOULD NOT DO THESE THINGS
I have not done these things and want to do them	I have not done these things and do not want to do them

If you are partnered, this exercise can be used for your own information, to share with your partner, or to explore your answers and edges together. It gives you a direct way to communicate clearly about what you want and don't want.

This exercise can help you see something you'd like to add to your sexual life. It can also identify what you want to subtract.

Let's Talk About Sex

Another aspect within the yum and yuck continuum that requires self-knowledge, agency, and communication is approaching topics like ethical nonmonogamy, sex work, porn use, and cheating boundaries. There are more hot-button topics, but I am most often asked to help people navigate these.

The skills you need to approach these topics are the same as what's required for almost any conversation about sex acts.

- Know yourself, your needs, your wants, your yucks and yums, your boundaries. Pay attention to opinions that seem clear but could shift if you see the topic on your own genuine terms rather than what you've accepted by habit or inheritance.
- Root yourself in the mindset of sexual agency and the skill of agency.
- Communicate clearly and authentically, and be someone that another person can show up to in authenticity without facing judgment.
- Establish the safety needs for all involved in the conversation with emotional vulnerability.
- Become well versed in seeking and giving enthusiastic consent and in knowing how to discern when it is not given.
- Identify when you are open to taking a "no thank you" bite.
- Be alert to what compromise you might make for a relationship and what would constitute a compromise of your soul.
- Keep criticism out of the conversation, and watch for nonverbal cues and tones of voice that communicate judgment or that "yuck a yum."
- Focus on what you want, why it is a yum, and be open to anything that could bring a similar excitement to you if your yum is a yuck to someone else.

- Consider the conversation dynamic, ongoing, and fluid. Revisit it often.

I once worked with a couple, Mark, a transgender man, and Grettel, a cisgender woman, who reported having a wonderful marriage aside from Grettel feeling desperate to connect with Mark more deeply in their sexual life. He said he was happy in their marriage and didn't understand why things felt lacking for her in their sex life. She didn't want to cheat on him to try new things sexually, but she also didn't want to settle for anything less than her sexual dreams.

As they described their attempts to communicate about their sex life, a pattern became clear. She approached him with new things she wanted to try, such as bondage, a sex swing, or watching porn together, as either a joke or in a coercive way that was off-putting to him. Mark brushed off her attempts as juvenile and not important to their relationship. He had built up feelings of annoyance and disrespect that she was prioritizing her needs over his or their joint goals, and she had a growing sense of shame and anger that he was not taking her needs seriously.

As we worked together, he found out that the things she wanted to add to their sex life didn't feel so far out there for him; they seemed interesting and fun. He realized he was reacting to how she approached him, not to the sex acts themselves. He liked the idea of watching porn together and thought that learning how to tie knots for bondage play would be fun. She learned that he had a richer fantasy life than she imagined and felt a renewed sense of excitement for their sexual connection. He told her his fantasy about having other people watch them have sex and the outfits he would love to see her wear. Grettel also realized that Mark had a harder time asking for things in a specific way. He learned that telling her "I want you to wear that red bra" was hot to her and not offensive or heavy-handed. He noticed that when he was specific, she could be clearer about her yeses and nos. They also discovered together that there were things they were doing out of habit that neither of them wanted to engage in anymore but hadn't known how to tell each other; for example, they didn't enjoy reverse cowgirl position because it hurt her thighs and he liked seeing her face. Grettel thought Mark loved it because he always sounded like he did, and he thought she liked it because she often initiated it. They both laughed at the absurdity that they hadn't talked to each other about this, but when the laughter subsided, they grew quiet with the realization that not communicating had cost them valuable time and opportunity. This vulnerable discussion led them into a deeper one. In this safe, connected, and agency-filled space, they recognized that many cultural stereotypes had seeped into their own relationship—what it means to be a man, a woman, a trans man, a cis woman, a married couple, and so on—and these stereotypes had manifested internally and played out in their sexual connection.

Mark said, "This feels like the mature way to handle our sex lives. We do everything else as a team, but our sex life felt like we were against each other." And she agreed, adding, "I have no idea how to have a team approach to sex because I've always felt like I was the gatekeeper of sex throughout my life, but I want to try. It would feel like a relief to unload the burden of what society says I should be like and what I have come to know." The safety they created for one another and the vulnerability they stepped into in that safe space allowed room for a new chapter of communication and team-based decision-making for their sexual connection—read: agency-based decision-making. When you know what you want and don't want, you create a safe space for others to communicate their yeses and nos. This is the sweet spot of fun, fulfilling, and exciting sexual connections.

Self-awareness, insight, and clarity *are* sexy.

EXPANDING your safety container is contagious. The opposite is the same. With that in mind, we are moving into a pillar that focuses on how your identity, life experiences, and context intersect with your sexuality.

REVEAL YOURSELF TO YOURSELF

- Try the Four Quadrant exercise and note in a journal: What insights pop for you? Where does context matter for sex acts that are maybes?

- How comfortable are you in sharing the information from your quadrants with someone else?

- What do you wish you had learned about sex acts growing up? What would you like to learn now? How will you seek out sources of quality information?

- How do you react when a sexual partner communicates wanting or not wanting to do specific sex acts?

- Describe your experience of your sexual debut.

- Make a list of your firsts with sex acts. Include details like time frame, who was involved, what you thought of it, sensual context, and pleasure scale. If you have done the sex act more than once, how has it evolved for you?

- Detail an action plan to use agency within acts and interests.

PILLAR 6
Intersecting Identities

WHEN MY SON, Jack, was young, my love, Chris, who was a wonderful male figure in Jack's life, died unexpectedly. The grief was overwhelming and took us a long time to heal from. When Jack was eight years old, I was ready to start thinking of dating again, and at that age, Jack occasionally asked to sleep in my bed—"The light's too bright," "I don't feel well," "I'm scared of the noises outside..." If you know, you know. I told Jack that he was getting too old to sleep in my bed and he balked, so I tried a different tactic. I told him that one day I would most likely meet a man, maybe marry him, and that Jack would not want to sleep in the same bed as us so we should start practicing that now. It was clunky, but I was scraping the barrel for ideas to wean Jack off the co-sleeping situation. He looked at me and sweetly said, "Mom, you don't know that is going to happen. You may marry a woman." And with that, I was thrilled I was raising a son who did not assume orientation, which felt like a much bigger win than getting him to sleep in his own bed.

THIS SWEET MEMORY is a very small example of how our complex and intersecting identities impact how we are viewed in the eyes of others and how we form our own internal beliefs, determine what privileges society bestows upon us, and influence how

Everyone is a color of the rainbow.

we relate to each other—how we connect, love, and care for one another. Though our world has progressed in many ways, there's so much work to be done to acknowledge and repair the divisive nature of identity, while preserving the community that shared identity can build. Early in my work, I called this pillar simply "identity" and focused mostly on gender expression, identity, roles, and sexual orientation. I now call it "intersecting identities" to encompass the influence of many more outside forces on our sexuality, as well as our influence over others. Holistic sexuality sees us in our entirety and in an interrelated context. We need to examine and articulate our identity, understand how it influences others and how it may interact with other aspects of our sexuality, and grow our understanding and care for those who have different intersecting identities than us.

Our identities are an amalgamation of several different aspects including our biology, gender, race, socioeconomic class, orientation, mental and physical abilities, and other circumstances we're born into (like culture, era, and religion). Our identities are also shaped by the world around us, how we're treated and supported, and our range of and access to privilege in spaces like education, politics, and family structures. Each of us is on a unique journey that combines with our identity to create the essence of who we are, which then interacts with, intersects with, and affects the world and people around us.

"Intersectionality" refers to the ways in which different aspects of a person's identity interact with societal and cultural forces, such as oppression and discrimination. The concept of intersectionality—first coined in the late 1980s by Kimberlé Williams Crenshaw, an American legal and critical race theory scholar—is vital to understanding yourself and where you stand in society. Core concepts of intersectionality include social inequality, social context, social justice, and power relations.

In this chapter, I address aspects of identity and intersectionality within holistic sexuality. But before we get deeper in, a few notes. This chapter has the most potential to age quickly as terms change and society shifts and constructs are dismantled. If I had written this book five years ago, this chapter would read very differently. And so I predict (and hope) that in another five years, it will read differently again. In general, we are just beginning to deepen our understanding of identity and intersectionality beyond academic spheres, and culture is changing because of it—*thankfully*. The mental health and sexuality spaces have long understood that our identity intersections are integral to our essence awareness, growth, healing, and integration.

People of all different backgrounds are drawn to my work, to this work, because agency is its foundation. I have a "come as you are" mentality in most cases. You do you. We will have differences in experiences and values, and opinions and reactions to difference can be wonderful and interesting and exciting. They can also be confounding, infuriating, and, at their worst, harmful. All I ask is that 1) you do the work to know who you are in all your intersections, and 2) you do the work to understand and respect the agency of others and their intersections.

As a well-educated white woman in the US, I have a lot of privilege, and privilege can lead to gaps in my awareness of and biases about the discrimination and oppression of others. Throughout my life, I've become increasingly aware of the need to learn, understand, and unpack my privileges and biases, and I acknowledge this will be a lifelong endeavor. While I write this book and continue my work with the best intentions to take ownership of what no one can or should do for me, I understand I may make missteps or be delayed in my growth. If I get this wrong, I humbly welcome correction—please know I am open to agency-filled conversations.

This pillar may stand out as unfamiliar or off-putting or "very American." At times, you may feel some dissonance with the framework or with me. There may be many reasons why my framework bumps up against your beliefs and values. I invite you to please work through the uncomfortable places and stick with it, particularly if your viewpoint differs from mine or if I get it wrong for you. Feel free to reach out and let me know if I did. I want to know about your unique experience.

One exception to my "We are all welcome at the table" viewpoint is this: There is no room for anyone who intentionally silences, ignores, discriminates against, or causes harm to others. Taken as a whole, our society has unfortunately not figured out how to eradicate oppression or marginalization, and it takes advantage of unearned privilege. Mostly because those with the most privilege tend to be highly reluctant to give it up. In the complicated webs of our identities and social relationships, there are times when, while watching the news or reading a headline, I think, "What a fucking shit show. Ugh." And other times I am filled with wonder and hope and see movement and growth that feels wonderful, even if way too long in the making. I acknowledge those opposing feelings as we move forward.

What Are Intersectionality and Identity?

Identity and intersectionality are interwoven, inextricably tied, and also uniquely their own.

Intersectionality considers multiple factors of advantage and disadvantage, which include but are not limited to gender, socioeconomic status, race, ethnicity, culture, education, sexual orientation, physical ability or ableness, religion, mental and cognitive ability, body composition, and physical appearance.

Social advantages and disadvantages overlap and cross throughout our lifespan. They can either empower or prevent access and experiences within power structures and societal hierarchies. They exist and are ever-present whether understood, acknowledged, or addressed, and they do not exist independently of one another. The effects of a person's advantages and disadvantages are experienced privately, in groups, and on a systemic scale.

Identity is the understanding of who you are and how others view this self-understanding. As humans, we are prone to assigning categories to normalize, group, compare, contrast, and belong. When we apply labels to others, we risk causing damage by stereotyping them or diminishing them. It is always better to listen to how a person identifies themselves and learn from the assumptions you may have made. Metaphorically, think of "intersectionality" as all the letters of the alphabet, and "identity" as every individual's unique word—the possibilities and combinations of words are endless, unique, and individual. Once you learn someone's "word," making a point to remember it and respect it goes a long way to creating safe, supportive, inclusive, agency-rich environments—something we all need more of.

Understanding Your Identity

With this foundational knowledge in place, let's dive into you. Who you are. The context of you. It is important to consider how your various intersections may shape your experiences, how you see yourself, and how you see yourself in the context of the greater world. Holistic sexuality asks you to understand your own identity, acknowledge how your intersecting identities have informed and interacted with your journey, and own how you have affected others' intersecting identities and thus their journeys. All three are powerful and necessary acts of self-development that help you learn how to better honor and respect the agency of others. And that is a powerful cornerstone of holistic sexuality.

As a vital part of self-exploration, I ask my clients to define how they identify, and I encourage you to try it too. Notice your sexuality first—your biology, orientation, and gender roles. Then name some ways these identities intersect, overlap, and diverge with other aspects of your identity.

You might consider how you identified at certain moments in your life (e.g., labels such as girl, nonbinary, working class, student, parent, genderqueer, convert to Judaism, etc.) or characteristics you were born with (e.g., female, male, mixed race, white, Black, and so on). You might be a Jewish trans man from an urban center. You might be a Japanese-Iranian, queer, immigrant musician. You might be a straight, white, nonmonogamous woman who is an accountant and uses a wheelchair. There are many, many ways to identify.

Once you have articulated how you identify, you can consider how social forces affect you and your experiences. For example, a client spoke passionately about how frustrating it felt to have others assume things about her character since she identified as a cisgender white woman from a middle-class, religious background. People assumed she was a prude, judgmental, frigid in bed, and racist and that she thought anyone who didn't attend her church was going to hell. Those labels didn't fit her self-identity. She felt the labels put on her limited her friendships, her dating pool, and her view of herself. She felt angered by what seemed a double standard of discrimination and judgment and felt the power to define herself was taken away by others who had already categorized her as harmful. She acknowledged there was truth to this viewpoint in general and understood some members of the groups she was associated with had done harm and that her association with these groups did inherently make outside judgments fair game. She was proud of her religious and conservative viewpoints and also felt healthy in her sexual expression. She didn't think the evolving world was leaving a place for her. Many of us, with different details, feel dissonance with identities people put on us versus the identities we resonate with.

Next, look into your history of experiencing discrimination, microaggressions (a targeted form of insult and/or language directed at a group of people based on their identity), and othering (being made to feel like you are outside of a group) because of your identity. Undoubtedly, you have parts of you that feel different from others or societal norms, that have been used against you, or that caused others to threaten you.

I want you to consider how you see your differentness as a part of your identity. How do you think you are different from others or from norms? Next, how do you feel about that? Go beyond categories and get specific.

I remember having a profound conversation with a women-identified college soccer team. They talked about the confusion they felt about their thighs. Within the context of their team, muscular thighs were valued. They were a visible representation of strength, working out, and honing soccer skills. They loved seeing photos that showed them kicking and their muscles popping. Then at night, they would put on clothing to go out in, and those same amazing thighs felt like liabilities. They were frustrated that they didn't fit into conventionally sexy clothing and heard derogatory comments about their thick legs. The dichotomy was deeply hurtful and confusing.

I also want you to consider how you see your physical and sensual ableness. Do you think your body functions to the norms of society? How do you feel about any differences from societally formed norms? A client, Ken, told me about the discrimination and limitation he felt in the dating world because he used a wheelchair. If he used photos that didn't make this obvious on dating apps, he had a lot of matches, but if he did, his matches plummeted dramatically. He also talked about the resentment he felt that most women didn't see him as sexual, let alone sexually desirous, and too many friends had asked him about "how sex worked." They didn't realize it was an offensive and invasive question to pose.

Further, a friend of mine, a person who is blind, told me about her frustration with dating. When dating a sighted person, it was hard for her to understand their visual aspects of sexual arousal and hard to describe her interactions with lights and shadows during sexual connection. She didn't want to only date those who were also blind but felt exhausted by having to share this part of her identity.

You, too, will have stories about your particular brand of you, your intersecting identities. Maybe you feel anger about being seen a certain way if you voice that you are conservative politically or a religiously devout person. Perhaps you are sick of people saying how thin you look and not recognizing that their tone isn't complimentary. Maybe you like to wear clothes that are different from other people's, or maybe you have many face tattoos or body piercings and get stared at a lot. The options of being different are endless, and our engagement with these differences as individuals and as a collective are endless too. Start with those differences that have wounds attached to them and then move into places where you are proud of your uniqueness—perhaps in some places they're the same.

Owning Your Shit so You Can Do the Work

In this work, you must do a thorough self-examination, asking yourself whether you have biases, prejudices, or unearned privilege because of your identity, and you must answer honestly. You might question whether you have discriminated against anyone or been discriminated against in micro or macro ways. Have you ever oppressed someone or been oppressed? Your reflections could take many forms. Perhaps you have always assumed your acquaintances' spouses are the opposite sex (a heterosexist bias) or the same race as their spouse (a race bias). Perhaps because of your race, religion, or gender, you have never had to worry about your safety while walking down the street. Maybe you are uncertain that every person you have had sex with has had the power to do so consensually (imbalances of power).

My education exposed me to conversations surrounding unearned privilege, discrimination, and racial bias, and when I moved into advanced degrees within counseling, my education went from a macro examination to a micro and deeply personal self-reflection. I did not want to think of myself as racist, discriminatory, sexist, or biased in any way, but I began to see where I held unconscious biases that influenced how I related with people and with myself.

I'll give you some personal examples in order to kick-start your work with unpacking your identity. It is hard to include these details for fear of perpetuating harm, but agency is about truth, and I aim to tell the truth, even when it is hard and embarrassing, messy and ugly. I hope I serve as an example of growth and as someone who wants to get it right and to evolve. These stories are from my history and I've grown well past them, but they are part of my journey so it feels critical to include as real-life examples. I humbly provide a trigger warning.

In my early days of college in the South, I attended a party advertised as "FRESHmen I want to MEAT." The poster included photos of freshmen women whom the hosting fraternity considered hot. At the time, I was amused and hoped to be on the list my first year, and now I find it horrifying. Back then, I was complicit in "casual jokes" and conversations that were harmful to my own gender and that created a hostile environment for most identities.

I sadly found that I used to have the ignorant mentality of "I'm not racist. I have Black friends." I was raised by parents who, in the South, were considered progressive. (Neither was Southern, with my mother being Canadian and my father from Detroit.) My mother and her friends held a sit-in at a country club that excluded women from membership. They sat, unwelcomed and unwanted, in the dining room, staring at paintings of naked women, and the club finally relented. But then one day, I was swimming in the club's pool with a friend who was Black, and a staff member asked my mother to get her out of the pool, saying that my friend's hair would ruin the pool. An incredibly disgusting thing to think and say. My mother refused. She moved her chair by the poolside in protection and defiance that day and wouldn't let anyone go near my friend. But after management did not back her up, we kept our membership. We erroneously believed that we weren't perpetuating racism or sexism and that we were fighting the good fight because of those small acts of rebellion. However, we never took further systemic steps that aligned with our sense of justice, nor did we make efforts to fully care for my friend in this situation.

In adolescence, I didn't recognize the harm done to a Muslim classmate who had to say a Christian prayer every morning at school. I didn't know how to protect my friend, who was a Jehovah's Witness, from being made fun of for not celebrating birthdays. I didn't stand up for my neighbors when others made antisemitic statements about them in casual conversations.

In graduate school, a classmate in my counseling program called me out when I said "That's so gay" to describe something I thought was silly. This was 1995. My classmate stopped in her tracks and said, "Don't say that. My father died of AIDS and was gay, and being gay isn't silly. You can't use those words synonymously." I was stunned back then, and she was right. Now it's not something I would ever think to say, and growth is good, but it is painful to see what was so individually and systematically missed in the past.

I have asked people in marginalized communities to teach me about their experiences, thinking that was respectful, when really it was wrongly asking them to do emotional work for me. I have been silent in public spaces and afraid I would say the wrong thing on social media—fearful of getting canceled. Unfortunately, the examples are plentiful. There shouldn't be an award for doing the right thing, and there is too often no consequence for doing the wrong thing. This work doesn't end with the self-awareness and accountability that we're seeking in this chapter; this is where it all begins.

Each of us has lots of examples of our unconscious bias, uncaring discrimination, and microaggressions. The goal here is to be responsible for your own examination, education, and unpacking of the harm you experienced and caused. The commitment to being evolved and holistic means going there and uncovering your story for the sake of your essence and the essences of those around you.

Holistic sexuality requires us to self-examine.

Agency demands we own our shit and take accountability.

This endeavor can be quite simple and obvious or complex and nuanced. You may be a member of a group that experiences marginalization. You may be prejudiced toward others within a community you identify with. You may be someone in a marginalized group who holds bias against your own identity. You may hold bias against other groups of people. Or you may view yourself as a fully enlightened being with zero biases... And if so, I'd love to sit with you as you uncover the biases that invariably are there.

Examining yourself in this way is uncomfortable at best, and it often can be devastating. However, do not back away from the examination. We need to feel remorse, rage, embarrassment, and, for many, fear of the consequences for things done and said in the past. By doing so, you arrive at insight, resolve, and action. Agency-driven action is the key to individual and systemic change—the change we all deserve. After you've spent some time with this section, let's go a little deeper.

Sexuality, Gender, and Identity

When asked to define their sexuality, people often begin with their identity in the form of orientation. Who are you attracted to, or more bluntly, who are you having sex with? But sexual identity through a holistic lens includes much more than sexual orientation. Identity within holistic sexuality includes seeing the fluidity and range of sexual expression. It is also about understanding how cultural norms influence our expression of our identity.

Gender is an integral aspect of identity. This includes biology, gender expression, position on the gender continuum, gender roles, and societal construction of gender—think of stereotypical displays of masculine and feminine, and consider if you feel aligned with being a man, woman, or somewhere in between. Where do you place yourself on the continuum of gender? How does this placement match or not match up with cultural expectations?

Note that when I talk about biology, I mean your reproductive anatomy, chromosomes, genes, hormones, and secondary physical features that develop in puberty such as breasts or a deepened voice. Biology, or your biologic sex, is often referred to as male, female, or intersex. When I talk about gender, I am talking about how you feel, identify, and relate or don't relate to your biology and to the societal constructs.

For many years, mainstream society only observed two genders: woman and man. Gender is now recognized, rightfully so, as a continuum and not a binary. Terms like "gender fluid," "agender," "androgyny," "nonbinary," "demigender," "genderqueer," "gender nonconforming," "cisgender," and "transgender" have entered into the vernacular. Trans and nonbinary communities have once again become the focus of social, political, and cultural polarity and debate. Governments pass policies that seem incomprehensible in their blatantly oppressive intent. Younger generations are embracing gender fluidity with such fierceness that adults need to look up new gender terminology regularly. Transgender representation in the media and entertainment is at new levels, but there is an equally sharp rise in violence toward transgender people. People are joining the gender conversation for the first time with heated opinions about transgender athletes, gender neutral bathrooms, and pronoun use. Knowing the correct terms helps with accurate self-examination and with advancing societal discussions and constructs. Staying up-to-date with language helps everyone evolve and change together. The impact of identity in a holistic sexual context is becoming more widely acknowledged, and by reading this chapter, you're deepening your understanding of how to be a part of the conversation.

You have a right to your view of gender, but no one has a right to dismiss, marginalize, oppress, or erase another's view of gender. That can feel complicated for people who are used to more traditional ways of thinking of gender as binary: "There are women, and there are men." To those people, I say you can disagree that there is a plurality of genders, you can state that you don't understand it, and it still can be real for others and thus worthy of the respect people deserve—that's sexual agency. If you think you are right, the decision-maker, and the authority over someone else's experience of themselves, you have stepped out of sexual agency and into sexual entitlement. If you feel an intense reaction to *anything*, it is surely something to reflect on. To find the edges of your bias, you can ask yourself:

- What emotions are attached to this reaction?
- Where does my understanding of my rights end and others' rights, experiences, expressions, and understanding begin?
- Do my reactions, values, actions, words, and/or behaviors marginalize others?
- What feels like a threat to me about this? What am I fearing?

You can use these questions to reflect after noticing an intense reaction within any situation, really.

With some of my clients and in my Revealed course, we do what I call a gender audit. It takes the topic of gender out of the macro and conceptual and into your personal journey and thoughts. Through this self-exploration, you may uncover aspects of yourself you haven't seen before or become even more sure of who you are and your gender expression. Either way, you will be developing self-knowledge and learning more about your essence. You can start by answering these questions:

- How do you see yourself as a gendered being?
- In what ways do you not conform to social stereotypes about your gender?
- In what ways do you conform to social stereotypes about your gender?
- How does your gender affect you in sexual and non-sexual contexts and relationships?
- How do you express your gender privately and publicly?
- How has society informed your view of gender and your experience of your personal gender?

Gender and biological sex are critical aspects of our sexual identity. Holistic sexuality places both within a powerful and impactful intersectional place of our identities inside and outside sexual connection.

What Is a Woman?

While I was filming woman-identified folks asking them "What is a woman?" my first participant was assigned male at birth and identified as and transitioned to a trans woman in adulthood. Isabella was formidable in appearance. She was six foot three, large-framed, and dressed to the nines in a fashionable suit. She identified as Latina, came from a traditional Hispanic Catholic family and community, was a corrections officer, and was five years post-transition surgery when I interviewed her. I asked her what it meant to be a woman. After a lengthy pause, she said, "Fear."

Then her eyes twinkled. "You can see I am quite the delicate flower," she said with a grin. "I am big. I am strong. I am trained in self-defense. I am proficient in the use of a gun and weapons. I have been around hardened criminals. For most of my life and career, people looked at me and were afraid."

Isabella grew up in a liberal town, but her profession was male-dominated. Her coworkers and boss supported her when she revealed to them that she identified as a woman, wanted to start wearing skirts and dresses, and eventually to use a women's bathroom and have a name change to reflect her needs. Her job was a surprising place of support and safety; her immediate colleagues protected her rights and her journey among the staff and inmates.

Isabella had identified as a woman in name and dress at work and had undertaken hormonal treatment for many years when she decided to undergo gender-affirming surgery. In so many aspects of her journey, she was already living as a woman. But, as she explained, something profound happened to her a few months post-surgery. She was leaving a group of friends after dinner, and having said her goodbyes, she walked by herself to her car. She noticed that the street was dark, isolated, and sketchy, and for the first time, she felt something stirring inside her—fear—because she knew others saw her as a woman and vulnerable physically. That was when she knew she was a woman. And then she cried and was full of swirling emotions. Her size hadn't changed. Her self-defense training was intact. Nothing had changed to elicit such deep-seated fear. Except one thing: looking and feeling like a woman.

Isabella shared another profound story that highlighted the intersection of race, gender, religion, and culture in her life. Her immediate family was strongly entrenched in the Catholic and Latine communities as well as being first-generation immigrants to America. When Isabella told them about her transgender journey, they responded by saying that while they loved her, they would only ever call her the male name she was given at birth) and asked her to wear only masculine or gender-neutral clothing around them and extended family members. She was devasted but chose to find comfort that they didn't excommunicate her.

Fast-forward a few years. Isabella had followed their requests and did her best to handle the disconnect from her family. Meanwhile, her father was hospitalized with a terminal illness that was in its final stages. She got the call while at work that it was time and she needed to pick her mother up on the way. In the emotional turmoil of the news, Isabella didn't notice until her mother walked outside to her car that she had forgotten to change out of her work skirt and heels. Her mother climbed into the passenger seat, saw the oversight, and sighed and shook her head. Then they raced to the hospital.

With each stoplight, the reality that her father was dying sunk in and panic ensued. Isabella knew that his room and the waiting room would undoubtedly be filled with extended family and that everyone would see her clothes. She was overwhelmed that at such an important event, her gender would be a distraction from her father's life-to-death transition. She was devastated and wondered if she shouldn't wait until her family left to go inside. She wondered what her father would want. Her mother said nothing, and the silence consumed her. Isabella found herself walking alongside her mother through the parking lot and into the ICU suite.

Gasps. Stares. Silence. A different kind of silence. But as she entered and clung to the side of the hospital room, her father stirred. He lifted his head, and they locked eyes. She was terrified to scan his face, devastated with the thought that her feminine outfit would crush him in his final minutes. Instead, he said *"Mi hija"* (my daughter) over and over again. With two words, he gave his blessing and his acceptance. She was no longer his son; she was his daughter.

Isabella's story shows how vulnerable and powerful it can be to live with agency and be supported around your identity, as well as how intersectionality plays into each of our lived experiences of our full, holistic sexual selves.

Orientation Is Dimensional

When first asked to define sexuality, a lot of people start with pillar 5, acts and interests, what people are doing with their body physically, and this pillar addresses the second part of the common answer—with whom. Holistic sexuality sees sexual orientation ("sexual preference" is not the currently accepted term) as whom you're attracted to and to whom you feel drawn within three categories: romantic, emotional, and sexual. Orientation also encompasses your sense of personal and social identity and community membership due to those attractions.

    A client in her late fifties came to me frustrated by the abrupt change to her sexual life when she began her journey in menopause. She was on top of all medical interventions to help with physical symptoms, but she was finding little support for her concerns about her desire, particularly with her husband. After months of sifting through possible desire impediments, she confessed she had a secret fear she had been ashamed to name. She did have desire, but it was very specific. She had fantasies about being with women. Emotionally and sexually. She had no problem feeling aroused and wanting to sexually connect with herself if she sunk into that fantasy. She wondered if that made her a lesbian and if it wasn't menopause but actually a new sexual orientation blooming inside her. We discussed the continuums and types of orientations and discussed loosening her grip on needing a specific label. Her acceptance of fluidity in her orientation allowed her to celebrate that her body was indeed experiencing desire. Pleasure was a new and powerful starting point to further explore the overlap with her experience of menopause and her marital relationship.

    Sexual orientation is different than gender identity, although it does address the gender(s) to which you are attracted in all three categories. They are separate aspects of being a person, and we experience them differently. For example, we often have a sense of our gender between ages three and five, but typically we develop an understanding of our attraction orientation as we age—often around adolescence—and understand what it means and feels like to be drawn to someone in multiple ways.

The sexual orientation continuum includes identities such as heterosexual, bisexual, monosexual, gay, lesbian, demisexual, pansexual, queer, asexual, and so on. If any of these terms are new to you, take the opportunity to learn a little more about them with curiosity.

There are multiple scales available to you to assess the complexity of your orientation such as the Kinsey scale, which asks you to rank attraction as exclusive, equally, or predominate toward an orientation, and the Klein Sexual Orientation Grid, which asks you to measure your past, present, and ideal attraction to things like sexual behavior, sexual fantasies, and social preference. There are outdated concepts within both of these scales, but they provide thought-provoking prompts to consider.

Sexual orientation is not only about sexual attraction; it can involve a range of connection, sense of self and identity, and may be privately felt and not publicly expressed. The continuum contains the options mentioned above, but an individual may also have different expressions of orientation emotionally, romantically, and sexually. For example, a client, Nicholas, was sexually attracted to multiple genders, romantically attracted to women only, and emotionally attracted to men, women, and nonbinary folks. A man in my Revealed course filled out the Kinsey and Klein scales and expressed confusion regarding his orientation. He wondered if he was not as exclusively heterosexual as he'd previously identified when he acknowledged he had included some sex play with men and nonbinary folks in his fantasy life.

Sexual orientation as part of identity is an integral part of holistic sexuality and has a stacking effect with the pillars of desire, pleasure, and acts and interests. Our orientation is fluid throughout our lifespan and ties into the upcoming pillars of relationships and connection.

The Core of the Issue

In the realm of holistic sexuality, understanding your identity and how it functions in relationships can lead to new levels of agency and therefore connection.

One couple I worked with, Janelle and Frank, had experienced infidelity multiple times. Through our work, we decided to explore their orientations and the concept of monogamy. After heartfelt and hard-won self-examination, they discovered that Janelle identified as polyamorous and Frank identified as monogamous. The realization that they identified differently in this sense reduced the judgment, hurt, and shaming, and they moved into a space of curiosity: "Hmm. Neither is right nor wrong, but neither of us can compromise about this. So now what?"

When they let go of the hurt and saw that each had a right to embody and explore their identity, they had to come to terms with the truth that their differences meant they would not work as a couple; they decided to end their relationship.

But the story doesn't end there. When they checked back in months later, they decided to reconnect with different boundaries and knowledge. They were friends who shared history, affection, and care but were no longer romantic or sexual with each other. This new relationship felt safe and wonderful to them both.

Sitting within a conflict of needs, wants, and identities without judgment or blame is no easy feat. But then neither is sacrificing the truth of who you are and who you discover you are over the course of time. I, for one, prefer the truth. To do this, we need to learn how to stay with the discomfort that arises when owning our identity (and agency) leads to major life changes. We also need to understand how our identity intersects with the identities of our partners and with the wider world. It's our right and responsibility to uphold the agency of others. This knowledge is vital for the responsible use of sexual power, which we'll look at next.

REVEAL YOURSELF TO YOURSELF

- How do you identify? Include your gender identity, gender expression, race, socioeconomic status, religious or spiritual views, sexual orientation, mental and physical ableness, family structure, culture, geographic location, nationality, physical appearance, and any other category that holds meaning for you.

- To what extent do you feel safe being in the world when you are expressing your identity in the way that you feel is most authentic? What places feel safe or unsafe?

- How has religion impacted your identity? How has it impacted your view of sexuality?

- How has your race and culture impacted your identity? Your sexuality?

- How has your physical ableness and appearance impacted your identity? Your sexuality?

- What gender(s) are you sexually attracted to? Is there a gender you feel safer or more comfortable with? Emotionally? Romantically? Platonically? Sexually?

- Where has your agency been blocked within intersecting identities?
- Now that you understand intersecting identities, go back through pillars 1 to 5 and consider how your identities intersect with each pillar topic.

PILLAR 7
Power and Trauma

ISABEL WILKERSON, the author of *Caste* and *The Warmth of Other Suns*, is a hero of mine. She has written one of the most powerful bodies of work on generational racial trauma I have read. She says, "In order to heal, we must confront the wounds of the past." She is speaking specifically within a racial context, that of identity, but the point extends to other forms of injustice and harm too. Individually and collectively, we must all reconcile with the legacy of power imbalances and work toward greater justice, a rebalancing of power, safe and inclusive spaces for people—and that begins with our sexual relationships.

There are parts of being a sexual being (a.k.a. a human) that are obvious: Don't ask a woman who looks like she may be pregnant when she is expecting; affairs with coworkers are usually messy; and don't say hateful things to your partner about how inadequate they are sexually and expect things outside that sexual connection to feel great. Other aspects are more nuanced. Throughout this pillar, I want you to consider the differences and similarities of intention versus impact on the emotional, physical, and sexual well-being of all people involved. As stated previously and particularly within this pillar, take care of yourself. The material in this chapter highlights the misuse and abuse of power and how that

Seduction, sexualization, and safety are potent.

leads to trauma, as well as where it can be sexy and enriching. Let's start with my personal experience.

My junior year in high school I had a huge crush on Justin, a senior. He was cute, popular, and fun. I wanted his attention, and though he seemed mildly interested in me, he was very into the hot senior girls, all of whom seemed much more sexually advanced than me.

I was inexperienced. One guy had felt up my shirt, and I had cried when that happened because it scared me to be intimate. I thought my mom would be able to look at me and tell, and it just felt vulnerable. I really wanted Justin's affection and attention, so I made the decision to try to emulate the seniors and offer him what I thought he wanted.

One night, I convinced my parents to let me go with a group of friends downtown to an outdoor festival, knowing he would be there. My parents were strict, so this was a victory for me on multiple levels.

When I arrived, I had one mission: Find Justin.

I found him. I flirted. He showed mild interest. I persisted.

I saw him looking at his friends to see if my interest in him was socially acceptable or not, and I guess it was because he didn't completely shut me down. He also didn't direct attention toward me, show me respect, or seem to care if I disappeared. Sadly, at that point in my life, that didn't matter to me. The only decisions I thought needed to be made involved whatever would get his attention and interest.

At some point between the cover band's rendition of "Don't Stop Believin'" and his third hot dog, something shifted. Maybe it was because Hot Whitney left. Maybe it was because he was a bit buzzed from the whiskey he had snuck in. Maybe it was because I was low-hanging fruit. Who cared? I was thrilled he was starting to show interest.

He asked me if I wanted to go to his car with him in the parking garage. Yes. In a nanosecond, yes. As we walked there, we talked some. Not about why he needed to go to his car. I didn't ask. I didn't care. I just wanted to walk anywhere Justin wanted me to go with him. I was so enamored that he wanted me to go with him that I glided over the concrete, flew up the stairs, and the next thing I know, Justin was opening up his car door. The back seat. And getting in.

I stood next to the car a bit puzzled. I had a sudden awareness that I *had* assumed we were walking together to his car to get something. Maybe alcohol. I felt ridiculous just standing there, so I popped my head in the door and asked if he wanted me to get in. He looked at me with slight disdain, swallowed it, and said, "Yes, get in."

My enthusiasm was dimming, but I remained optimistic. I thought, "Maybe we will talk? Maybe kiss? Maybe this is good. He must like me, right? He will like me if I get in. Don't be difficult. Don't act childish. That would be a turnoff. All the girls in his circle would know what to do in this situation."

He kissed me. It was pretty dreamy. I just kept thinking, "*Justin is kissing me!*" I felt him shift a bit, heard his pants unzip, and then he grabbed my hand and put it on his dick. That was a first. It was odd. I remember thinking that. Hard and warm but also soft to touch. "So this is a dick. Interesting."

I was curious, but I did not know what to do with it, and I am sure whatever I did do, I didn't do well, but I tried and he seemed to like it. I was in and out of my mind and body, watching myself from above. I was slightly into the newness but very much with a running commentary of self-doubt, fear, and uncertainty. I wanted his interest in me, but I didn't want to be doing that. I was happy, from what I can remember, that he wanted me above anyone else at the festival, but I wasn't getting anything out of it. He didn't touch me. He didn't check in with me. I was there for him.

He grabbed my head, and the next thing I knew his dick was in my mouth. He moved my head, teaching me in a way. I was wide-eyed and trying to catch up to what was happening. I did enough right because he orgasmed. Just as fast as it started, it ended—without a word in between. He was zipped up and out of the car before I could say anything. I don't know what I wanted to say, but I wanted to say something.

He didn't. He was impatiently waiting for me to get out of the car. He said a few things I don't remember, but he didn't check in with me, debrief, clean up much, ask me out or anything I really wanted to be asked. We walked back to the festival and I felt very different, but it seemed to have changed nothing for him.

Back then, it didn't feel like anything close to an assault had happened. The experience felt consensual and wanted, just bumbling and fast. I felt empowered. I felt like I was choosing to do whatever it took to get his attention. At the time, it felt like a victory and validation of being wanted. Desirable at last. When you read it now, the truth is clearer. An adult lens shows me a very different dynamic. I did not have a hold of myself or my agency throughout most of that experience. This is the story of what happened through my viewpoint and memory, and in my work, I discovered quickly that there is often a vast difference in how two people experience, interpret, and describe a sexual exchange like this. The sometimes-murky view and interplay of consent, self-awareness, regard for others, mood-altering substances, naivete, self-esteem, agency, and power all have an impact. If Justin was to write his version of the story, if he even remembered it, he may present a very different tone and interpretation. Or not. Maybe he would remember it the same way I do. Power, trauma, and sexuality are a complicated and impactful trio and important to holistic sexuality.

WHEN I STARTED LOOKING at the interlocking aspects of sexuality and power, my gut reaction was "yuck" and avoidance. The vestiges of trauma fluttered inside me, trauma I have witnessed myself, experienced through my friends and family, and heard of as a therapist. But I knew how important it is to tackle this subject head-on. I have seen the immediate aftereffects of sexual trauma in multiple ways: while assisting a sexual assault response team evidentiary medical exam, sitting through a review board of sexual violence reporting, and having heard countless stories of abuses of power in many contexts throughout my career.

Sexual violence has generational ripple effects that are both immediate and longer lasting. I've talked with fathers when they found out their child had been raped, and they are ravaged with guilt and tormented by their desires for justice and to ease their child's pain. I've worked with spouses trying to be supportive of their partners when their past sexual trauma shows up in their current relationship. I have also worked with those who have committed sexual violence. I've seen the pain of someone's horror when they recognize what they have done and also sat with those who have little remorse for their abuse of power. The essence of someone bubbles up involuntarily in discussions of power, violence, and sexuality.

Spend time examining the powerful force of sexuality. It's an energy that can be accessed for good (pleasure and connection), for manipulation (flirting, seducing, or coercing to get something you want), or for violence (abuse and various assaultive behaviors). Most people can remember when they first noticed the palpable presence of sexuality. I recall when I started to notice men looking at me. One specific moment stands out: I was on spring break in high school with a friend and her family. We were at the pool, and a man the family knew casually waved my friend and me over. He put his arm around my waist and pulled me to his lap. I didn't like it, but admittedly I was also flattered by this older man's attention. At the time, I didn't know why I was flattered; I just felt confused. But I know now it was that taste of sexual power.

He whispered to me that I was hot and he could tell I didn't realize how beautiful I was. Those words were like magic. How did he know that's how I felt? Invisible to my peers and not beautiful compared to other girls my age. As I sat silently in his lap, he lowered his voice and said, "But you'd be even sexier if you took out a few of your pubic hairs I know you have hiding under that suit." I was stunned and instantly felt the danger of sexuality's power—his and mine. We were surrounded by adults watching him. His wife was sitting one table over, but no one said a word, including me.

Something changes when you are sexualized and when you are witness to or an orchestrator of sexualizing another. According to the APA Task Force on the Sexualization of Girls from 2007, sexualization happens when someone places a value on another for their sexual appeal or when they are viewed as an object for sexual use or when sexuality is inappropriately imposed on another. This definition still stands decades later and extends to all genders and ages.

The pillar of power and trauma involves how we use our sexuality—and its inherent power—in relation to others, as well as how others use sexuality to influence, control, or manipulate. This includes a variety of behaviors and elements such as flirtation, seduction, media messaging, political bullying, withholding sex, sexual harassment, coercion, consent, sexual violence, and trauma. Traumatic events and intensely good experiences both impact our personality, perspective, trajectory, and essence, and the stories I share in this pillar highlight both. The examination of power and trauma includes all the life experiences that have influenced you in a powerful way—how you came to be here and where you want to go.

Sexual Currency's Exchange Rate

Like all things sexual, power is not benign and everyone has their own history, interpretation, needs, and perspective on it. In the context of sexual connection, people often see power as dangerous, and it can be at times. Power within sexuality can also be a sweet exchange, such as flirting with a stranger in a grocery store for a few minutes or seducing a long-time partner as a way to keep a spark of wanting alive. Some sex acts access power as a central factor in the sexual connection. Sub-dom scenes are often centered on a consensual imbalance of power that brings pleasure, joy, and ecstasy to both involved.

A couple client, Gennie and Rob, hired me to help them find their edges in seeking power differentials. They wanted support in consent-seeking and skills in sexual acts like role playing professor and student, sensory deprivation, and taking submissiveness to a sex handmaid. They also wanted guidance to increase their level of safety in debriefing to help refine their sexual connection. The notion of power was an intensely arousing and pleasurable experience for both of them. Power in their sexual connection was hot, safe, and expanding.

The term "sexual currency" lands deeply with me as it describes a crucial way that we experience the power of sexuality collectively. "Sex sells." How many times have you heard that? "Sex appeal" and "sexiness," as defined by the media, show up in places where the connection is tenuous—such as advertisements for car wash companies or hamburger joints or tennis shoes.

Sexual currency is experienced individually. As I've aged, I've noticed people do not turn their heads to look at me in the same way they used to. When I was younger, older women warned me that this would happen. I remember thinking, "Well, I don't like it when it happens now, and I don't gain much from it, so I will welcome this when that happens." But when it did start happening, I didn't like it. Hello, ego and irony!

In retrospect, I did get a charge when someone checked me out. It was currency, a deposit in my bank account of sexuality. Of sexual worth. Someone's stamp of sexual value onto me. And when those deposits became less frequent, the absence was more powerful than the charge. This wasn't a huge thing for me, but I did notice it and was surprised that I needed to adjust. Today, when I am with a young woman and see how frustrated she is by relentless staring and constant comments, I feel protective of her. This is not about what I no longer get but about the damage this sexist dynamic does to all of us. A similar dynamic also exists within same genders; jealousy and feeling threatened morph into critical gossip and rejection. The experiences of having or feeling like you have never had sexual currency, of being overlooked or shunned, and of not having any options for sexual connection are equally and profoundly impactful.

The continuum of power and sexuality goes from flirting and seduction all the way through to sexual trauma and violence. That range includes things like coercion, sexism, sexual discrimination, harassment, assault, rape, molestation, incest, and many other things in between. Everyone has a story of sexualization. For some people, the experiences are obvious and clear. For others, these events are subtle and confusing and closer to microaggressions than one overt act. Death by a thousand cuts rather than a record-scratching moment.

Our society has inconsistent messaging about, understanding of, and reactions to experiences of power and sexuality. This can confound your perception of things that you've experienced and their influence on your journey. But although it's important to examine micro and macro experiences of power and sexuality, I would caution against categorizing micro incidents as having only minor impact and macro incidents as having macro impact—all interactions of power and sexuality matter and affect us differently.

When Hiroto, a forty-six-year-old cisgender man, took my Revealed course, he didn't think this pillar would be relevant to him—until he recalled a story from his youth in Japan. In the sixth grade, the mother of one of his friends took a shine to him. She told him he had the most beautiful, mesmerizing eyes. She would arrange to pick him up and take him home from school and was in charge of his group during field trips. He started feeling uncomfortable and told his parents about it. His father dismissed Hiroto's concerns, and his mother was incensed. She ended the carpool, and she insisted to the school administrators that Hiroto not be placed in the woman's group on field trips.

Two years later, when he was in eighth grade, he was with his father in a movie theater and they ran into the woman. She made a highly inappropriate comment to his dad in front of him. "Your son is so hot," she said. He was thirteen. Finally, Hiroto's father understood and told her to stay away from his son.

Hiroto had been traumatized by the lack of safety and by his father's initial dismissal of it. A pervasive attitude is that men—and even young boys—should be flattered and built up by sexual attention from women rather than threatened or victimized by it. He was supposed to be the guy who gets high-fived in the locker room, even as a young boy.

Upon reflection and after processing the experience, he took away a sense of pride that he had stood up for himself—stood in his agency—and told his parents, and that his mother and eventually his father had protected him. How many children never receive that protection? So many are told, "This is just life. You have to learn to deal with it, forget about it, and move on." Or they aren't believed. Or they know it is not safe to share, so it remains a secret. Until we sifted through this pillar, Hiroto wasn't aware he was still carrying the residue of that experience inside or that it had contributed to his pain as he entered adulthood. Coming to terms with the way he had been sexualized and working through that experience were steps in his journey to reclaim his sexuality.

Coercion, Harassment, and Marginalization

For some, the experiences of coercion, harassment, and marginalization will have a profound effect, like a constant drip that slowly erodes you to the core. For others, these experiences are more like a flood that comes out of nowhere and instantly wipes out who you know yourself to be in the world. Much of how an experience affects us has more to do with how we process it rather than the "bigness" or "smallness" of an incident.

Early in my career, I was second in command in an office setting. My boss was a man, and we had an easy rapport. There was absolutely nothing sexual between us, no flirting, no weirdness, no tension that I was aware of. I had looked for the signs: a lingering look, eye contact, staring at my chest, flirty jokes that weren't really jokes. Nothing. Ever. Everything was platonic and professional. I felt fantastic that I didn't have to worry about him hitting on me or about feeling tempted myself. I felt relieved that he was a married man and self-professed devoutly religious man, and I felt safe within a dynamic that I knew had the potential for a lack of safety. Since it checked out, I let my guard down.

I was in a good place in my life, happy in my relationship, confident in my skin, liking my work, and excited about my future. I felt like I had great sexual agency, thriving in my confidence, and my job opportunities were taking off. But then, because of some changes in my family, I needed to step down from my position at work and shift into a part-time situation elsewhere. Our office had a tradition of send-offs, and I tailored mine to fit my personality. We held an Office Olympics. It was a blast. We finished the games, laughed, said our individual goodbyes, and hugged, and it ended. My boss didn't give me a send-off toast or thank-you speech at the conclusion of the party. I was a bit surprised and disappointed, but it was not his style, so I didn't make too much of it. I started packing the rest of my belongings and finished up briefing my replacement.

In my final hour, my boss took me aside and asked if we could talk privately and ushered me away from the group. His demeanor was happy and cheerful. "Oh," I thought, "here is the 'thank you and you will be missed' talk." Private and reflective did seem more his style. We stepped outside where we could be seen but not heard by people in the office. He looked at me and said he wanted to tell me something. I nodded and waited.

His special thank you? He said, "I had a sexual dream about you last night."

Cue screeching tires! "Wait... what?!" I thought.

"Do you want me to tell you about it?" he asked.

I snapped into reality and realized he was serious. I wanted to run, but instead I laughed weirdly, like a hyena. My face got splotchy, and I said something like, "Oh, stop it, that is silly," and walked back into the office. Reeling from the shock of his admission.

He didn't say anything more. For the rest of the hour, he acted like the interaction hadn't occurred. At five o'clock, I said a few final goodbyes, got into my car, and drove away.

As I drove home, I began processing what happened and then I cried. I cried because I didn't get thanked. I cried because he ended our professional relationship on something so bizarre. I cried because I didn't call him out. I cried because I had fled instead of standing my ground. And all this because of one sentence.

Over the days and weeks that passed, I thought about this incident and my reaction to it a lot. I know women who would have put him in his place. I know women who would have filed a harassment suit against him. But not me. I froze and then I felt sorry for myself and cried. A slew of uncomfortable questions followed. Why did he say it? Why then? What did he expect to happen? What did he want? Was he trying to hit on me? Is that sexual harassment? Do I care? It had been one hour before I did not work there anymore. If he had given me a glowing toast publicly and then said that privately, would it have felt different?

Had I been that blind? I never once felt anything awkward sexually with him. Was I being sensitive or thin-skinned, or was I being naive and afraid? Was I being too timid? Why hadn't I filed a complaint? What was the line between a socially awkward misfire and sexual harassment? And then it hit me: I was judging myself for *his* decision. His action. His words. What he said was about him. The meaning I made of it was about me.

Further context informs the complexity or lack thereof. This incident took place long before the #MeToo movement and within a conservative environment. At the start, I had contested my salary for the position, which was his former job. I was offered a salary almost twenty thousand dollars less than what he had made, although our résumés were similar. When I questioned the administration about the discrepancy, a woman told me that many others would accept my pay, and if I tried to claim gender discrimination, I would lose and the job would be offered to someone else.

I'll never know what his motive was for saying what he did, but what I do know is that his statement was not a reflection of my worth or my work value. He said it. I reacted. It was done. Although I'm still not great at coming up with zingers when I'm taken by surprise, I now know how to set a boundary because I've had some practice. I've been through a lot of harder things than that incident, and this was a reminder to reflect and grow.

If you were in the situation I was in, you would have had a different reaction and your meaning-making afterward would be unique. You may have another take on why he did it or what I could have done about it. You may identify more with him than me in that situation. After it happened, I received all kinds of advice. People told me I needed to report him because if he did it to me, he would do it to someone else. People told me not to tell anyone because I would be blamed. People said it was a terrible way to end my work there, and others felt it was no big deal. It all felt so complicated, and these kinds of incidents that involve sexuality often are.

Too many people take the power they have in one context or aspect of a relationship and extrapolate it to another area, thinking there is implicit consent in other areas. Know the difference for yourself when you witness interactions between others and monitor how you use your own power.

Enthusiastic Consent

"I want you to stay at the kitchen table until I tell you that you can get up."

"Yes, ma'am. Thank you."

"Do you want me to feed you, or do you want Rebecca to feed you?"

"You will walk in with black stilettos wearing this black lace panty and bra set, straddle the chair, and keep your eyes closed while I drip wax on your body."

Clients Oliver, Rebecca, and Elicia were in a consensual triadic relationship and long-term members of the ethical nonmonogamy community. The basis of their relationship was consent, trust, and proactive communication. They were also drawn to power play within their relationship inside and outside sexual connection. They found their high level of consent and communication a powerful container for safety and, because of that, felt freedom to find their edges within kink and power exchanges. Each described one of their top turn-ons being enthusiastic consent from another. They came to me looking for support in how to expand their ideas in positive power play sex acts and to deepen their understanding of the complexities of power exchanges in all aspects of their relationship.

Consent addresses power dynamics within a sexual exchange. In the traditional definition, consent means that a person voluntarily and willfully agrees with something someone else proposes.

The person consenting must be capable to do so, determined by criteria such as age, mental capacity, level of intoxication, and freedom from coercion, misrepresentation, or fraud. In looking at the definition, the baseline conditions seem straightforward, but in real-life scenarios, consent can be complicated and murky.

I like the term "enthusiastic consent." It speaks to a vibe you are looking for that clarifies potential muddiness in real-world situations. Enthusiastic consent means you give or receive a clear, verbal yes for each new addition or level of sexual activity. For example, if you want to move from kissing mouth to mouth to putting a hand down the pants, you seek consent first. Clear, definitive yes. You are looking for the embodiment of yum. The person moving the sexual connection to different levels is the one responsible for seeking consent and waits until receiving it to progress. If the response feels weak or if there is no response, keep things at the current level. I love hearing client stories about a sexual encounter where there was a seamless progression of consent that felt fun, sexy, reciprocal, and ease-filled.

What does unenthusiastic consent feel like? Imagine calling a pizza place that picks up and says, "Hello, can I put you on hold?" Before you respond, you hear an abrupt click followed by Muzak. "Can I put you on hold" is a statement posed as a question. There was no intention to be flexible to the answer because the question was a social script rather than motivated by true consent-seeking. This happens in sexual connections too. Consent is threaded throughout each holistic sexuality pillar in the practice of self awareness and communication of yeses and nos.

There is a lot for you to examine within consent as it relates to holistic sexuality and sexual agency. The skill and interaction of consent happen inside and outside the proverbial bedroom. I've experienced intense reactions because consent can be both straightforward and obvious or at times nuanced and situational. The latter is where emotions and consequences intensify. For example, I've heard many frustrated arguments that someone is trying to do the right thing with consent but finding it can ruin the mood and flow.

An unnecessary disruption. The details of the scenario are usually something like they were hooking up with someone and their partner told them that repeatedly asking for consent was amateur and annoying or their relationship was well past needing consent. Yet the need for consent is clear because there are many instances when there is a vastly different view of a sexual connection's yeses and nos. Some individuals don't feel safe enough or don't have practice in stopping an undesired sexual act or progression so their silence could seem like consent but is actually people-pleasing, insecurity, or acquiescence. In some circumstances, they may think they are okay with a sex act until they are in the middle of it and realize it has moved from a maybe to a no and it is "too late." The opportunity for harm and agency removal without clear consent is plentiful. Granted, few people would describe their own behavior within a negative sexual connection as an assault, and in my work, I typically see people willing to describe an incident only as a mixed message, as in "The person didn't say no" or "They seemed super into it and then changed their mind." This is where the conversation about the difference between mood and assault and rape must shift.

When you seek consent with an understanding of how and why to do it, it ends up being a turn-on rather than a buzzkill. You create a deeper connection and a sexier trusting exchange of communication. I am grateful that a deepened understanding of consent continues to be included in sexual education curriculum. Enacting consent is a basic life skill. You need to know how to ask for, give, and receive consent. You can learn consent from all angles and practice to refine it and fine-tune it.

Often missing from the education, though, is how to accept a no—that is, how to respond to a partner's boundaries in an affirming and validating way. Feeling disappointed, embarrassed, or confused about a no is okay. But you must know how to feel those feelings and still respect the response. You cannot fully accept a yes from someone until you can fully accept a no from them as well.

Seeking consent requires effort. I've worked with people who are neurodivergent, and for some of these individuals, reading social cues, especially within the context of sexual consent, can be confusing, even if understanding the value of it is not. I have listened to many heated debates about partners sending so-called mixed messages, how consent changes when mood-altering substances enter into sexual connection, and how you prove consent or lack of consent when it is one person's word against another's.

Consent is a part of every sexual connection. Examine how you value consent, your experiences in giving and receiving consent, and the meaning you make of any instance where you violated consent or where your consent was violated. Consent intersects with safety, vulnerability, pleasure, and agency. The kink and sadomasochistic communities offer a great example of how to do consent. Although not everyone gets it right, in general the people who play in the space of power, dominance, submissiveness, and kink root their activity in consent. It is seen as integral to the experience, making it both safe and a turn-on. In fact, it is a requirement for most people's desire to play and for arousal in the exchange.

I was on a trip to New York City to meet up with friends and colleagues, and a friend had an extra ticket to a pop-up VIP sex club in a Manhattan warehouse district. I jumped at the opportunity, though I was a little nervous. My first surprise was how soon and how often consent was addressed on the website's rules and practices pages. Admittedly, when we pulled up in our Uber, the pop-up club seemed a bit shady, but my friend who had been to many sex clubs was nonplussed. I was so grateful to be there with a couple of trusted and experienced friends. After we opened the door, the first thing I saw was a dark room full of sex toys and neon signs that read "Stay sexy" and "Fuck yeah." Interesting, but not what I expected.

A good-looking man dressed in white and wearing wings checked us in and directed us to our safety angel, another cutie wearing all white and wings. The first topic: consent. He explained that patrons wore all black and safety angels wore all white. If we felt uncomfortable, we were to find an angel who would support us. He explained the first room was the shop for toys, condoms, and lube, as well as lockers for our personal items and/or clothing. The second room was the clothing-optional room, bar, and initial group gathering. The third room was lingerie only or nude, no watching, only playing participants allowed. The fourth room was anything goes and all nude only.

We walked into the second room, which was filled with huge black pleather ottomans; the music was loud, and the bar was self-serve. The lights were dim, and it smelled of a mixture of cologne, lube, and possibilities. People wore sleek all-black outfits and were seated on the ends of the ottomans or were lying on their sides chatting. Some were alone, some were in groups, and some were coupled up. The atmosphere was chatty and sex-filled, although no sex was happening. Everyone was clothed, but the extent of coverage varied. One couple was wearing elegant and sexy club wear. One couple was in matching leather harnesses, with the male in a leash and a woman leading him around. Several men in couples were shirtless wearing pants or stylish boxers.

At a sex club for the first time, I admittedly lost my grown-ass-woman confidence and felt like I was at a grade school dance. My friend guided us to three chairs in a corner, and we had barely sat down when someone approached us. We weren't interested in engaging. His move felt invasive so soon after we arrived in the space. An angel followed him over to us and asked us if we needed any assistance, if the man's presence had been consensual. I was stunned because that level of protection and supervising of consent were new to me. I have felt that lecherous feeling from so many men over the years. The ones that come at you right away. The ones who won't leave. The ones who dominate and don't read the room. This club didn't have any of that, and that took some time to get used to. I know other genders experience this as well with a variety of contextual details.

I watched the man to see if he was embarrassed or upset, subconsciously assessing if things were about to get awkward. To my surprise, he said he was happy to meet us and perhaps connection would feel better timed later. His reaction felt classy and freeing, and our reaction felt quick and defensive.

Remarkably, a similar scenario repeated several times. Men approached us and either asked if they could join us or said a few things and then asked if they had consent to stay with us. After a while, our nos felt more comfortable. When we moved to room three and then four, the consent vibe was the same. I heard things being said to people like "Is it okay if I sit here close to you three?" "I would like to give you a massage. Would you like that too?" "I want to invite you into the backroom. Does that excite you?" and "Can I watch you two?"

Consent is indeed sexy. Safety is an incredible turn-on because it releases a level of vulnerability and opportunity for risk-taking that opens only when no energy is being spent in assessing and monitoring emotional, physical, and sexual safety. Sexuality and power do not have to cause harm and can create safety and ease. But when they do not, you need all the agency you can muster.

When Agency Is Compromised

The last element in this pillar of power and trauma is agency and sexual violence. When I teach the concept of agency, one question that often comes up is "How do you have agency when someone takes it from you or disallows it? Isn't this victim blaming?" When you have experienced the violence continuum of someone taking your agency, the notion of embracing the concept of agency can feel scary. Even offensive. If you believe, as I do, that agency is foundational to holistic sexuality, then you understand that there are power structures, communities, experiences, and people who do not want agency to exist or do not respect it; it doesn't serve their motives, behaviors, or intentions.

The world is wildly inconsistent regarding the safety of people reporting incidents of sexual violence, supporting victims emotionally and logistically, spotting the signs of unreported sexual violence, and outlining and enforcing consequences for violence. Even in the most advanced institutions and communities that have evolved policies and laws, most victims do not report feeling safe, validated, or valued in the legal process of reporting violence. This creates an environment where people opt not to report, privately or publicly. Many people end up feeling as if their experience does not matter, that they are invisible and must suffer in silence. For those who do choose to pursue legal action, the impact can be soul-crushing and painful as many parts of the system vary and are influenced by privilege, access to legal support, local and state laws, and social connections.

Society has done an awful job with accountability after the fact, and an even worse job with the prevention of sexual violence. Enter holistic sexuality, and what we as individuals can do to make a difference, one person at a time. When I was working in a college setting, the counseling center partnered with an organization called the Red Flag Campaign. It targeted students who thought a friend may be in an abusive relationship. It was based on research that many don't self-identify as being in an abusive relationship, but if information was given in the context of prevention for a friend, the information was often better received. I loved the idea, but the campaign didn't get traction because, unfortunately, prevention and violence are hard topics to fund and to get participants to want to engage in for any period of time.

When your agency, especially your sexual agency, is taken from you in any form, it affects you to your core. You need to sort out where you and your agency end and an external force or person's harmful agenda begins. If you have experienced sexual violence like assault, cyber assault (for example, revenge porn or the sharing of sexual imagery without consent), rape, incest, or molestation, the interplay between sexuality and power will have both direct and indirect impacts on you. Integration of what happened, how it happened, and what this means for your view of yourself, the world, and sexual connection can be intense, lifelong, and even inherited by the next generation. If you have been the target of violence, a qualified mental health professional whom you feel safe with is a good place to start or continue processing the experience. It's never too late.

FURTHER EXAMINATION is important. A holistic approach to sexuality requires you to reflect on 1) anything of significance that has happened to you, 2) what you have experienced, and 3) what you have done to others within each pillar. This trifold way of examining your life is particularly necessary for this topic. People often find the first two points clear. The third point, however—what you may have done to others—can feel tricky. But it is critical.

Every interaction involves the interplay of power, so you will probably be the person in the power position at some point. At times you will use this power for good, and other times you won't whether inadvertently or intentionally. Recognizing this in yourself takes a tremendous amount of honesty, courage, and fortitude, and it is critical to your self-knowledge. Start by being brave in your self-reflection.

Let's look at an example. In your lifetime, it's likely that you have coerced someone. You know what to say, how to say it, and when to say it to a certain person to get an outcome you want. Although it may not be harmful, this is a use of power. Start here and then consider this scenario in a sexual context. For example, have you withheld sex or offered up sex as a way to motivate someone to do something for you? Or to punish them to make a point about something you didn't like? Have you pushed a sex act on your partner, knowing they were lukewarm about it, but you wore them down until they did it with you? Maybe at your job, you flirted on purpose to get a better tip? Or maybe you pushed a sexual connection with someone without any clear idea if you had consent? Or maybe you knew you didn't? Your history could include sexually abusing or sexually harassing. Go there. We stay stuck where we keep secrets.

One of my clients, Cheyenne, wrote a story about a time in college when she had sex with a guy, knowing it was his first time. She wondered if she had coerced him into it. She assumed any guy would want to make his sexual debut, especially if it had not happened by the time he reached college. But she remembered that they had not talked directly about having sex and she felt his hesitation. He didn't seem happy or into it that night. Because they never talked about consent, she looked at herself differently afterward.

Naming and acknowledging experiences of harm are important parts of the journey to holistic sexuality. Sometimes asking others what they remember is part of the process, as is looking at an experience from a different angle.

Here are some questions to broach the multiple sides of the topics of agency and violence for yourself. If you have not experienced sexual violence personally, you can change the wording to be generalized into the context of society or to ask someone in your life.

How Did the Reactions of Others Affect You?

People respond differently to experiencing or learning of sexual violence. If you have experienced sexual violence, you have probably had to choose, if not immediately, then possibly years later, whether to share it, how to share about it, with whom to share it, and what you want them to do with the information. If you did not share, perhaps feeling that you do not have an option to share, this secret-keeping, however necessary for emotional safety, will have a profound effect on you, your relationships, and your essence integration. If you did share or the information became public, how friends or family reacted, whether medical care professionals or law enforcement believed you, who supported you, and how the journey resolved in terms of accountability—it all affects you. It is critical to examine the impact on you.

How Have You Used Coercion?

As you review what violence you may have been subject to, you must also turn the mirror on yourself. Every single one of us has coerced someone. By a young age, we learn how to work caregivers or peers to get something we want—a toy, food, a reaction, a hug. To qualify as coercive, a behavior need not be ill-intended. Examine your history of coercion with bravery, authenticity, and strength. Look at multiple relationships, different times in your life, and inside and outside sexual connections.

Have You Harmed Another?

For yourself and for whomever you may have harmed, be accountable for your actions. Now is the time to consider whether you have ever committed an act of violence, however big or small. Here is a hint: Most people have. Your self-review should be a powerful and releasing experience that allows you to own behavior that has harmed others. Doing this will affect your transformation, growth, and essence. Conversely, consider how you have used your power for the greater good—to help, to speak for others, to help others feel powerful as well. Review how you have employed your power to help someone else feel validated, safe, or confident.

How Have You Responded to Violence?

Sexual violence affects those experiencing it directly and also affects bystanders. Have you ever witnessed violence first hand or been told about violence after the fact? How did you respond emotionally, verbally, and nonverbally? What effect do you think you had on the person sharing with you? Now explore how hearing about the experience impacted you personally: Did it create bystander trauma, or did it grow your insight, compassion, or awareness?

What Negative Events Have Affected You?

The pillar of power and trauma also considers big life events other than sexual violence that have affected your essence and thus you, holistically. Some events will have an obvious impact on your sexual connections, such as a loss that made you want to have more or less sex during your grieving, cancer treatments that changed your body so that you could not physically engage in sexual penetration, a job loss that made you angry and sad, or preoccupation and depression while dealing with an existential crisis.

From years of hearing stories, I realized power and trauma outside a sexual context hold relevance to your holistic sexuality because traumatic events, regardless of context, change life courses, alter worldviews, and impact your essence. You see yourself, the world, and relationships differently. So, as we finalize a 360-degree review of power and trauma in your journey, consider 1) personal experiences of things like crime committed toward you, a terrible divorce, bullying, an unstable home life growing up, severe social isolation, losing your home, chronic illness, death of someone important to you, terminal diagnosis, profound change of physical ability, food insecurity, pervasive mental illness, domestic violence, childhood neglect, and narcissistic abuse and 2) more communal, cultural, or societal traumas like genocide, terrorist events, political aggressions, natural disasters, economic collapse, election trauma, refugee experiences, war, and government-led sexism or discrimination.

How we experience, process, and integrate trauma and power differentials in all contexts profoundly affect our holistic sexuality and the essence of who we are.

List what has happened in your lifetime, and label the level of intensity, duration, and how it impacted you.

What Positive Events Have Affected You?

Positive events may also impact your holistic sexuality. As with the negative, list personal and global events; note the level of intensity, duration, and how they impacted you. These could include things like a move to a school that supported your learning style so you could flourish, a marriage that you find fulfilling and affirming, a job that opened career and financial doors, a trip to another country that expanded your view of the world and your place in it, political or social justice movements that brought about desired change, peace between warring countries, and scientific advances.

The key is identifying positive events that were not just wonderful but changed your life. Sometimes the intensity of the goodness or the positive impact isn't noticed immediately; it requires reflection. Those events are important in this exercise as well. To help us learn and avoid reencountering dangerous things, the human brain is wired to easily store negative experiences. For our survival, we need to know what could harm or kill us. We do not need happy or positive events in order to physically survive, but in modern society, we have learned that positive experiences enhance human existence and relationships. So we must anchor these positive experiences in our soul to create a balance.

I included examples above of how reflecting and deepening self-awareness can sound and look. There are many other types of questions to explore that can take you shooting down tributaries of your self-knowledge quest. They are good to ask, but do not stop at the asking. Answer them and use your answers as calls to action for you individually and collectively in relationships and your greater community.

POWER IS COMPLICATED, inescapable, and multifaceted. You no doubt have benefited from it and been hurt by it. We have all had access to and been denied power, inside and outside sexual connection. The flow of power between people in relationships influences how you see yourself, the world, and your safety within it. And with self-reflection and courage, you can address the places where an imbalance of power has caused you to shut down or freeze in your relationships and embrace a new position on your sexuality. We are all here to do better and make the world a better place. Power can be a ticket to change not only how you feel, but also how you make others feel, and you have the power to make the world safer for us all.

REVEAL YOURSELF TO YOURSELF

- How comfortable are you flirting with or seducing someone or being flirted with or seduced?

- Have you been coerced into doing something sexually you didn't want to do?

- Describe a situation where you have coerced someone inside or outside a sexual context.

- Have you ever withheld sex as a punishment or offered it up as an incentive to get something you wanted?

- How would you describe your sexual currency? Explore your past and present.

- What is the relationship of agency, power, and trauma in your journey?

PILLAR 8
Relationship

ANAHIT HAD SPENT a lifetime taking care of her parents who struggled with drug addictions. She also was a go-getter and a doer with a generous heart. She was a steady force and the calm in the storm for many people, friends and family. She often attracted unsteady, unaware people who preyed on her caring nature. She knew what to do with that sort of person because of her history with her parents: care, listen, and support. Wash, rinse, and repeat. The dynamic was leaving her exhausted and feeling like her needs always came last, if they were recognized at all.

After she left college, she began an impressive career that quickly snowballed into new experiences, countries, personalities, people, and relationships. During this time, she realized that she always felt safer with and more cared for in her relationships with women. Her relationships with men puzzled her. Anahit had a knack for choosing men with a lack of drive, who were comfortable with complacency, and who would plug into her giving, open, and loving nature. Over time, she gravitated toward seemingly gentle, emotionally tuned-in men, but even then, she faced adversities. I met her soon after a former boyfriend had raped her during a meetup years after their breakup, an experience that left her with a confusing, tangled web of questions such as "Did I do something to

Soul-to-soul
encounters change the
quality of your life.

trigger it?" and "Am I overreacting?" and "How is it that I still care about his feelings after he did this?"

Although the sexual violation was the initial focus of our work, I noticed that Anahit spoke about one friend, Daphne, more than the rape. She was grappling with something in this friendship more than she was with the assault. The assault was horrifying, but she had clarity about it; her feelings for Daphne were ambiguous. So, we turned our focus toward exploring orientation, love, relationship, and sexualization. Not long after we talked about what Anahit was looking for in a relationship, she said, "I think I am in love with my best friend."

Eventually she revealed her feelings to Daphne, and it turned out the feelings were mutual. She told her parents that she had found her soulmate who moved cities so they could be together. Her parents were not supportive and expressed their hope that Anahit would "realize this was not love." Still, Anahit and Daphne's relationship grew in depth and length; they bought a house and got a dog. In therapy, Anahit mapped out previous relationships, childhood relationships, friendships, and more. She dissected past romantic relationships, including the relationship with the man who had raped her.

All this reflection flooded her with information about what it means to be in a relationship, where she ended and another person began. Agency became a centerpiece in her growth. She started talking differently about herself, and even the quality of her voice changed. She became comfortable with making choices that were unpopular to some but in support of her own life. I will never forget the day I asked her what relationship had the biggest impact on her, and she answered simply and profoundly, "Myself." The times when she abandoned herself, the times she lost herself in caregiving, the times she dissociated to benefit someone else, and the times "doing" served her more than "being" had been abundant. But when she found out that her most important relationship was to herself, she began to live the life she had always dreamed of but had not known was possible.

Anahit's story points to a place we all must get to at least once, if not multiple times in our lives: understanding that sexuality is an individual journey experienced collectively and within relationships. You can learn some things about yourself only by being alone, and some things you can learn only through relationships. You learn more about yourself, your essence, and your dreams through relationships, which makes them a catalyst for great change.

IN THIS PILLAR of relationship, I ask you to consider not just a primary relationship but all relationships that have had a significant influence on you. This includes sexual relationships and those you have with yourself, your family and friends, work colleagues, spiritual companions, and community, whether they are long term or short term.

When I am first working with people, they often describe their sexual journey through their relationships, and that's a worthy starting point, of course. But relationships viewed within a holistic lens begin with yourself and then extend out to when you've given and/or received emotional closeness to another human. This closeness includes caring, sharing, loving, liking, disclosure, trust, and authenticity, and these things matter very much to our human experience.

Whom you sexually connect with typically does impact you, but I am careful not to focus on the "body count." The who, how, and why are more important than the how many. For some, reflecting on the number of sexual partners and connections adds some interesting context but a focus on "the number" tends to be used for meaningless comparison and harmful judgment rather than for insight. Viewing your sexual partners through a holistic, evolved lens is more relevant. Some sexual relationships will have affected you, and some will not have; some are positive, and some are not. The focus needs to be on what the experiences were like, your agency within them, and how they influenced your path and your essence.

Here are some key questions you can ask.

- What did that relationship or sexual partner mean to my journey?
- How intense was it? What kind of intensity was it, and how did it affect me? (Go into detail here.)
- How did this relationship impact my view of myself in a relationship?
- What did it teach me about relationships in general?
- Did the relationship help me understand what I need and want in other relationships?
- Did the relationship intersect with any of the other pillars of holistic sexuality?
- What are the lighthouse moments (regrets, joys, lessons) about this relationship?

After examining obvious and traditionally defined sexual relationships, it's good to look at your relationships that are not traditionally sexual but more soulful. As humans, I believe we are meant to be connected to something or someone outside our inner world. This drive to connect has a profound impact on our essence and our holistic sexuality, depending on the quality and nature of these connections and relationships and the meaning we make of them.

Relationships are a source of learning who you are and how you relate to others; they are a mirror of you. Relationships influence your view of yourself in the world, and the way you show up in relationships impacts others. Examine the types of relationships you engage in, how you show up for others, as well as any patterns that support or thwart your essence, your purpose, and your intentional growth.

Intimacy is an important aspect of relationships that I will explore in more depth later in the chapter. But I wanted to be clear that "intimacy" is not a polite synonym for "sex"; it refers to an emotional and soul-deep connection, to opening your soul to another, and the exchange that ensues. You have your own intimacy style, and you experience various levels of intimacy in different relationships. How you are intimate is important to understanding your relationships overall, whether they represent a singular moment or a lifetime of connection.

The Long and the Short of It

Many types of relationships—not just lifelong ones—can affect your understanding of yourself. I once interacted with a man for only five hours during a volunteer shift at a concession stand at my son's ball game. We were serving together, and we talked to each other casually to pass the time. When we were busy, we entered a seamless groove of communication. I observed how he treated people and heard his life philosophies. Up to that point, we had hardly ever talked. I remember seeing him once before that shift, and I only saw him briefly afterward. But this short-lived relationship had a significant impact on me for several reasons.

He embodied partnership in the way that I like and had never experienced with a man at that point. He had zero agenda with me beyond showing up for the job. He also shared some gems about life that effortlessly spilled out of him but felt so well timed, even though he had no idea they would be relevant to me. Our interplay as a cisgender heterosexual man and woman in a platonic partnership was positive and so different from what I was experiencing in my personal life at that time. I was partnered with a man who found it impossible to collaborate with me in many mundane domestic tasks. He also blamed me and my flaws for the upheaval in our relationship. And while I take accountability for the self-improvement work I had to do, there was a futility to the relationship that wounded me at my core. This brief interaction at the concession stand with a virtual stranger, who exhibited nothing but ease as we worked together, healed some of that wound.

Although that relationship wasn't one in a traditional sense, and certainly was not sexual, it makes it onto my list of relationships with impact. This connection showed me that my partner and I had a profound mismatch. Spending a few hours with the father of a boy on my son's ball team spurred a lot of reflection and action in me, and I bet he doesn't remember me or that day at all. Your details may be different, but I am certain you have experienced these kind of relationships as well. When they appear, they expand your definition of "relationship" and open you to insight. Be aware of them because they matter as much as the obvious long-term ones.

You will experience both positive and negative relationships that either change or strengthen your self-purpose. Note which relationships informed you in positive and negative ways. Reflecting on these relationships can point you to your behavioral patterns, illuminate your strengths, and highlight your unmet needs, which in turn may suggest some of the reasons for your needs and wants. This self-knowledge will bolster your authenticity and inform your agency.

The first few times I went through the self-examination of relationships, I noticed two obvious trends. The first was that I attracted strong personalities in both friends and romantic partners. I was flexible and didn't have tons of opinions, and people saw me as easygoing and approachable. I was even directly told by some strong personalities, and particularly women, that they saw me as someone who wouldn't bump up against them much, and if I did, I was manageable. It took me a long time to realize the implications of that assessment of me and my part of that pattern.

As I learned more about my pattern, I saw I wasn't being fake. I earnestly didn't have a strong need about most things and was happy to go where other people wanted, to do what they wanted to do, and to focus on their interests. In some circumstances, I found that if someone sounded certain and did not include me in a decision, I did not have the awareness or skill to assert myself if I did have a differing opinion. I didn't have the awareness that is the first step of agency. But invariably, I would reach a point where I did care and said so, and it was often rebuffed due to the way I clunkily asserted myself or because that wasn't within the unstated agreement of our relationship. My unexpected pushback often resulted in massive arguments or profound and lengthy silences from the other person.

What I know now is that in these relationships, I had unconsciously made agreements to stay quiet and to back down if my needs were inconvenient to them. I went on a journey to realize I wasn't a victim; I had an active role in this pattern, and I was the only one who could disrupt it. However uncomfortable this self-review felt to go through, and frankly however cringey as well, it was my only path to insight and eventually to growth and change.

The second unwanted trend I noticed was that I valued being a chameleon in relationships. I saw my personality as having multiple facets that could appear and disappear at will in various situations. I thought this behavior was valuable, worthy, admirable even. I would describe myself as someone who could be comfortable anywhere and fit into just about any context or group of people easily. But then I started to see how this chameleon quality was more harmful than helpful.

Often my shifts in behavior led to self-abandonment, which led to poor decisions and people-pleasing. In other words, if you think I am describing myself as an easygoing person who was taken advantage of and a victim, I wasn't. People-pleasing can harm the people you are "pleasing," and my "not having an opinion" demeanor was most assuredly annoying and burdensome. Also it was disingenuous. How could someone really know who they were connecting with if I changed depending on my environment? Worst of all was my pattern led me to feel resentful and then angry. My fuse was long—it took quite a bit to get me mad—but when I was angry, I was a scorching villages kind of angry. It was strongest when someone lied to me or took advantage of my laidback nature, or when I felt a high level of injustice. I realized I believed that because I didn't feel invested in "my way" often, when I did want or expect something, my will should be followed. Which felt like an abrupt and unexpected vibe shift for a strong personality who hadn't signed up for my opinion being invited into the room. I opened up only to a chosen few. And I had rules: Be honest, be loyal, be trustworthy, be dependable. If I chose someone, I depended on them to consistently embody all those qualities. But it rarely felt reciprocated. If a person let me down, my hurt was deep. And my reaction strong. Too strong.

Truly, though, my anger was fueled by outrage at myself for not showing up for myself. I was angry at myself for not investing in relationships with people who saw and valued me and for choosing unwisely when it came to opening up, especially in romantic relationships. I was angry that I had gotten good at hard. The people in this pattern with me were not interested in agency-fueled relationships; examining my relationships showed me how much that affected me. But I also saw that I was not great at opening up or even knowing what I wanted to say. If I wanted my relationships to change, I had some major mindset shifts to make, and I needed deep resolve to change my part in this pattern. It was hard, but I made the changes.

Noticing these patterns helped me look at the relationship between safety, vulnerability, and intimacy from a fuller perspective.

Safety, Vulnerability, and Intimacy

I have mentioned him already in this book, and finally it is time for me to talk more about Chris and how our relationship changed my life.

I had been in love before Chris, married and divorced. I'd had close relationships and friendships, a few sexual partners. But I had never experienced a relationship with the level of intimacy I had with him. It started with intrigue, big dreams in common, and insane chemistry, but it was destined to be more. Chris had an interesting mixture of complete and utter confidence and fragility that was earth-shattering and that I felt I shared. We fell in love and lived in a whirlwind romance. We lived a dichotomy of rock shows, tour buses, and crowds of thousands and graduate school, private family life, and domesticity. The relationship was imperfect, but it was also next level.

In many ways, I wasn't prepared for Chris. I didn't know crucial parts of myself that I needed to know to show up for this depth of intimacy. He was patient. He opened me up to a completely different world sexually, emotionally, and relationally. The band often called him a bull in a china shop, but he was also a teddy bear. And that's how he showed up for me. Sometimes that was confusing, but mainly it allowed me to figure out my intimacy style. Chris knew who he was—especially within a sexual and romantic relationship—and he expected me to know as well. When he realized I didn't know myself well in this context, he provided a safe container for a self-guided exploration of me within our relationship. He didn't take it over, he didn't answer for me, and he didn't let me get away with deferring to him. I discovered the power of feeling safe within a relationship and stepped into my sexual power. Chris saw me, understood me, and valued me. I felt a different brand of safety with him. I learned more about my responsibility in showing up for someone so that the intimacy flowed both ways.

I had always seen myself as a great friend and listener. But in my relationship with Chris, I realized an obvious fact that had been lost on me: People need different types of closeness and different levels of intimacy. This was in the early 2000s and well before this was common relationship lingo. We had different safety needs. I needed a wide berth that gave me time to show up for myself or I would let a bigger personality take over, and I also needed encouragement and reassurance with a gentle touch and tender demeanor. He struggled with anxiety and past trauma and needed stronger, quicker reassurance when anxiety took ahold of him; he needed direct guidance and hands-on care. Further, I saw I needed a variety of things to be present and feel comfortable being emotionally intimate with someone. Not just a good listener and not just someone who cared genuinely. And I needed to be able to look for those qualities when getting close with someone and to communicate those safety needs when partnered. Feels obvious now, but it wasn't until I met Chris. We all get to our own safety needs differently. Most people find it through a combination of solo time, relationships that don't work, and healthy ones that do.

This was the first relationship in which I needed to learn how to match the energy and potential of the relationship. For the first time, I felt I was sharing myself and connecting soul to soul consistently with someone. He became my first true lover, my trusted heart source, and that connection allowed me to take emotional risks. I felt like he knew every inch of my soul, heart, and body. That was special. Even though I was thirty, I felt myself shift from a girl to a woman in this relationship. Perhaps because I had been married before with a good man and was a mother, I was readier for that shift. Maybe how he interacted with me and who he was prompted me. Or perhaps it was the internal shift that happens after a divorce. I was open and hungry to change and to feel differently. Most likely it was a combination of all these factors.

PEOPLE OFTEN seek safety in their relationships, or experience a lack of it. Safety represents the parameters, behaviors, words, energy, actions, or context that need to be present so you can open up to emotional vulnerability. When that happens, you are ready to gain insight, repair harm, or grow. For most individuals I work with, safety leads to intimacy, pleasure, surrender, and connection (something I will talk about in the next pillar).

Vulnerability can be soul-altering as it shows up in long-term close relationships or in interactions with people who are only in your orbit for a short time, like at a support group or personal development retreat. It can happen in a one-night stand when the tone is about showing up authentically in a momentary and mutual celebration of wants and needs.

Many people think and feel that sexual connection is the ultimate act of vulnerability. In some circumstances, I think it can be because sexual connection has the potential to incorporate safety, vulnerability, and intimacy within a variety of sexual partners and contexts. What matters most are your answers to these questions: 1) How do you relate to these terms? 2) How do you think they relate to each other? 3) What need and comfort do you have with these terms? and 4) How much do you understand that others may conceptualize them differently than you do?

When I looked up the definition of "vulnerability," I was honestly shocked by the answer. One definition from *Merriam-Webster* was "openness or susceptibility to attack or harm." I was surprised violence was the leading reference. It gave me pause to celebrate that because of my work in holistic sexuality, I do not automatically connect vulnerability to danger. I see vulnerability as the potential to be deepened in one's own knowing, in being known by someone else, and for risk-taking with the hope of a positive connection. You may have a vastly different reaction to vulnerability; know where you are and what you want your relationship to vulnerability to be. In vulnerability, there is an inherent sense of not knowing how you will be received, perceived, or reacted to. I experience this when meeting new people, in expanding my professional reach, and sometimes with posts on social media—even with writing this book.

It is impossible to explore vulnerability without bringing up another heavy hitter: trust. People respond visibly when trust is brought into a conversation. I've seen people melt with the memory of being held in trust completely. Conversely, I've witnessed people bristle, become defensive, or even attack in reaction to broken trust. Infidelity and abuse are two examples that tend to evoke the latter response. We've all experienced the pain of being made vulnerable by our circumstances, identity, history, or by choice. I want you to experience the *joy* of being made vulnerable by our circumstances, identity, history, or by choice. Feeling safe is crucial where nurturing vulnerability is concerned. And as I have said already, to me, safety is the number one aphrodisiac.

When I became a listener (a.k.a. a budding and then professional therapist), I perfected the art of being witness to other people's stories. I deeply value the stories shared with me, and I love that my profession revolves around people sharing. But being a great listener is a double-edged sword. When you are the listener, you tend not to be as vulnerable and less often share and trust other people with your stories. But when you practice vulnerability—practice *being* vulnerable—the feeling of safety in relationships grows. It must be reciprocal to deepen the connection of the relationship in the long term.

SEXERCISE: Safety, Vulnerability, and Intimacy

When talking about safety, vulnerability, and intimacy with my clients, I often take them through this exercise, either individually or as a couple. Use a journal or paper and pens to record your responses.

Defining Terms
1. Consider the terms "safety," "vulnerability," and "emotional intimacy." Define what they mean to you. Don't think too much about it; just write down what first comes out of you.

2. Check in to see if you have a gut-feeling reaction to any or all three words.

3. Draw a shape that represents how you experience the three relating to one another.

4. Write an explanation of how the three concepts relate to each other and how they need to be present for you to feel connection with someone.

Deep Dive on Safety
You can take this exploration further, diving into safety. You can do this with a partner, but you must start by tuning in to what you know you need to feel safe and what lessens your feelings of safety. Ask yourself three questions:

1. What do you need from the person(s) you want to experience emotional intimacy with?

2. What do you need from the environment in which you will be opening up to emotional intimacy?

3. What do you need to feel grounded and emotionally regulated for intimacy?

If you are partnered, share your insights with one another, and be open to what your people need. When safety is met consistently, relationships deepen significantly, and the positive effect on each person is visible.

Bonus Questions

Here are some additional contextual questions to consider about safety, vulnerability, and intimacy to ask outside and, if relevant, inside a sexual connection.

1. The person. Do you feel at ease with your partner at the moment? Do you feel connected, or are you harboring resentment from an unresolved fight or something else?

2. The situation. Is the environment one that you can relax into the discussion or experience? Does it feel safe, supportive, and not distracting?

3. Your health. Are you feeling connected and well within your body, your health, your emotional well-being, and your spirituality?

4. The level of consent. Is any trauma being triggered? If this is a sexual connection, do you have a say in what behavior you are engaging in? Do you believe you can voice a desired behavior or stop a behavior with this partner? Do you know what it is like to be with a partner who honors consent and communication and wants to engage in mutually pleasing behaviors?

Making Safety Tangible

One couple I worked with through these questions found them critical to changing their intimate exchanges. Previously, many of their conversations had been wrought with tension and often ended in conflict and hurt feelings. As they answered these questions, they each recognized the role of safety in fostering vulnerability and intimacy, and they learned to look for solutions together so that all their needs were fulfilled. They figured out how to name their differences and see them as needs for safety, not as critical or dismissive of each other, but as an investment in their relationship.

When I learned my relationship patterns and identified the relationship between safety, vulnerability, and intimacy, I could name what I needed to feel safe. This led me to much better discernment in my intimate relationships. I examined how I showed up for others in their vulnerability and what safety I provided them in intimacy. Once I knew better, I needed to end relationships that didn't meet those parameters and avoid investing time or intimacy in people who were incapable of providing that for me.

That process was not easy. The strong personalities in my life reacted strongly to my nos. Life showed me a big gap between ending relationships that didn't serve me and finding or deepening relationships that did. I had to make a leap of faith many times as well as face loneliness and self-pity. I needed to do some risk-taking when investing in people; I wasn't sure how they would show up for me or how they would react to me showing up for them. But in the end, it was worth it—and it will be for you too.

Intimacy Styles

One triad relationship between safety, vulnerability, and intimacy is that safety fosters vulnerability, and the two feed into intimacy. People express intimacy in different ways. Some, for example, need lots of physical distance when talking to someone; others are "close talkers." Similarly, people have different entry points into intimacy. For some, it is a slow burn; others are quick to share or to want to deepen a relationship. For some, intimacy comes with ease, and for others, there is hesitancy or reticence. Some believe that most people can be trusted with and are capable of intimacy. Others need people to prove they are capable and can be trusted. You will be drawn to different intimacy styles to varying degrees, depending on your life circumstances and who you are relating with. However, you will likely have one favorite or most ease-filled way to connect intimately with someone.

Physical intimacy focuses on vulnerability through sharing your body with mutual consent and pleasure. This does not include overt sexual connection through sex acts but means spending time in physical proximity and doing things like hand-holding, snuggling, hair brushing, massage, talking, and sitting closely. This can happen in all types of relationships, such as with friends and family.

Sexual intimacy takes place when you share your body with another or others through overt sexual connection and sex acts. Arousal and desire are often present. This occurs only with sexual partners.

Emotional intimacy is experienced through emotional vulnerability, such as sharing feelings, needs, wants, and insights. It is experienced when you feel safe to let your guard down.

Intellectual intimacy results from the vulnerability of sharing what we are curious about, when we admit that we don't know something, and when we share self-reflections and self-knowledge.

Spiritual intimacy focuses on respecting someone's right not only to an individual identity but to their own beliefs about and understanding of religion, spirituality, and otherworldly or human existential questions.

Another factor intersects with intimacy: self-worth. How you feel about yourself, how you feel about someone knowing the truth of you, and how you regard your life's journey influence your access to and quality and expression of intimacy. When you feel relatively secure, confident, and comfortable with who you are, instances of conflict, discomfort, or disconnection are less likely to rattle you deeply.

There is no right or wrong or better or worse style, type, or approach to intimacy. It is, however, important to understand your own relationship with intimacy and how that manifests when you form and grow relationships. Just as vital to understand is that other people have their own relationships with intimacy as well. Sometimes differences of intimacy style between people can be misinterpreted. That's when the questions in the sexercise above will be extremely helpful.

"Intimacy" Does Not Mean "Sex"

Our society is confused about what "intimacy" means. Many people use the word "intimacy" as a euphemism for sex. This is troublesome because it implies that there is a right and wrong kind of sex, that closeness is the same thing as sex. Or that it is the "right" kind of sex, which leads to people thinking that sexual connections without intimacy are "wrong." The type of sexual connection you want may line up with this view of sex, which is great, but the term only captures that one kind of sexual connection.

Understanding intimacy is knowing that there is an array of options for intimacy in relationships. Some people see intimacy as meaning physical closeness. Some people view kissing as the most intimate sexual act, while others see penetration as the ultimate act of sexual intimacy. Still others see oral sex as the most intimate exchange people could experience. But of course, not all sex acts require physical closeness. Cybersex has zero physical proximity, and neither does listening to audio porn or phone sex. Yet some people describe those experiences as deeply intimate while others couldn't imagine feeling close to someone during those sex acts.

Several sex workers have told me that their cisgender male clients say they hired them initially for the sexual release but then realized it was mainly for the emotional closeness of the conversation. Not all pleasurable or desired sexual connections include emotional intimacy. Some people don't need or want emotional intimacy to find pleasure or enjoy sexual connection. And some people experience sexual connection as emotionally or physically unsafe.

Emotional intimacy is the interest you (and someone else in return) are willing to take to expose and connect on a soul-to-soul level. It is the embodiment of vulnerability, trust, and safety. It is about being willing to share the hard stuff, the deep feelings, the wounds, the dreams, the things you worry others won't understand or accept. Still, intimacy is a critical aspect of sexuality because it expresses and influences your essence.

When intimacy needs are met, individuals and couples experience greater satisfaction, trust, and support in their life circumstances and their relevant relationships. When intimacy isn't present or is inconsistent, this can damage the relationship and negatively affect the mental health of those in it. Healthy and intimate relationships foster positive regard for the other's intentions, a feeling of safety, a team approach to the relationship, and a common commitment to conflict repair. But if you were raised in an environment where the people surrounding you were not emotionally trustworthy or nurturing, intimacy can feel confusing and unsafe.

The dance of intimacy outside direct sexual connection is confusing for many and even more so when a sexual connection is in the mix. For some reason, we think we are going to walk into a sexual connection and magically nail intimacy. We get naked, messy, exchange noises and fluid, and are faced with a different type of intimacy. After we get dressed and cleaned up, we walk out into yet another version of intimacy. Intimacy is complicated. Beautiful but complicated.

In the tender territory between two or more people in close relationship, intimacy can be greatly affected by words. I have seen a shockingly high number of couples who become certain about things—that their partner doesn't love them, that they just need to be free, that they'll never get what they want from the other, sexually or otherwise. And they are about to break up. But when I work with them to decipher what the fight is actually about, we discover it is rooted in misunderstanding. The problem is not value differences or differing needs or wants or a lack of intimacy.

If you find yourself in such a situation, choose your words wisely in intimate conversations. Make sure you are saying what you mean. Check in to make sure what you are hearing and understanding *is* what your person is trying to say. Briefly discuss details, but as quickly as possible move to a conversation that is soul to soul.

SEXERCISE: Talking Soul to Soul

When you are in a heated exchange that has triggered something bigger or a matter that is a pattern that just won't go away, try this exercise.

1. Write down your partner's side to this argument or issue—both what they've expressed and what you think is their point of view.
2. Write out your point of view.
3. Consider the relationship as a third party in this exchange. What does this relationship need you to know?
4. Answer these questions: What is the soul-to-soul truth of this matter? Underneath the layers, what is this really about?

Intimacy and Trauma

Trauma can affect all styles of intimacy, and the impact of trauma on relationships can be permanent, fluid, temporary, instant, or long-standing. When someone is fighting for their life with deep depression and considering suicide, human intimacy and connection can be desperately desired and seem abhorrent at the same time. When someone is fighting a terminal illness, deep and intimate relationships may be critical to enduring the experience. But they may not have the energy to put into relationships, and that is when the people around them need to take up the slack where intimacy is concerned.

When I work with those who have experienced sexual violence, they often see a direct change in themselves regarding physical intimacy: drawn to more sexual intimacy or repelling it. The impact on other types of intimacy may not be as recognizable. For example, they may lose trust in their religious worldview (spiritual intimacy); they may not be comfortable taking a stance of knowing on a subject (intellectual intimacy); they may find that accessing emotions is harder for them (emotional intimacy); or they may feel a loss of trust in the judicial system or the people who didn't show up for them (worldview intimacy).

I experienced domestic violence, and afterward my emotional needs around trust changed dramatically. I kept to myself and held back vulnerability until I tested someone's reactions to shocking information. I lost faith in my own judgment and my sadness leaked out of me without control at times, and I did not know why. Sometimes I wanted to pass out a manual about how to show up for me, so that I could feel safe enough to open up to the intimate relationships I desired.

Trauma, particularly violence, affects intimacy, vulnerability, trust, and safety on profound levels inside and outside sexual connection. But it does not have to mean the end of a relationship. I worked with a couple, Bonnie and Tayrone, who hadn't experienced a fulfilling sexual relationship for over ten years. During our work together, both of them revealed that they had experienced profound trauma in their sexual journeys. Tayrone talked about the domestic violence he witnessed between his mother and stepfather, and then experienced himself. Bonnie revealed she had been raped in high school, which resulted in a treatable STI and a pregnancy that ended in an early stage miscarriage, something that she had never told anyone, not even Tayrone.

Both of them felt activated in their trauma when retelling the stories, but they also described feeling a release from sharing them and felt more compassion for each other. They both recognized how the experiences were still active in their bodies and souls. Tayrone made the connection first; touch felt triggering for him rather than intimate or arousing. He felt numb, which then made him feel angry. Bonnie had never told Tayrone that she sometimes had flashbacks to the rape when they had sex or that she felt intense guilt when people around her talked about her "first pregnancy" with their oldest child when she knew that hadn't been her first pregnancy. She had worried how Tayrone would react if she ever corrected the misbelief and felt she was trapped in that story.

Bonnie and Tayrone began to rebuild connection using mindful touching exercises to ease their anxiety around physical touch. They discovered what they liked and didn't like and worked on new communication skills to support pleasure and emotional intimacy. Once they were both feeling safe and comfortable in these new skills, they progressed to using them during sexual connection. In the end, they found cocreating a new sexual relationship gave them new spark and excitement. And each of them felt more fully known by the other because their secrets had seen light.

Letting Go of Inhibitions

There are varying opinions on the benefits or problems associated with using mood-altering substances in a sexual connection or when opening up in intimacy. I've seen substances like alcohol and cocaine cause a tremendous amount of damage and prevent a person from accessing their agency. These substances can also alter your ability to accurately read the behavior of others and your own behavior.

One of my clients once dated a man who told her he had a secret, but he could never find a way to tell her. This felt scary to her, and she found it odd that he kept telling her he had something big to share but then wouldn't tell her. She tried everything she knew to help him feel safe enough to open up to her, but nothing worked. One night she went to his place for a romantic dinner and to play music together. Predinner drinks led to dinner drinks led to after-dinner drinks led to waking up the next morning with a lot of foggy hangover vibes.

As they lay snuggling in bed, he kissed her and said, "I am so glad I finally told you. Thank you for handling it so well. You are the best." She had no idea what he had told her. Zero memory of it. She asked him several questions designed to get him to reveal the secret again: "What would you say were the highlights of the story in your eyes?" "How do you want us to incorporate this into our relationship now?" But he never answered in a way that explained what the secret was.

Later, she had an uncertain laugh about it and wondered if he was messing with her. She also felt sad that he had not felt safe enough to open up in sober moments, when the exchange could have built a foundation of emotional closeness. We also talked about her regret that she could not tell him that she did not know what his secret was, if he had indeed spilled it out. Their relationship didn't work out. Not because of that instance in particular, but most likely related to the dynamic that arose from a lack of good communication.

I've listened to substance-using clients who regret behavior, exhibit remorse over what they've shared, or are fearful because they have no memory of what happened or what they said. Regret and damage can shut down intimacy profoundly. Substances can make you feel like you are lowering your inhibitions and allow you to engage in a sex act or a conversation you couldn't make yourself do while sober. A false sense of agency. But since you are not doing it coherently, the meaning-making process of it is thwarted, which further inhibits intimacy.

People say drunk people tell the truth, in vino veritas, without thinking through or caring about consequences. I've seen this to be true. If you can't consciously think through the consequences of your actions or words, the aftermath can be confusing, confounding, and misinterpreted. There is a high potential for someone's agency (namely considering the consequences of one's decisions) to be compromised when mood-altering substances are present. Substance use also heightens the likelihood for a lack of judgment, misinterpretation of or disregard for social cues, and toxic inhibitions to be unleashed during sexual connections. Potential danger and peril lurk in mixing sexual acts and intoxicants—and also greatly impact our capacity for intimacy. Lowering your inhibitions with mood-altering substances is not the same as actively deepening intimacy when you are conscious and sober.

Still, I have seen mood-altering substances help people open up to intimacy. In some instances, and with comprehensive education, professional support, advanced communication skills, and the absence of addiction, the consensual use of some mood-altering substances may be pleasurable. I have seen substances like marijuana, MDMA, and psilocybin open people up to deeper levels of physical, sexual, and spiritual intimacy. Some have described their sexual experiences as otherworldly, not just in pleasure but in intimacy. Ashley Manta, an expert on cannabis and sex who coined the term "cannasexual," describes the benefit of using cannabis in sexual connection as a way of heightening sensation, enhancing pleasure, and promoting mindfulness to create deeper intimacy.

A client of mine once used mushrooms with her boyfriend. They had both used them previously, had a reputable supplier, sought professional oversight, and had a detailed safety plan. They knew how to handle themselves and each other in case the trip took an intense turn. Their relationship was in a healthy place, and each had a steady sense of self and strong communication skill set. During this experience, they had a mild trip and found it brought out the playfulness in their connection as they danced and held each other most of the night. They shared insights about their sexual relationship that they had not articulated before and enjoyed the levels of mindful play.

Using mood-altering substances can be a fun and fulfilling option for some people, but for others it can be dangerous and damaging. As with many aspects of sexuality, the variables in any situation must be considered so that people's agency is protected and they make choices that are safe and purposeful. Everyone's story is different. But when it comes to the use of mood-altering substances and intimacy, serious harm may result if the intent isn't consensual or if the people involved do not have a conscious relationship with intimacy going in. Using these substances is an individual choice, and when the choice is made with intention and purpose, you are likely to get a better result.

ROBUST INTIMACY is a major factor in the strength of relationships, and strong relationships support many physical and mental health benefits. You don't need a ton of healthy intimate relationships to experience the benefits, but you do need at least one and preferably two. When you are fully embraced by someone you feel close to, regardless—or perhaps because of—the details of your life, your self-esteem improves. This may boost your desire to reveal more of who you are to yourself and to other people. And that can transform your relationships for the better.

I have an unlikely set of friends called the Van Clan (named after the caravan of vans they drive to the designated football game of choice for the season) who demonstrate this point. Now in their eighties, the Van Clan were in their sixties when our paths first crossed. After I graduated from my doctoral program, I went to an alumni event, and one of the clan, Susie, jokingly directed me to commandeer a bottle of wine from another table and give it to them in order to sit with them. I did, and twenty years later, this crew of about twenty people and I have gathered many memories together. A mutual love of football and the College of William & Mary fuels our friendships. We've traveled to games together, tailgated, and watched highlight reels on the Mondays after the games. We have also shared stories and life wisdom.

As the youngest member, I paid attention to this rowdy group of retirees, philanthropists, and good souls, I listened, and occasionally I shared. They took genuine interest in my kids and career, made me laugh until my sides hurt, and cared for me deeply. I felt like a favorite niece. They weren't responsible for me, but they cared. I ate up their stories and advice, like know your blessings and give back to the community, have fun and be where your feet are planted, sit at dinner parties with people you don't know instead of who you came with, and so much more. I was lucky enough to have Don, the Van Clan "leader," become a dear friend, and I had a front-row seat to his processing of life changes, loss, and celebrations and many late night heart-to-hearts. Our connection met a need in me to be cared for and platonically valued by a healthy male friend.

I always left my time with the Van Clan feeling wanted, valued, and lucky that this powerful collective of souls welcomed me into their group, even though I was almost thirty years younger than they were. It was like having a whole lot of extra parents. Over time, the Van Clan has lost members one by one, but the feelings remain deep and strong. Relationships change, but the depth of connection in relationships like these remains solid and meaningful to me still.

REVEAL YOURSELF TO YOURSELF

- Consider several significant relationships, those with sexual connections and those where there was not or is not a sexual connection. Describe them and their impact on you (positive and negative). Are there any themes or patterns?
- In what ways are you someone that others feel safe enough with to open up to and become emotionally intimate with?
- How much do you monitor and control people getting close to you and knowing the truth of who you are?
- Do you care how many people you have had sex with (however you define "sex")? Do you know how many people that list includes? Would that list change if the context was one of sexual connection creating a deepened sexual intimacy?
- How do you think your sexual debut impacted your relationships at the time and your subsequent sexual history?
- How has agency aided your relationships?

PILLAR 9
Connection

I'VE WORKED with a company called Campowerment and its trusted leaders, the mother and daughter duo Tammi Leader Fuller and Chelsea Leader Gold, for many years. The organization brought women-identified folks together with a focus on self-knowledge and growth, fun and connection. We met online, at rustic camps, and at a fancy boutique retreat.

One of the other Campowerment experts, Anne "Sussy" Sussman, coined the concept of Bliss Buddies. (She has a book titled *The Bliss Buddy Project*.) The point of a Bliss Buddy is to create a connection with someone to share moments of bliss with, to promote joyful experiences and a mindful approach to daily life.

At a fancy camp event, I decided it was time for me to try this Bliss Buddy thing myself. I told myself I would leave the event with one. But who? I knew whom I was drawn to, but I didn't know her well as we hadn't interacted much. Did she want a Bliss Buddy? And what did she think of me? I felt like I was twelve years old and hoping to be picked early for the cool kids' dodge ball team. But I trusted my instinct, and I went up to her.

When I introduced myself and asked if she was interested in becoming my Bliss Buddy, I felt so awkward and vulnerable and weird. But happily, she said yes, simply yes, and our connection began. Years later, we remain Bliss Buddies, and Barbara and I

The reason you
are here is
beyond words.

share our bliss or missed-blissed moments. Our connection has been soul-filling, meaningful as women, single parents, and entrepreneurs. Our connection involves laughter, lightness, hard truths, helpful advice, and "you matter" vibes.

This small moment of forging connection has opened up whole worlds to me. Through short texts every day, we have told each other things that people in our inner circles do not know. We expanded our definitions of bliss. And we learned a lot about ourselves in the revelation of patterns of bliss and its absence. Our relationship grew in connection so uniquely. It was deep and fun, real and flexible. It is a testament to how wonderful it is to have connections that start in different ways, have unusual forms, and allow other sides of you to be seen and wanted. And our relationship has persisted because we have both put in the effort, carried each other at times, and let space grow when needed without fearing the connection had lost importance.

ONE OF MY STRONG BELIEFS is that we are all here to connect. Connection is the ultimate purpose in life—it is universal—to connect with something outside yourself, whether that is a person or a pet, a friend or a parent, or a lover. The list is long. Connection lets us know we matter.

Through my work, I have seen another truth: People can live a long time in pain, but they cannot survive long without purpose. Connection is the ultimate definition of purpose, and it's what every person I work with is seeking on some level. Love is a unique type of connection and one of the ways we explain attraction to people and things.

The final pillar of holistic sexuality, connection, requires the deepest and most profound level of self-knowledge and fearless, authentic self-reflection. That's why it is last for us to examine. The push and pull between connection and love, vulnerability, intimacy, and safety are inescapable. But in a way, the pillar of connection is a culmination of all the pillars. One of the essential meanings of life is to connect: with others, with our purpose, within ourselves, with a power higher than ourselves.

You and Your Story Matter

In my office, I have a sign that reads "You matter" and another that reads "Your story matters." They both are powerful and true and describe slightly different aspects of connection. When I ask my clients, "How do you know you matter?" some know instantly, some don't know what the questions means, and some answer that they do not matter at all. It is a powerful starting point in therapy and self-reflection. Connection to yourself matters to your mental and physical health; it is critical to your understanding of how you fit into the world; it is delicate and substantial. It has to be respected, tended to, and protected.

Connection serves as a protective force against the negative things we all encounter in life. Connection increases feelings of self-worth, belonging, and confidence. I have seen, over and over again, that it's less about the number of connections you have and more about the quality, consistency, reciprocity, and meaning of them.

After working together weekly for over a year, a college-student client and I talked about reducing the frequency of his sessions down from weekly. He looked at me and said, "You are the only one who knows I exist week to week. My sessions with you remind me it matters that I am on this campus. No one eats with me. No one talks to me after class. No one talks to me in the dorm hallway. No one lives with me. No one even acknowledges me when I smile at them as we pass on the sidewalk. The one thing I have each week is an appointment on Monday afternoon at two. I check in with the receptionist, and she says hello to me with a smile; I sit in the same seat as I wait for our appointment to start, you come and get me, and you care what I have to say and how I feel for one hour. I am not ready to give that up." We kept the weekly sessions until he graduated.

That conversation, which happened almost twenty years ago, is when I put up the "You matter" sign in my office, and I started hanging out in cafeterias, looking for people who were sitting alone and making my introverted self ask if they would like me to join them. I couldn't bear the thought of anyone feeling that isolated and unsure that anyone would notice if they were there or not. And yet so, so, so many of us live daily with that dread and that feeling. Suffering from the torment of loneliness and lack of connection.

There are many connections that matter. There are many ways to know you matter. Sometimes it is a therapy session. Sometimes it is a routine with one person. Another client once said to me, "So I just realized I pay you to be my best friend. How sad is that?" From sitting in this space with other clients and wondering it myself with my own therapist, I replied, "I see it as a victory. You invest in yourself by being consistent with someone you trust who genuinely cares about you and reminds you that you matter." And I know it is true. I know I am a really good therapist rooted in theory, techniques, and experience, but there are times that I know the most powerful thing I do for my clients is show them how deeply it matters that they are here and that they and their stories matter. Connection is as deep and as simple as that.

In the years following the height of the global pandemic, we have a different view of the importance of connection. The CDC describes connectedness as "the degree to which a person or group is socially close, interrelated, or shares resources with other persons or groups." During the pandemic when we were practicing social distancing, I wished we had used the term "physical distancing," because although it was understood that we needed physical distance to slow the progression of the disease, we needed social connection or closeness to survive the isolation and mental health consequences of the pandemic.

Seen, Wanted, Valued (a.k.a. the Trio of Love)

Dr. Brené Brown brought to the popular lexicon an important trio that the mental health community had taught for years. We all have a trio of needs to feel connected. She lists them as to be seen, heard, and valued, and she describes them as an energy between people and a source of safety, acceptance, and relationship strength and sustenance.

I have used different word combinations (seen, wanted, valued, understood, loved, safe, appreciated) to get into a deeper layer of connection, but I (and my clients, for that matter) most often land on seen, wanted, and valued. They appeal to aspects of your essence: being known and shown authentically, desired enthusiastically and entirely, and held as sacred and important. This is about seeing and being seen, soul to soul.

To understand this at a physical level, a visualization can help. Imagine me (or someone you love) sitting across from you with my hands folded over my heart. I open my palms, and a beam of light extends from my chest, as if my essence is reaching out to yours. You might imagine my hands based near my sternum and palms wide open for a long time or a short time or anything in between that represents the amount and length of access to my soul or yours. What is shared is the feeling of soul-to-soul connection, of being seen, wanted, and valued.

Being seen for the truth of you is powerful. An example of the gift of connections that make you feel seen and understood came from a college friend. I went to a very small college for my undergraduate degree, Centre College. When I attended, the enrollment was 850 students total. Tiny. That meant we knew or knew of everyone at the college, creating a unique web of connection. The uniqueness of our collective experience persisted over the decades. I have a core group of friends of mixed genders who gather once a year. We do things like attend sporting events, rent a house, cook together, drink too much, play flag football, share current life stories, find moments to share pains and worries, and relive college stories one too many times. One particular gathering, over candlelight and amazing food, the shit-giving tone shifted as one friend, John, stood up and talked about how stressful his day-to-day life is, how his high-level job zaps a lot from him, how he is trying to be a good husband and father but feels like he fails a lot. It was real. It was relatable. The connection in the room felt like a thread we had woven through each of us with two simultaneous versions present—our college-aged selves and our current older ones. His voice cracked, and he thanked us for giving him a space to not be anything but him. The purest form of him. Not the college kid who made dumb mistakes. Not the high-powered guy who seems like he has it all. Not the dad who needs to be smart and on it for his kids at all times. But just John. We saw his soul. He explained how it filled him back up to be seen and not need to give anything in return. It is a rejuvenating experience when your essence is seen, when the good and bad parts of us are wanted, and when our value isn't in what we can give, our roles, or our résumé, but in our connections individually and collectively.

However you find it for yourself, make the idea of connection tangible in some way as you explore it further and particularly when you get specific about being seen, wanted, and valued. I ask my clients how they know they are seen, wanted, and valued. One client answered: "I know I am seen when my body relaxes. I don't feel triggered into emotional dysregulation. I don't feel defensive. I know I don't need to overexplain myself, and I'm not thrown into an aggressive stance. It isn't about someone agreeing with me; it is about them honoring and knowing the details of my identity. When I feel that someone sees me, I notice that they highlight, talk about, and protect parts of me that I value as much as they do and that not everyone notices."

I know I am wanted when I get that buzzy feeling that someone is digging what I am saying, how I look, my verve. It feels as if a string is connecting us, drawing us toward each other. I know I am valued when I feel a sense of protection. This isn't about someone thinking I am entirely wonderful but about seeing the whole of me, which means my flaws or challenges don't diminish my overall worth.

One story from my own life is a clear example of feeling seen, wanted, and valued. A week after I was first introduced to someone, we started writing long emails to each other. Both of us were reluctant to begin dating after separating from difficult spouses. Neither of us loved talking on the phone with people we didn't know well, and texts were just too short. So emailing it was. That is how our love connection began.

We wrote to each other constantly. We couldn't ask enough questions of each other. Our emails were like a living memoir. They were flirtatious but much deeper. We felt like we had known each other for years. We discovered that we had often been in the same cities or places but had never met. We found we had the oddest people in common, but we had never heard of each other. The connection deepened with each email. At one point, he did a word count of all our emails from the first year. The number was enormous, higher than most novels. And that was well after we had moved to talking on the phone and seeing each other in person.

This connection was a pure exercise in being seen, wanted, and valued both with physical distance and emotional proximity. It was safe to be "seen" through my words and not my verve or career or looks or trauma. It was exhilarating to be wanted for my soul, my humor, my way of seeing the world and not just my body, my work with sexuality, or my newness to him. It was validating to be valued for my essence after being through a brutal divorce, as a mother, as a woman, as an evolved and communicative soul.

The nature of our long-distance relationship and our life circumstances forced us to live in a protective bubble, but it also gave us freedom to meet soul to soul more readily. I had experienced this type of automatic soul connection one other time, with Chris. But now I had a maturing relationship with agency, and that grounded me in meeting this man—and I'd had enough healing time after Chris's unexpected and tragic death. Although parts of me remained altered from that trauma, a large part of me was protected and buoyed, and my new connection really valued those parts.

When we finally did meet again in person, our soul connection translated fiercely to sexual and romantic connections. To be seen so deeply, to be wanted so passionately, to be valued authentically, it was intoxicating and grounded simultaneously. For years, strangers, people we hadn't even noticed, would stop us to comment on how our connection and love looked. We would see them smiling at us and giving us a thumbs-up, or they would want to share their own love story with us.

HOW DO YOU KNOW when you feel connected with someone through how they see, want, and value you?

There are some relationships where you may feel all three. Put those in the inner circles of your life. They are your soulmates, besties, twin flames, your doubles, your mini mes, your trusted mentors, your life-changing teachers or coaches. Then there are relationships that hit one or two of those parts of connection. They don't necessarily mean less, but they are different. However, the nature of the connection can indicate why some relationships last for a season and others are lifelong, and why some don't work at all. It also may explain those relationships that start with a bang and the magic is palpable, but then the connection ultimately feels empty.

Pay attention to how you show up for others in connection. How do you show people you see them, you want them, and you value them? The answers may vary from person to person and based on context. You may, however, see patterns that shine light on your power, challenges, and needs of connection. This awareness may help you enrich your connections. It may expand your experience and investment in connections.

Connection and love are not the same thing. Connection and intimacy are not the same thing. But these qualities are interwoven inescapably and powerfully.

Boundless Possibilities for Connection

The skill of connection includes presence of mind, expressions of empathy and compassion, agency, accountability, and social-cue awareness. Connection is the ultimate binder of sexuality, relationships, intimacy, and self-knowledge. It is the truth of who you are versus the mere summation of your circumstances. Connection has context, substance, motive, and outcomes.

Earlier, I asked you to examine the relationships in your life that have the most impact on you positively or negatively. When you were doing that, you were also subtly examining your connections.

I would like you to directly consider those relationships again in the lens of the three parts of connection that resonate most for you (being seen, wanted, valued). Examine the presence and absence of those elements in those relationships. Be mindful these types of connections come from a place of self-worth and self-knowledge rather than unhealed wounds and unconscious insecurity. Look for patterns and insights—the lighthouses—that are shining for your deepening self-knowledge. When you look at those relationships through the perspective of connection, does the list change or shift?

Connection is mostly about relating to something outside yourself. There are times this means connecting with a person, but it won't always. Look at other connections that matter to you beyond human relationships. It could be a community, an organization, a spiritual belief, a pet. What connections give you purpose, tie you to something outside your internal world, and imbue your life with worth, belonging, meaning, and a knowing that you matter? When I started writing this book, I did not predict that I would write about my dog. But here we are.

I've loved pets for my whole life, but the last two dogs in our family turned me into one of those people who talks to my dog and considers them family members. My current dog, Flash, is a little fur soul who has taken hold of our family with the sweetest connection. We like to joke that Flash needs skin-to-skin contact at all times. His little pug-mix face is full of expression, and he is often instigating playful contact. He is quite the extrovert and very social. So is my son, Jack; my daughter, Annalise, and I are more introverted.

Jack and Flash are a match made in heaven. Flash came into our lives originally to be a companion for Annalise. However, the timing coincided with Jack transitioning from college to home and his first career-focused job after a scary accident that took six months to recover from and an almost career-ending injury the week of his college graduation. Jack was feeling sad and lonely, leaving his college friends to come back home for surgery and recovery, and he was worried about falling behind in starting his career. Flash just wanted to connect with him. He read Jack correctly and nestled in with him, mirroring his energy and giving him lots of snuggles. He slowly started getting Jack to play tug-of-war with him. That led to running and chasing.

As Jack's sadness lifted, he grew closer to Flash and was more open to the dog's happy enthusiasm. Jack found a purpose in caring for Flash and, through him, found the synergy of connection and happiness. They are the best of buddies, and the amount of joy Jack has with Flash is palpable.

Do not discount the value of connections with pets or through other connection points like sporting teams, love of a musician, or a hobby community. The community of connection Taylor Swift has cultivated in her fans is a clear example. Or football team fans. I've seen people find meaning in observing a raccoon family that came to visit their backyard every year, the fun of a men's-only pickleball group, or the relationships with birds that frequent a garden feeder. These connections may not hit the magical trio of connection, but they can provide a meaningful stacking effect of feeling seen or valued or wanted even in a moment. Just like moments of bliss, moments of connection can make an enormous difference in our experience of the world. Connection is a reminder that you matter.

Connecting Sexually

As noted earlier, I use the term "sexual connection" rather than "sex." People often use "sex" to refer to sexual penetration, whereas "sexual connection" encompasses many aspects of pleasure, options, and interests, including but not limited to penetration.

Sexual connection refers to a variety of things. It can be a sex act or a deepening of intimacy, relationship, and knowing. Sexual connection can occur privately through solo sex or with multiple partners. It can be meaningless, profound, or harmful. It can be privately or publicly known, and it can be a deepening of intimacy and a strengthening force within a relationship.

Some people describe sexual connection with others as a beautiful, transformative, and even as a transcendent energy exchange. Others see it as a momentary, pleasure-filled connection—brief but positive. And some find they are distracted and dissociative, or perhaps neutral during sexual connection, and some feel it is actually disconnecting. A person can experience all or any combination of these variations. I have found that those who describe a particular sexual connection as "soul connecting" or "soul building" often say authenticity, safety, sexual agency, and an equitable exchange are parts of the experience. Something quite powerful happens when people want, see, and value themselves and another (or others) from a place of truth, authenticity, and openness to the exchange. Seeing a sexual connection as a dance or a flow can also enhance the connection.

Everyone ought to choose the verve and type of sexual connection they want to engage in, and my recommendation is to play with various types or personalities of energy when exchanging sexually. There are yucks and yums in sexual connection too. Build upon the yucks and yums from the pillar of acts and interests, and deepen them with a variety of energy exchanges, vibes, and verve of sexual connections.

Connection is a potent aspect of human existence, an expression and experience of our essence. Prioritize understanding connection. Build that skill. And increase the quality of connections in your life. Inside and outside overt sexual contexts.

What's Love Got to Do with It?

We need to add "love" back into the equation of sexuality and connection, specifically within sex acts. Although love isn't always contextually relevant within sexuality and sexual connections and some have negative histories with love due to trauma, religious trauma, or sex ed messaging, love does have a valuable presence within holistic sexuality.

People use different terminology for it. We "have" sex, but we "make" love. And "fuck" is its own noun and verb. I like the term "love fucking" to capture the passion and vibe of "fucking" someone you also feel a love connection with.

But what is love? Who the hell knows. As a culture, we are obsessed with love. We have a history of reality shows and TV dramas focusing on (something like) love: *Love Is Blind*, *The Bachelor* and *Bachelorette* series, *Love After Lockup*, *Bridgerton*, *Grey's Anatomy*. We can take any topic, any era, and any context and put love into the mix. We have professions devoted to it: wedding planners, dating coaches, matchmakers, and therapists. We have theories and tips and tricks of how to fall in love, how to stay in love, how to grow love, and how to keep long-term love.

Over the centuries, humans have tried to capture what love means through songs and plays, poems, literature, and novels. Writers and musicians and poets and artists are all trying to help us describe love in digestible soundbites so we can wrap our heads around something we (arrogantly and perhaps erroneously) think that only humans experience. And yet we aren't satisfied. We haven't said enough about it. We haven't figured it out. We haven't been satiated individually or collectively.

Some cultures and languages have multiple words for different kinds of love, but by and large, English speakers haven't figured out the nuances of the word "love." We often speak of it: "I loved that concert!" "I love you." "I am in love with that shirt of yours." "See you later, love you, good night." "I love you. Will you marry me?" "I love that you are my son." But what are those different usages referring to? The word has a different connotation in each context and for each person who uses it. So, how do we understand "love" collectively? We can't get any further into the discussion about sex, sexuality, and love without coming up against that issue.

Is it chemistry? Is it butterflies? Is it long-term knowing? Some liken love to certain types of tenderness, warmth, or fondness that "is just different." Or they call up "passion" and "adoration." Some are trying to tip their hat to the kind of devotion that results from a deep and enduring emotional regard and connection with another. Again, similar to the Supreme Court's ruling on pornography, sometimes you just know love when you see or experience it. For most, the experience of love is positive, if not wonderful. It is important to acknowledge, though, that love also has negative aspects to it. Maybe not the expression of love itself, but the potential for love to be used negatively with ulterior motives, carelessly, or as a weapon of judgment, manipulation, or control. Love hurts. Damage can come from a lack of reciprocity or even resistance to receiving or giving love. Love hurts when it is lost, faded, or morphed into something else through discord or death. Love is complex in its beauty and its power. It is potent. It is important.

Scientists have tried to explore the science of love by focusing on neuropeptides and neurotransmitters and hormones. Scholars and philosophers have written theories about love. Robert Sternberg's triangular theory of love includes eight types of love based on variations of passion, commitment, and intimacy. Some religious and spiritual practices split love into different types. Love, it is posited, helps us survive as a species and is a critical factor in our mental and physical well-being. There are interesting things to absorb in all these views, and they fill in parts of the picture. No single perspective completes the definition of love.

Because love is a noun, an action, and a feeling.

Love is a science and an art. It is palpable and ethereal, clear and confusing. Defining love is like trying to nail down jelly. It will always jiggle free. The elusiveness of love becomes part of its definition as well.

I do not profess to define love better than anyone else, but if I had to give it a shot, I would say that generally, I see love as a concept, as different types of love, and that there are different ways to experience and give love. Love is a feeling of wholeness. An embodied, pleasurable sensation related to the person or object of love. Love is a powerful urge toward connection, openness, and reciprocity. It is a dogma, a belief, an unveiling. Love is trust in the wanting, in the transformation, in the powerfulness of the affection, tenderness, or passion. Love is an exaggeration, and it is the truth. It is our greatest expression of hope. Love is a choice and involuntary. Love tells us that we matter somehow to someone and to something. Love is being seen, wanted, and valued in the vastness of humanity. Love is the pinnacle of feeling, connection, and knowing. It is the pathway and the expression of our essence, like our sexuality. I believe it is inextricably tied to who we are and why we are here and that it is threaded throughout holistic sexuality.

Types of Love
A complete list of types of love seems impossible to make as the variations feel endless. We love in so many ways within many different contexts and with varying degrees of intensity.

But let this pillar be the place you examine the positive and negative messages you have received about love's place within holistic sexuality, and identify what place you would like it to occupy. For reference, here is a quick list of types of love, just for the love of it.

- Romantic love: love that may lead to being committed partners or spouses.

- Self-love: love for yourself emotionally and sexually.

- Spiritual and religious love: love from another source (God, Allah, Mother Earth, goddess, energy, and so on) and your love toward that source.

- Familial love: the love that ties us to what and who we consider family or genetic relatives.

- Friendship love: love we have for our chosen family and inner circle of confidants.

- Parental love: love for and from those we raise or have influence over in their journeys and for those who guided and parented us in our journeys.

- Global love: love for a community, culture, country, and humankind.

- Sexual love: love making, love fucking, sexual connection, and lovers.

- General love: love for things such as pets, sports teams, a type of music, or a type of clothing.

What Does Not Make the List

One kind of love you don't see in the above list is unconditional love. This may be a perplexing or unpopular opinion. Yet I stand firm on it. Here is why I find this phrase troublesome: I have seen this phrasing used as a weapon against healthy boundaries and the activation of agency. "If you fully accepted me and loved me unconditionally, you would accept this behavior." Saying no is translated into not unconditionally loving someone, and so someone is faulted for their boundaries. Let's look at parenting as an example. When you are correcting the behavior of a child, it's better to distinguish not liking the behavior from not loving the child. This is because in their developmental life stage, children often hear the criticism and the emotion behind the correction or punishment as directed toward who they are as a person rather than the behavior. This happens with emotionally immature adults as well.

If you want or need to be experienced as someone who loves well, the concept of unconditional love has the potential to be misconstrued, flipped around on you, or could be a sign that love is being defined by a vastly different viewpoint from yours. I have seen this concept do deep-rooted damage because a huge part of love is safety. A good kind of love and a healthy person can absolutely have conditions for loving the behavior, the relationship, and the person. You can love someone and not stay in a relationship with them, and your love for someone can diminish or end because of how they acted toward you or others. You can love someone for who they are and not accept some of their behaviors or beliefs. Love isn't less if it has conditions. Love can have an opinion, needs, and wants. Saying no does not mean love ceases to exist.

One participant in my Revealed program, Beatrice, shared this story with me about seeing a text exchange between her boyfriend and his mother. Her boyfriend was writing to his mother about a conflict between the couple. Beatrice couldn't believe the spin he put on it in the text. He took no accountability for his actions and exaggerated her reaction to something he did. Beatrice sat spinning, floored, but she continued reading. The mother's text in response explained why her soon-to-be ex-boyfriend took such little accountability in their relationship: "I don't think Beatrice is capable of giving unconditional love."

A lighthouse insight came into view. Beatrice had spent so much energy and time in a string of relationships trying to be a good partner, a good girlfriend, to be seen as loving and benevolent, that she had abandoned herself continually in an attempt to love unconditionally. She knew she wanted to be with someone who felt that the action of love, the commitment to love, required a reinvestment on an ongoing basis. She resisted the urge to defend herself as a good person who loves fully and freely, and she sat in a place of knowing that "unconditional love" meant something different to her. She had standards, boundaries, and behaviors that had to be met for her to actively love another person. And she realized the unconditional love conversation between her boyfriend and his mother served as a way for him to not be accountable for his behavior.

This point about unconditional love became clearer to me when I heard and then subsequently gave the best advice I know: Children of all ages know you love them. Telling them one hundred times a day won't ensure they have good self-esteem or make them feel wanted, seen, or valued. They think you are supposed to love them because you are their parent. It certainly matters to say it and for them to hear and feel it. But in a healthy family, parental love is a given. This belief is unconditional adjacent. Continue to tell your kids you love them, but it's also powerful to tell your kids you like them and what specifically you like about them. This advice extends to friends and those who matter to you as well. In this context, like and love have many overlaps.

Be specific about what you like about them. When I started saying this to my children, I noticed a difference immediately in our relationship. I would say things like: "I really like you." "You are my favorite person to hang out with." "I really like how fun you make our walks." "I really like that I learn so much from you." "I really like the kindness I see in your heart." The reception was much different than when I said "I love you." Those just seemed to bounce off them or were absorbed quickly; when I told them I liked them, the difference was shocking. It felt energetically differently. This hit hard at first and then it felt like a superpower. Everything in moderation and in authenticity, of course, but I have heard the same feedback from clients who made this shift with their kids too. Being seen, valued, and wanted within a relationship of safety and love was a powerful formula.

So why, in this context, is "like" more powerful than "love"? Why is this not a chapter on liking someone? I think it is about the power of choice, the myriad of definitions of love, and the hurt we all know and want to avoid when we feel a rejection of our essence on a soul level rather than a superficial one. The answer is also in the power of being or not being seen, valued, and wanted. That is the trio of the ultimate connection: love. And isn't that lovely too?

There is no consensus on what love is or why it is such a powerful force. The list of the many attempts we as humans have made to capture and celebrate the gravity, longevity, and importance of love is long, but one person, for me, has solidified the concept into the most poignant and cherished simple statements. Within her masterpiece *All About Love*, bell hooks, my all-time favorite visionary, writer, activist, and feminist, writes the following:

- "The essence of true love is mutual recognition—two individuals seeing each other as they really are."

- "When we choose to love, we choose to move against fear, against alienation and separation. The choice to love is a choice to connect, to find ourselves in the other."

- "To truly love we must learn to mix various ingredients—care, affection, recognition, respect, commitment, and trust, as well as honest and open communication."

- "Of all the definitions of love that abound in our universe, a special favorite of mine is... 'the will to extend one's self for the purpose of nurturing one's own or another's spiritual growth.'"

Your Longest Love Relationship

Your most important, most influential, and longest relationship is with yourself. Self-love gets a bad rap as bumper-sticker psychology, which is unfortunate because how you love yourself makes an enormous impact on what you think of love in general, your access to love in action, and your ability to incorporate it into who you are and your sexuality. It's a truism: If you don't love yourself, you cannot love another. I do not think it is so cut-and-dried, but I do believe how you love yourself compared to how you love other people is vastly different in motive, verve, and energy reserve. Love is a guiding force that you feel is a birthright and a responsibility to keep when you make and feel the connection to self-love and authenticity.

When it comes to love, some of us hit the jackpot with a great family or incredible romantic partners. But some of us do not. Hitting that jackpot, or missing it, isn't a representation of your worth or of your ability to love or be loved, but it is often seen and felt that way. You can access something more powerful, though, something much more potent and reliable than the love jackpot, and that is you.

If the term "self-love" makes you squirm or recoil, or you are desensitized to it, find another word that feels better, although I acknowledge it may not be easy. I looked up words that I could offer to you instead of "self-love," and I was floored by the negative synonyms for this word: pride, conceitedness, egocentricity, pomposity, smugness, vanity, arrogance, self-satisfaction, and complacency. Nope.

Other definitions for self-loving were confusing: self-satisfaction, self-sustaining, self-confidence, peace-loving, self-determination, self-esteem, and loving. Self-love is perhaps all those things and more. What I do know is that self-love is more than a media campaign; it is foundational to essence-based authenticity and connection and agency.

Megan, a cisgender woman and colleague in her mid-forties, is a powerful and unique example of this assertion. Her details will differ from yours, but I want you to apply the thread of connection, love, and agency in her story to relevant parts of your story. Do not compare the details of her life to yours; pay attention to the presence of and relationships between love, connection, and agency.

Megan lives in agency consistently and upholds holistic sexuality in so many areas of her life that it leaves me breathless. Her mother died at an early age, and her father died while she was in her formative years. She had a sibling, but they were long estranged, a death of a different sort. Megan essentially raised herself. She alone made key decisions about her life, education, career, living situation, and relationships without family guidance and, at times, without generational wisdom or values to guide or limit her with boundaries. She described herself as having a base of love from childhood but not a deep, replenishing well.

She had, in some way, no choice but to find agency. Ultimately, Megan decided to forge a fearless relationship with love and connection. She made her own rules and explored boundaries in extraordinary ways. She asked for what she needed, and she refused to say yes to things that didn't serve her purpose or needs well before this was cultural vernacular. She sought relationships that gave her profound love and connection. She was true to herself along the way. Self-love was her guiding life force.

Her path involved often being the third in polyamorous relationships. She was a sex worker and frequently a dominatrix with conservative-identified men. She wrote publicly about her views on sex education and specific sex communities, and she told stories about her sex life that made me laugh until my sides hurt. I have the utmost respect for her authenticity. She is the author of many of my favorite sex stories and is one of the few people who has gotten outrageous sex stories out of me in return. When you are in the company of someone living their truth and who values connection and love in her life as fervently as Megan, you want to meet her at that level. She doesn't need people to have the same story as her, to approve of her, or even give her an opinion. She wants love and connection with you—whether as a friend, a lover, a boyfriend, a girlfriend, a client, or someone in her trusted circle.

She has chosen her family through friendships and romantic relationships and built a love reserve in those connections. She is crystalline on how she wants to be seen, wanted, and valued and on how she sees, wants, and values you. She hears what others want and it matters to her, whether you are a paying client or a friend she has flown across the country to see and either check out a sex club or an Eagles game with. Megan makes you feel both loved and in connection.

If you are an asshole landlord who doesn't treat her or others with respect, you are going to hear it, and she will move on from negativity without transferring the effects of this experience to the next encounter. If she is feeling lonely and vulnerable on Mother's Day and Father's Day, which are triggers for her, she will ask for extra texts and calls that day or ask you to respect that she doesn't want any contact.

If you want to date her and she agrees, you will be a part of her relationship world. This may include single dates. You may be one of four in a day. You may be a double date with a couple she is dating. If you want her to be the girlfriend to your couple's relationship, she will want to date both of you individually and together. Some of this will involve sexual connection, but there will be love connection too. If you are a sex work client, she gets very clear, very fast about how you want her to talk to you, what role you want her to play, and how you want to feel in the interaction; she is equally clear on her boundaries of what she will give and exchange with clients and what she will not. Without exception, she will require you to respect her agency and will give you big love when you offer an exchange or a relationship rooted in agency.

On a recent birthday, she put up a post on social media asking for specific ways to show her love and appreciation. She got what she needed because she knew what she needed, because she knew herself and because she lives her life that way. Megan conserves her connection energy and depth of love for those who give back in ways that nurture the connections she seeks.

Your details will most likely be quite different from hers, but her framework, the framework of love through agency, can be replicated with a multitude of life details and in your life. Her lack of traditional familial love and connection both forced and allowed her to define love and connection in the ways that serve her soul. And she is loved deeply by friends, colleagues, lovers, and clients. Her remarkable authenticity, her brazen honesty, and clear boundaries are backed up by how she gives of herself. Her truth feeds this level of love and connection in a synergistic way that is beautiful to behold. Love combines agency, self-knowledge, and self-compassion. As bell hooks writes, "When we can see ourselves as we truly are and accept ourselves, we build the necessary foundation for self-love."

REVEAL YOURSELF TO YOURSELF

- What is your definition or concept of love? Define self-love, spiritual love, friendship love, sexual love, and romantic love. Write about how they have or have not manifested in your life.
- With sexuality as your essence, how does your essence love? How has your essence been loved or not loved?
- What makes you feel seen, wanted, and valued?
- At what stage do you feel most connected in relationships? What does that mean for you?
- How has connection shown up in your sexuality?
- Can you think of times you had sex, made love, fucked, or love fucked?
- What do you think is the relationship between agency and love?

TUNED IN AND TURNED ON
You on Agency

AGENCY FIRST CHANGED my life and then it saved my life, and it never stopped evolving along the way. In my relationship with Chris, I thought I had found my true agency. We had a beautifully consensual sexual relationship, we had deep emotional intimacy, and he wanted to know what I wanted and needed and who I was authentically. I later realized, however, I had learned *more* about agency and what it means to me, but I actually hadn't integrated it fully. When Chris unexpectedly died five years into our relationship, this truth crashed into my awareness. My own agency needed shoring up, because I had tied it to him. My agency felt powered through my relationship with him, so after he was gone, I grieved the tragedy and I lost the grounding I had felt so secure in. A new level of understanding agency opened for me.

I felt lost because I could not tap into resiliency, and I lost faith in how the world worked, and that trickled down to me losing faith in my decision-making. I didn't feel unsteady only in life; I felt unsteady in the world—it was a true existential crisis. So I began there. I looked at the meaning of my life, my place in it. On any given day, I vacillated from "Life is short—do it!" to "Fuck it, who cares, we are all going to die anyway." And my decisions at that time reflected that confusion.

Activated agency is a superpower.

The journey with agency is cyclical for everyone. As I've grown into a deeper understanding of my agency, I have not always prevented hard things from happening; I have not always been the "Queen of Agency." But I have learned how to recognize when I am not acting with agency and I course correct more effectively now. I can now spot people, relationships, and organizations that are not agency-driven and protect my energy or remove myself from those connections faster and more effectively. Within sexuality, I can advocate for my needs and wants at an advanced level.

Though agency will not and cannot solve all our problems, it bolsters us, sustains us, and fuels us in the moments when the dust settles and we must pick ourselves up and choose which way to go. Though agency isn't a magic wand that effortlessly tidies up the messy parts of life, it offers us the rubber gloves that fit perfectly, the bucket and mop, our favorite music, the time to take matters into our own hands and to build confidence in ourselves, and the tools to make the work easier—10 percent more enjoyable and 100 percent on our own terms. Agency is for you, from you, within you, and around you anytime you need it, and its reliability, strength, support, and power are unparalleled.

At first glance, the concept of agency seems almost insultingly simple when it's promising such big results. But once you begin working with it, you realize how complex it is, the patience it demands, the perseverance and skill it requires. The more you think you know about agency, the more questions arise. So buckle up!

You want to be loved and to feel true connection—we all do. Within an overt sexual context and outside one. We want connection holistically. To feel the connections you crave, you must bring your authentic self to the relationship. And to present your authentic self, you must know who you are. To know who you are, you must have agency. And to be in agency, you must self-reflect; face the light and dark, the strengths and weaknesses in yourself; hold yourself accountable and also forgive yourself; heal and accept; and find a balance between resilience and self-protection. You must also be able to do the following:

- see multiple perspectives;
- strengthen your tolerance for ambiguity;
- draw boundaries for yourself and others;
- learn the difference between empowerment and entitlement, as you grow in empowerment and dispel entitlement in yourself and others;
- embrace the understanding that empowerment is individual while agency is relational;
- see the complexities of intersecting identities within it;
- find your voice and create safe relationships, communities, and environments in which to exercise it; and
- dedicate yourself to making decisions that are aligned with purpose and intention.

That's a lot, I know. How are you supposed to do all of that and shower? Agency is not something you can do 24/7, so instead see it as both the road and the destination. You will meander. You will veer off course. The terrain will vary, and at times the destination will be unknown. That is okay. Some of the work is to be okay with the ambiguity of the journey. Agency will be there for you to keep coming back to.

An Idealistic View?

I hope you agree that one of the best ways to know who you are is through holistic sexuality—the final frontier of self-development. You know now that sexuality means so much more than what kind of sex you have and with whom, and that it can have an enormous impact on your well-being. You will build upon your definitions of agency and sexuality again and again, redesigning, relearning, and deepening your understanding of you, your choices, and your life, sexually and beyond, for as long as you continue to work with them.

Sometimes people ask me, "So, holistic sexuality is really just a path to knowing yourself, and you are replacing spiritual growth or another psychological theory with sex?" Yes... and no. A holistic view of sexuality has been forgotten, overlooked, misconstrued, and diminished. Yes, I do think having great sexual connections—great sex—is amazing and valuable and worthy of time and effort. I think it helps in the moment, stacks upon itself internally and within relationships, and builds positively over your lifespan. To be clear, I am an advocate for great sex in your life.

It is a both/and. I value that, *and* I want you to see sexuality as a path to your truest self, your essence, and a medium through which to express your endless potential. Will your life be shit if you don't adopt this point of view? No. But can it be better? *Abso-fucking-lutely*. Much more fulfilling and peaceful. I want this for you so very much. For your well-being. To deepen the well of your mental health, physical presence, and most importantly how you see your place in the world. Yes, I do believe holistic sexuality offers this improvement.

Can we vastly improve our sexual culture and social structure if we collectively adopt this viewpoint? Yes, so very much, yes. It may be idealistic to dream as big as I do about it, but I do so because I have seen the transformation that happens individually and within relationships when you shift to agency, when you see people healing from past wounds and changing their lives so rapidly, as they move away from pain and harm toward pleasure and connection. I do firmly believe that the ways sexuality is weaponized and controlled in cultures bleed into all areas of our lives to our individual and collective detriment. I also firmly believe this is preventable. The problems in our sexual culture can be healed and prevented simultaneously. It is hard not to dream about what this would mean on a larger scale, even though I am quite aware of the incredibly powerful forces that would never want this to happen and the enormous hurdles to be crossed from here to there. Still, I dream. It is possible. I've seen it happen and know it is worth it. The beauty and power of those more private victories fuel my dreams on a bigger scale, and I hope this will happen for you as well.

When I worked with a football team at a university, one of my roles was to lead a talk that aimed to meet a Title IX requirement of sexual assault prevention. I had a tough audience as I was the only woman in a group of male players, coaches, and administrators; not one of the one hundred men wanted to be in that room. My approach was to present the information in a way that assumed positive intent and behavior and to bring them all into solutions instead of assuming they were the problem. There were particularly impactful learning moments that highlight what holistic sexuality can do for a culture at large. One addressed the concept of coercion. I gave all first-year players a toy firefighter and instructed everyone else to do all they could to coerce them to give up their toy. Throughout the talk and over the course of a couple breaks, everyone either worked hard to protect their toy or weaved coercive webs to get their teammates to give up their toys.

After what seemed to be an innocent game, I had the first-years talk about how the others had emotionally and physically manipulated, overpowered, or threatened them for the toys. Coaches used their power to blame them for something they didn't do and threatened to make the team do laps. Players lied about the meaning of the toy and convinced them I was the one tricking them. Staff would team up and distract them and take the toy off their desk when they weren't looking... The list of tactics was seemingly endless. It didn't take long for a rich discussion to emerge about how coercion can happen in any relationship, can be subtle or overt, and can change the vibe very quickly. The severity of the subject became easier to navigate when they were experiencing it firsthand.

With an open, understanding, and engaged group, the second teaching moment unfolded, which addressed power and violence. Each player wrote on separate index cards four people who mean a lot to them, and then I had them rip up one card at random, signifying the statistics of violent sexual crimes. The horror of personalizing the statistic caused linemen to tear up, coaches to shake their heads, and a quarterback to stand up and say, "We are going to be a team that changes the statistic." *This* is what I mean when holistic sexuality changes culture.

Agency-rich culture began to grow as the team held each other up in their individual agency, and the ripple effects were noticeable among the team. They joined marches, they sat on panels, they advocated for change in policies. Women's groups joined up with them. Fraternities started changing policies, and I heard multiple stories from other students of how the hookup culture changed. Like agency, the journey isn't perfect—it meanders—but its progression toward safety, care, and connection for individuals and the collective greater good is never a bad thing.

Now, imagine the power we could cultivate within society if we had the support and ability to enact changes like the football team did. I can imagine that, and it is what fuels me when the bigger picture feels hopeless. Each one of you, by reading this book, is joining a community and movement aimed at changing the statistics together with agency. We *can* begin to progress toward a culture that does not cause inherent harm with misinformation, lack of education, and fear-based propaganda around sex and sexuality.

It's Hot to Show Up

In our current society, we don't have a lot of space to talk about positive experiences of sexuality. We need to explore positive and negative stories, stories of celebration and healing, in order to get in touch with our essence, to learn, and to continue to evolve alongside our agency. When I started doing this work, the unspoken rules about sharing our sexual stories and journey became clear. I knew people shared their stories of sexuality, but it was never cohesive, consistent, or rich in context; it was usually confined to specific moments and spaces like on a night out or with golf buddies drinking after eighteen holes. You could tell this story to that person but not that story to this person. You couldn't bring the mood down with a traumatic story or trust that a story of exploration would be kept private. When we impose rules and limit our spaces for sharing, we lose the chance to gain insight and learn from each other and ourselves.

In that spirit, I'll share with you a story of celebrating my own journey with sexual agency that I once told to one of my closest friends, Steph. I showed up for myself, and I said yes to the yum of it and was fully aware of the limits to the experience and felt fine with them. I said yes with purpose and intention to an experience with someone new on my sexual journey. I share this with you to inspire you to show up for yourself (and others) in the way Steph did for me. As you read it, pay attention to how you feel about my activation of agency in this one story as practice. Allow yourself to read it as a witness to my journey, and at the same time compare and contrast it to your own life, values, and choices. Explore how it feels to be in your agency as you read about me being in mine.

"So... Hawk and I met up last night."

Silence.

Then: "Whoa, how did that happen? When? We just talked at six last night, and you were headed home. Give me the details. Now." She had a tone of hesitancy because this was far out from typical behavior for me. Until recently. There was also a tone of "Who is this new Juliana?"

The setup: Hawk had been in my orbit for many years. No real relationship potential, and although we had strong chemistry, there had never been an opportunity to act on it—until there was. He was part of a team that was turning a historic building into an event space.

The story: We had been audio texting, and I mentioned I was driving through his town. He said, "Drive back. Let's have dinner." (I read, "Drive back. Let's fuck.") I may have left tire tracks on the pavement as I turned around.

Agency activated. I was clear that I wanted to have a chance to take flirting to another level. I had thought through the consequences many times. I knew I could handle them and adapt to any unexpected ones. I also knew I was at a place where I could say no or leave at any point if I felt an ick. I had zero need to impress or compromise myself for him or the situation. I didn't want this because I felt empty or lonely. I wanted to experience him. I felt confident and interested in him sexually. I didn't want anything else with him, which was atypical for me. I had a pattern of assessing marriage potential quickly when I met a possible partner. Not in this instance, and that felt good. My car may have carried me there, but my agency directed me.

We did all the niceties. Good to see you. You look great. Laugh. Drink a drink. Brush hands. He asked me if I wanted a behind-the-scenes look at the construction site. Clearly that was no coincidence as he had suggested a bar near it. As he guided me around, sharing his site plan, I saw that the place was in the middle of demolition. Hmmm, not necessarily a sex zone. I was problem-solving on the fly and not really listening to him. Near the end of the tour, we stopped in the future lobby and stared at each other. After a decade of sexual tension, we sprung at each other. There was passionate kissing, something murmured about his office being upstairs. We ascended the staircase as we took each other's clothes off. A jacket there. My purse there. His phone fell out. My bra splayed at the top of the stairs. We went to his office, and it was like an oasis: clean(ish), a desk, a chair, gorgeous floor-length windows.

We devoured each other, and it was better than I dreamed. Seamless in our chemistry and skill and wanting of each other. We exchanged consent between breathless nibbles, uttering "At last" over and over. He put on a condom that appeared out of nowhere, thankfully, and then he turned me around, naked, and pressed me against the windows. We stared at the city skyline as we had sex, and it was magical, hot, and pleasure-filled. We could have fallen out the windows, and I'm not sure we would have noticed because we were in a different time continuum. Hawk was attentive, directive, skilled, confident, and playful. Yummy. I met that energy and reciprocated.

As I finished recounting the story in my sex bliss, Steph broke the spell with "Well, shit. I'm wet now." We laughed hysterically. She celebrated my story, my pleasure, my agency. She knew this was unusual for me and liked that I had taken a risk with this one. She wondered if I would shame-spiral afterward. (I didn't.) She was happy I had been treated well. (She didn't necessarily love him for me relationship-wise.) She supported my journey and gave me space to have my own experience and decisions and meaning-making. She was safe to share all of that with. And she would have been there if I regretted it or did it again or the condom broke or whatever ripple effect could have occurred. She would have celebrated this story regardless of the outcome, and yes, we found joy in the fun and pleasure of the experience, but more importantly, we acknowledged and celebrated my sexual agency.

The point of sharing this story isn't to say, "Agency means having more sex and saying yes to it all." Actually, I have found agency often means saying no more often. No to the real nos. And many more discerning yeses. My story of agency is that I paid attention to what I wanted. It would be a story of equal celebration if I had responded with a no that night and driven on home with my music blaring and my heart singing. It isn't about the what as much as the why and how. It's about purpose and intention rooted in deep self-understanding. My relationship with Steph was rooted in agency because she had room to ask questions and give her opinion, which differed from mine, and also had space to hold what felt true to me without oppressing me. And she would have no matter the details because we had a refined relationship of agency. We have worked on our relationship agency as well as our agency as individuals.

Holistic sexuality asks us to support others' agency and to create relationships and communities of agency. One story, one person at a time. It isn't easy. Your wounds can bump up against each other, your needs can be in conflict, and you may have different values. This isn't always easy. Still, agency carries us and helps us to remain relational through those challenging dynamics. When we are relationally focused, we protect and expand connection. Our essence is strengthened and upheld through connection when rooted in sexual agency within holistic sexuality.

YOUR PEOPLE AWAIT YOU

WE ARE ALL STORYTELLERS. And to be able to tell a story that matters means that the teller has lived a life. As a man in Afghanistan told humanitarian activist James Orbinski, "No scars, no story, no life."

Life may harm and scar us, and these scars become ways of telling our lives to ourselves and to others. Life also bestows us with beauty and bliss and joy and crowns of flowers. We bob and weave peaks and valleys, hurdles and buoys. Stories aid understanding; stories create empathy. Stories create the same physiological changes in a human as do the experiences that create memories. As bell hooks writes, "Contrary to what we may have been taught to think, unnecessary and unchosen suffering wounds us but need not scar us for life. It does mark us. What we allow the mark of our suffering to become is in our own hands."

Stories matter; your stories matter.

Stories of suffering and stories of utter joy.

Holistic sexuality offers you a gift. The gift of knowing yourself so deeply that you are able to stand strongly in yourself, with yourself and with others; you are able to ask for what you need, offer what you can to others, and choose how you allow suffering and joy to impact your life. Holistic sexuality is both the expression of your essence and the pathway to it. It is the gift to yourself of being safe, seen, and cherished while being in connection outside yourself.

If you connect with someone else who has also done the work within agency and holistic sexuality, you are two whole people. Two people who are whole unto themselves and can maintain their agency while nurturing each other's growth, safety, and essence without losing themselves. To me, that is the gold standard of connection and the reason why holistic sexuality is a necessity and not a luxury.

When you have a deep holistic understanding of your sexuality as well as the skills to communicate this understanding to others, you have the key to achieving your needs and desires. As you examine, reflect upon, and strengthen your connection to your essence, you can express a deeper level of authenticity of who you are. When you know your essence, you can show up for others as your true self too. When you connect soul to soul with another, whether this connection is simple and swift or deep and long-lasting, a strong sense of your essence reminds you that you matter. You know how to give yourself the gift of being seen, heard, wanted, understood, and loved for who you really are. And because you show up authentically, you can accept being seen, heard, wanted, understood, and loved at ever-expanding levels. Due to the complicated, interwoven, and interactive nature of human sexuality, finding your essence here beams it out into the rest of your life. The ripple effects are enormous.

In community, side by side, there is a growing movement of people ready to meet you in your agency, listen to your stories, witness you along your journey, and offer compassion when you don't get it right, change your mind, or have different needs.

The decisions you make with your life matter, both inside and outside the bedroom—and your sexual stories matter. They should be shouted, whispered, revered, and celebrated. They should be revealed. Your sexual journey is an important one and no longer needs to be hidden, sanctioned, or portioned away from the wholeness of you. Your sexual stories are the summation and reflection of the truth of who you are, your essence, and your soul. Sometimes the biggest changes in life can happen in the smallest and most courageous of moments.

At the end of a Revealed journey, I remind participants that there are people all over the globe waiting for them, who have done this work before them. These people cannot wait to meet you, celebrate you, and welcome you. Like I do, they know that our world needs you to do this work, so that we can all heal, one person at a time.

From my essence to yours, welcome.

THANK YOU

FIRST TO MY FAMILY. Annalise and Jack, thank you to my little one and not-so-little one. This book is for you and the world you are growing up in. I thank you for your patience, understanding, and support when it was hard to see me leave one more time with my laptop to write. Thank you for teaching me about your way in the world and choosing me to be your mama. Thank you for letting me tell some of your stories by me sharing some of mine. I love you beyond measure and am so proud to be your mom. I adore your dear souls deeply.

Mom and Dad, thank you for letting me run around naked without shame when I was little, for fostering my love for tree climbing and my insatiable curiosity. Thank you for braving the judgment that has come your way for the work that I do. Thank you for giving me your heart and guidance along my journey and for loving me through the times when our journeys intersected and pushed and pulled us. Mostly, thank you for giving me a front-row seat in your love for each other. Mom, you have been my biggest fan, forthright "feedback giver," and social media follower. I am profoundly grateful for the lessons you have taught me about friendships and love. Your momma bear energy has been a lifelong gift to me. Thank you.

Gayle, thank you to you, my sister, for sharing so much of our lives together. We are different in many ways and yet share so much in common. I love knowing our different vantage points of many moments and treasures along our journeys help us know exactly what each other sees and means without having to say it. You not only taught me the best college music when I needed to feel cool, but had some of the first and most important sexual conversations with me. I am so glad I got you as my big sis. I am proud of the woman and mother you have grown into.

Samantha, Genevieve, and Sophia, thank you, my three nieces, whom I learned so much from through seeing my sister transition into motherhood, witnessing your individual and collective journeys through childhood and adulthood, and receiving many laughs and insights on how holistic sexuality intersects with generations, family, culture, and three very delightfully different and remarkable young women. I love each of you and am so lucky to be your auntie.

To the Dr. J Team.

Kaitlin, thank you for tirelessly supporting my wild and unexpected internal and logistic journey in writing this book. I am profoundly grateful for your intuition of knowing when I was struggling, of writing me texts I needed that validated how hard it was to figure out how to write as a solo mother working full-time, for remembering my stories, for knowing my work so deeply, for reminding me over and over and over again that this book mattered and I had to finish it. I am also so aware of how much easier I slept and breathed knowing you were at the helm of the business, keeping it afloat while I was hidden away at yet another coffeehouse writing. Thank you also for your editing talents and wisdom within these pages and for knowing my work so well you help deepen it. Finally, thank you for being a powerful woman who shared her stories with me along the way. You are an inspiration to me. This book wouldn't be in anyone else's hands but for you being in my life. I am beyond grateful for you, for Becky, and for both of your gentle and powerful ways in the world.

Deneen and Jennifer, your presence in my life and business helped me keep the plates spinning while I plugged away or recovered from writing. I thank you for caring for me and my work. I thank you for taking care of my clients, my to-do lists, my kids, and my home life so that I had some semblance of order in the midst of a very disorienting experience. Thank you for the words of encouragement, for reading the manuscript and giving your thoughts, and for lending me your stories along the way. I am so grateful to have such quality, powerful, and good-hearted women surrounding me in my inner circle.

To my initial editors, Jay, Anita, and Richelle.

The version of the book you possess is born from three other versions. One I wrote totally alone. One that Jay Bonner had his eyes, ears, and heart on. We spent hours in Asheville, North Carolina, debating points within my work, infusing literature into the conversation, dissecting my sexual journey, and eating a lot of great NC barbecue. Your expertise, male perspective, and support of my work were invaluable. You pushed me to finish the first true manuscript that had both original thoughts and memoir content in it. Thank you for helping make a painful process see sparks of joy. Thank you to Alex Martin for introducing me to Jay.

Anita Mumm, you took my immense manuscript into a process of self-reflection and practicality that was transformative and wholehearted. Your experience with the course Revealed and your unwavering support of the value of my work and ideas buoyed me when I had an unending stream of self-doubt. You also helped me be brave in expressing riskier thoughts and sharing more personal stories. Thank you for seeing the author in me and helping me see a "real book" was a possibility and inevitability.

Richelle Fredson, two unrelated and amazing colleagues told me about the amazing book proposal editor they had worked with and insisted I meet. You. Kismet. Thank you for whipping my book proposal into shape with enthusiasm and precision, for validating my work and ability to be a "real author," and for cheering me on well after our one-on-one work ended.

To the Page Two team.

Jesse Finkelstein, thank you for believing in me and bringing me into the Page Two fold, giving my book a home and my writing process support and new life. I will never forget the positive energy and stress relief our first meeting gave me. Thank you for giving me, the topic of sexuality, and my work a chance.

Adrineh Der-Boghossian, Carmen Ho, and team, thank you for project-managing this book and me as a first-time author. It was no small feat. All the emails, meetings, behind-the-scenes wrangling, detail-keeping, and deadline hopscotch helped bring this book from an idea into a tangible body of work. I am so grateful to each of you.

My esteemed and unafraid editors, Sarah Brohman and Kendra Ward and Crissy Boylan, I walked into this process thinking I understood what it meant to have an editorial team. I did not. I am so grateful for your patience, guidance, enthusiasm, and comments. Thank you for being brave in walking into the topic of sexuality with me and for having such gentle and firm hands in making sure we did sexuality justice. I am grateful to Sarah and Kendra for both of your expertise and good hearts. Kendra, you walked off the cliff with me into the depth of my sexuality story with respect, fearlessness, and enthusiasm. Your patience, intellect, and kindheartedness were profoundly helpful. Your journey and interest in this book and my work are infused throughout each chapter. Thank you for walking alongside me as a cheerleader, idea bouncer, and expert in how to get the ideas from my head onto the paper and into a form readers will consume.

To my College of William & Mary students.

Each of you is the foundation of this book. I will never forget the early days of my work with you. Thank you for signing up for the class and validating my work for the very first time. Before my degree, before I really knew what I was doing, before I had research and clients and experience to back up my theories, you were in the trenches with me. Your trust in me and your unyielding dedication to revealing your own sexual journeys inspired me beyond measure.

Thank you for filling the room when I defended my dissertation. This book would never exist without each of you.

To my clients.

From the halfway house to the university counseling center to my private practice with clients all over the globe. Thank you to the clients who trusted me with their stories for this book and to those who trust me with their stories privately. You mean the world to me, and I am continuously honored to be able to walk alongside you for some of your journey. Your bravery and work toward healing and evolution fuel my work when I am exhausted and in self-doubt. I am an incredibly fortunate therapist and counselor to work with such soulful, evolved humans.

To my Revealed people.

Thank you to the amazing folks in over eight countries and all over the United States who have taken the Revealed course with me and to my certified Revealed facilitators in person and online, DIY and guided. Thank you for prioritizing sexuality in your life. Thank you for doing the work. For yourself and for the ripple effects your work does for the world. "I believe you." "I honor your bravery." "I am in awe of your strength." (IYKYK.) The course Revealed is the springboard for this book. Each one of you shaped, strengthened, and informed the course as it evolved and grew. Each of your stories is indelible in my heart and within the movement. A select group of you helped me reach a personal career highlight—teaching Revealed in front of my friend and mentor Betty Dodson. Thank you deeply for jumping into that incredibly soul-lifting experience. That afternoon changed my life. Thank you.

To my Revealed facilitators.

Dr. Karen Beale came up to me at Betty Dodson's ninetieth birthday conference after I presented my work and told me I had to teach her Revealed so she could bring my work to Maryville College in Tennessee. COVID hit, and I was swamped with frontline mental health work. Dr. Beale persisted, and the first official Revealed facilitation certification was born. Thank you, thank you, Karen, for your friendship and persistence and for joining me so beautifully on this journey. (So many entries for the play...) Thank you to the other powerful facilitators. During the pandemic, we worked through the material and dreamed of changing the conversation about sexuality around the world. We had five countries represented in that first group alone. Bless the early adopters. I thank you deeply for trusting me with your stories and for your belief in my work. Loudly and in grand fashion, I thank you for your calling in the sexuality space. It is a special person who is interested in sexuality; it is a brave person who is willing to stand in the fire and help others heal and grow and evolve within sexuality. Your presence within sexuality is incredibly needed, and I am deeply grateful you find my work worthy of your time, work, and income. Revealed wouldn't have a community or movement without you. Thank you for your creativity within Revealed, thank you for bringing it to your communities, and thank you for your positive presence within a topic that is wrought with negativity, fear, and judgment. Your strength and resolve strengthen mine.

To the RAC—Revealed Advisory Council.

Dr. Karen Beale, Emmy O'Hare, and Liz Meir were the earliest of early adopters of my work. Thank you for your unwavering belief in me and the work of Revealed. Thank you for the countless volunteer hours you gave to Revealed by meeting, writing, reading, giving advice, and dreaming. Each of you had such an invaluable role in making this book come to life and transforming Revealed from a course I came up with in grad school into an international community and movement. Thank you for your financial investments. Thank you for giving so freely of yourself. Special thank you to Dana Kaluzny for helping RAC develop into a group of colleagues who each have an integral role in evolution, shared growth, and innovative design.

To the early readers of my manuscript.

Ashley Greathouse, Shuntella Whitfield, Victoria Carling, Scott Andrews-Weckerly, Laurie Marvald, Emmy O'Hare, Dr. Karen Beale, David Bertram, Aydian Dowling, Callie Little, Kaitlin Voellinger, Jennifer Entwistle, Deneen Zimmerman, and Russell Schaumburg. Sending an unfinished manuscript with known holes and problems out into anyone's hands is an endeavor of vulnerability. Sending it to these souls made it so much easier. Thank you deeply, each of you. You took my words, my work, and my manuscript into your heads and hearts and gave me your unique perspectives. I loved the suggestions and the compliments. I will forever remember: "It was so good, I was annoyed when people were interrupting me while reading at work" and "I never sit and just read, and I had to pee for two chapters but didn't want to get up." Thank you for following my request to not kiss my ass and for also giving me hope that this book may help others.

To my colleagues.

I am blessed to have colleagues who are doing amazing and powerful things in the world, who have believed in me, and who believe in the premise that we all rise together. Too many to name, but some I want to highlight: Betty Dodson, Carlin Ross, Dr. Lindsay Byron (Lux ATL), Lily Womble, Dr. Vonda Wright, Michelle Hope, JJ Miller, Emily Bina, Emily Powers, Sigga, Dogg, Mariah Freya and Beducated, Dr. Jen Gunsaullus, Dr. Jenn Caudle, Katrina Marie, Sarah Chadwick, Chrissy King, Allison Mandell, Rachel Rodgers, Ashley Manta, Barbara Carrellas, Robert Hartwell, the Bodysex community, H.C., Shuntella Whitfield, Katie Fogarty, Mike Watts, Erin Keating, Gerie DiPiano, Caitlin Peterson, Meryl Russo, Anne "Sussy" Sussman, Cam Fraser, Dolphin Kasper, Catherine Balsam-Schwaber, Lyndsay Wynn, Rachel Ford and the Souldust community, and Tammi Leader Fuller, Chelsea Leader Gold, and the Campowerment community.

Betty Dodson: You changed my life immeasurably with your spunk, pioneer spirit, unapologetic, and no-fucks-given way of showing up to all conversations. Thank you for paving the way for all of us in the sexuality space with blood, guts, and orgasms. You healed me continuously. Teaching Revealed in front of you was a career highlight and personal moment of immense joy. Thank you for your Betty stamp of approval (turning me around and humping me).

Carlin Ross: Thank you for taking Betty's work into the world so others could meet her and be taught by her. I thank you deeply for your invitation to teach at Betty's ninetieth birthday celebration.

To my friends, helpers, and those who took a chance on me.

This book began in the woods and whispers of Williamsburg, Virginia. Enid B. and Amanda J., the dearest and most loyal of friends, who were there in the initial stages of my work and my rebuilding era. Bless the friends who are by your side through thick and thin and with large sticky notes and Southern quips (Enid) and reality-giving sarcasm and fun distraction (Amanda). They both held open the door to my home as groups of women came and went through the various versions of Revealed and sat with me in the circles gathering stories and honoring the journeys of the first women who went through this course. Thank you for loving me, liking me, and giving me a lifetime of rich connection, laughter, and tearful hugs.

Jen MacNiven and Rachel Ford. Thank you, Rachel, for answering my random email asking if you would ever need a sex expert and inviting me into your magic on the Souldust Morocco retreat. You invited me into a space of expertise during the hardest chapter of my life. Your belief in me changed my life. Thank you for being ahead of the wave, for seeing me when I couldn't see myself, and for giving me the coolest yurts to teach in and for always saying yes to my out-there workshop ideas. You also brought Jen MacNiven into my life. Thank you, Jen, for being the fiercest of friends, for making the best playlists, and for teaching me how to take a new angle on every walk and photo. Your friendship is deep and soul-filling, and it has enriched my life in so many ways. Thank you for capturing me in your lens like no other and for flying across the country to protect and celebrate me.

My time with Camp Souldust led me to send another cold email to Tammi Leader Fuller with Campowerment. Thank you, Tammi, for being another person who took a chance on me and for raising me on your platform and into your powerful Campowerment community. Our professional connection transformed into a personal one, and I am grateful for your friendship, guidance, belief in me, and for confiding in me. I think you are magic. Thank you for introducing me to powerful and amazing women; for running through countless workshops, media, and speaking ideas; and for the many hours of laughter and spicy fun. The amazing Rebecca Powers, Meryl Russo, and Sussy are in my life because of your magnetic orbit of drawing quality women to you. I'm grateful to you for them and for many others, but I must highlight my intense blessing of you bringing my Bliss Buddy Barbara Palmer into my life. Thank you, Babs, for your unwavering support, bliss moments, words of wisdom that hit like no others, and times of endless fun, laughter, and mama bear worries. You get it. You get me. I am so profoundly lucky you said yes to being my Bliss Buddy.

My Kentucky circle, Suzanne Shaffer, Liz Wright, Haley Winkler, and Cacey Nardolillo. Thank you for your friendship, for getting what it means to be a mom who wants to be the best mom and also have ambitions in her career. Thank you for being women who allowed me to write with ease because I knew Annalise was safely with you. I am forever indebted. Thank you to my mom and Jack for giving me countless hours of writing time and business-building time without complaint and with loyal support of me and the greater good I have been trying to help.

Cathy May and my Soul Spark women—Karen Harvey, Lisle Foutz, Victoria Carling, Shuntella Whitfield, Ashley Issacs, Angelia Hunter, and Brenda Ward Spedding. Thank you for knowing the essence of me, for rooting for me emotionally and logistically, and for opening your trust to me in my backyard, fireside chats, and zany activities I came up with. I adore each of you. Thank you also to Jennifer Davidson, Laura McNeill, and Karen Crupi.

JJ Miller, you heard me as a fake guest on the amazing Michelle H.'s audition and took a chance on me. And kept taking chances on me. Your unapologetic opinions, splicing wisdom, and zest-filled social justice heart are such beautiful additions to my personal and professional worlds. Deeply and wholeheartedly, thank you for walking alongside me and saying I matter and my work matters over and over again to me. Thank you also for introducing me to the amazing Emily Bina, who has brought unparalleled elegance, support, and savviness.

Juli Nadler: When I had no money, had no understanding of how to grow my career, and knew absolutely nothing about PR, you took a chance on me and brought me into a new stratosphere of media. Thank you for enthusiastically reciting the words you loved as I was starting to have the bravery to speak publicly and for putting me in front of people who could elevate my voice. But mostly, thank you for seeing who I was and the potential impact I could have in the world.

As mentioned in the book, Centre College had a vast impact on my life. My friendships and experiences there were the fertile soil the premise of this book grew in. From my education to the opportunities to the relationships I built there. To this day, attending Centre was the best decision of my life. I am grateful for my group of friends and roommates, my Theta sisters, my Deke brothers, my professors, and the longevity and expansion of connection to Centre Alumni College and my core group of friends I still hang with and who have known me for thirty-five years.

MoMoMo. Seryna Myers and Kari Driskell. Thank you, thank you, thank you. Our mastermind group was a lifesaver, a soul-giver, and a wisdom tank. You had front-row seats to my business, my book, and my life and still stayed! I thank you for your good hearts and wise discernment. This book wouldn't be here without you two. Thank you for being beautiful souls and for doing such good in the world.

Auburn was the first place I found "my people." Other counselors and therapists. I began breathing easier when I worked through my master's there. Jenny Filush, Heather McPherson, Michaux Dempster, Brett Vicario, and Dr. Jamie Carney helped firm up my love for mental health and confirmed my decision to leave elementary education. My time at the College of William & Mary was another good decision in my life. My WM cohort and professors were integral to the professional life I have now. Dr. Rick Gressard, Dr. Victoria Foster, and Dr. Rip McAdams pushed me to levels I needed to be shoved into and supported my unheard-of idea of creating a sexuality class for my dissertation. Dr. Foster, you took me aside and told me that once in a while, a student comes along interested in sexuality and that I needed to pursue it. You seeing me helped me have the audacity to follow this passion. To my friends, confidants, partners in crime, and dear, dear friends Dr. Ed Cannon, Dr. Laurie Craigen, Dr. Angela Holman MacDonald, Dr. Dennis Frank, Dr. Kylie Dotson-Blake, Dr. Gerard Lawson, and Dr. Bacardi, thank you for all of the musings, tears, intellectual debates, and conference antics and for cheering me on through my dissertation while you were in the midst of yours. Thank you for the powerful work each of you do in the world on behalf of mental health.

Thank you to my FB and Insta families for encouraging me to continue writing and promising me this mattered. Thank you to those who wrote me privately and publicly, cheerleading me week after week and through every missed deadline. I kept each of your messages in a Google Document labeled "Write for them." Thank you, Marvin B., for the amazing playlists. Thank you to all who jumped on Zoom calls with me so I could be held accountable to writing and not get away with watching Netflix instead.

To the loves along my journey.

S and B. S, you were my first love and met my seventeen-year-old self full of naivete, insecurity, and sarcasm. You jumped into marriage with me, and we went feet first into parenthood together. Thank you for giving me a loving, kind, and safe foundation for my sexual journey. Our love was meant to transform into a thirty-six-year friendship and twenty-sex-year co-parenting partnership. I'm so lucky I was loved by you and cherish how we have stood by each other through all the unexpected and imperfect twists and turns of our lives. Our college selves would be proud of us. B, thank you for stepping into our lives, loving Jack as your own, loving Annalise like the best big sister, and for bringing sweet K into our lives. I am so glad you are in our family, and thank you for your kind, warm-hearted relationship with me and for making S a happy man.

Chris. Our lives crashed into each other, and I marvel at all we shared together. You brought fun to a new level and brought colors into my life I didn't know existed. Our souls were intertwined the moment we met. Thank you for giving me such a powerful introduction to sexual agency, for seeing me as a sexy woman, and for inviting me into a fun, playful, love-filled relationship. Thank you for loving me in your indescribable way, for the meaning of the last song you sent me, and for bringing Jack on stage with you and into your heart. He is a part of your legacy. You will forever be the drumbeat in my heart. You are missed and forever adored.

R, you came into my life with shocking commonalities and ease in a very unease-filled time. I thank you for seeing the good and power in me when I was having trouble recognizing it myself. Thank you for meeting me in a sacred space in my sexual journey. Our connection was unparalleled and profound. A losing-time-and-space kind of connection I wasn't sure I would ever get to experience until you. Your "fierce and fragile" assessment of me came at a time when I needed to understand that level of seeing of me. Thank you for loving me in a fierce and fragile way as well, for loving my little (and big) ones, and for walking alongside the journey of this book in a very real and unwavering way. This book wouldn't be here but for you in so many ways. Your editing skills, your questions, your insights and your highlights elevated my work and helped bring in a cis het perspective in a deep way. You've always understood and heralded me and my work to a level and with a verve no one else could match; your interest in and championing of my work matter more than I can express. I am better having been loved by you.

To the unnamed and protected.

I thank the many people along my journey who had positive and negative impacts on my life. Some are highlighted in this book, some remain anonymous, but all helped shape me into who I am today and informed my work so I could give it to you.

Thank you to the people who left me, hurt me, grew me, stayed with me, saw me, fucked me, fucked me up, fucked me over, and loved me for a reason, season, or lifetime. Thank you. There are things I have experienced that are profoundly sad and horrific that didn't fit into the purpose of this book but impacted me in ways that at some point I will share even more than I did in my TEDx talk. I do not believe in searching for the silver lining in tragic or criminal acts, but I see worthiness in seeking how to protect the strength that helped transform me into a "surthriver." All of you made me who I am, informed my stories, and allowed me to grow into a woman who can stand strong and say things others cannot or will not say. Your relationships with me helped me understand others' experiences beyond a professional lens. Thank you for my sexual guides, for my sexual teachers, for my sexual playmates, and for my soul lovers. You are infused throughout my work. Thank you for the ones who stayed when I was the one making mistakes and causing hurt. Thank you for the ones who left when leaving me was the healthy decision. Thank you for the ones who didn't choose me because I wasn't yours to choose. Thank you for those who taught me lessons in accountability and self-awareness. Thank you for all kinds of love and connection.

To Flash. Your cute little puggy soul saved and filled the hearts of my most cherished—Jack and Annalise. I never thought I would have a little pug potato enter our lives in such a serendipitous way and warm and expand our hearts daily.

NOTES

So Much More Than Sex

p. 7 *Sexuality is not static:* Juliana J. H. Mills, "The Effect of a Deliberate Psychological Education Model on the Ego Development, Moral Development, and Sexual Assertiveness of College Women" (PhD dissertation, William & Mary, 2005), dx.doi.org/doi:10.25774/w4-xrg8-tz20.

Sex Expired: Why Take a New Position on Sex?

p. 23 *When societies deny their citizens:* Nicholas D. E. Mark and Lawrence L. Wu, "More Comprehensive Sex Education Reduced Teen Births: Quasi-Experimental Evidence," *Proceedings of the National Academy of Sciences* 119, no. 8 (February 2022): e2113144119, doi.org/10.1073/pnas.2113144119; "Federally Funded Sex Education Programs Linked to Decline in Teen Birth Rates, New Study Shows," news release, New York University, February 14, 2022, nyu.edu/about/news-publications/news/2022/february/federally-funded-sex-education-programs-linked-to-decline-in-tee.html; American College of Obstetricians and Gynecologists, "Comprehensive Sexuality Education," Committee Opinion no. 678 (November 2016), acog.org/clinical/clinical-guidance/committee-opinion/articles/2016/11/comprehensive-sexuality-education; Barnett B., "Education Protects Health, Delays Sex," *Network Research Triangle Park N.C.* 17, no. 3 (Spring 1997): 14-15, 18-20, pubmed.ncbi.nlm.nih.gov/12292388/; Rebekah Rollston, "Comprehensive Sex Education as Violence Prevention," *Perspectives in Primary Care*, Harvard Medical School Center for Primary Care, May 29, 2020, info.primarycare.hms.harvard.edu/perspectives/articles/sexual-education-violence-prevention; Action Canada for Sexual Health & Rights, "Sex-Ed: Preventing Violence and Increasing Safety," updated May 7, 2019, actioncanadashr.org/resources/sexual-health-hub/sex-ed/sex-ed-preventing-violence-and-increasing-safety; Rima Al-Mukhtar, "Sex Education 'Can Prevent Abuse, Divorce,'" *Arab News*, February 6, 2014, arabnews.com/node/521411/spa/jserrors/aggregate; Sara Tonekaboni, Ramazan Hassanzadeh, and Sedigheh Ebrahimi, "The Effect of Sex Education on the Marital Satisfaction," *European Journal of Experimental Biology* 3, no. 6 (2013): 427-31, primescholars.com/

articles/the-effect-of-sex-education-on-the-marital-satisfaction.pdf; Eesha Pendharkar, "LGBTQ+ Students with Affirming Schools Report Lower Suicide Risk, Survey Finds," *Education Week*, August 24, 2023, edweek.org/leadership/lgbtq-students-with-affirming-schools-report-lower-suicide-risk-survey-finds/2023/08; "Let's Teach Sex Education!" Wyoming Health Council newsletter issue 9 (September 2020), myemail.constantcontact.com/Recovery--Sex-Education----Suicide-Prevention---September-is-a-busy-month.html?soid=1133471738111&aid=m221v3KZ0eg; Jo Yurcaba, "Sex Ed That Excludes LGBTQ+ People Is Tied to Worse Health Outcomes," *Forbes*, October 14, 2020, forbes.com/sites/joyurcaba/2020/10/14/sex-ed-that-excludes-lgbtq-people-is-tied-to-worse-health-outcomes/.

p. 26 *"Be the change you wish to see":* "Quote Origin: Be the Change You Wish to See in the World," *Quote Investigator*, October 23, 2017, quoteinvestigator.com/2017/10/23/be-change.

Holistic Sexuality: Stepping Into Your Essence

p. 37 *In 1981, Dailey published a graphic:* Dennis Dailey, "Sexual Expression and Aging," in *The Dynamics of Aging*, eds. F. Berghorn and D. Schafer (Westview Press, 1981), 311–33.

Agency: Doing It on Your Own Terms

p. 56 *When I was researching for my PhD:* Mills, "Deliberate Psychological Education Model."

p. 56 *Several important points related to sexual agency:* I want to acknowledge that there are multiple biases including gender, race, orientation, and socioeconomic within this research and its results, which is a reflection of how people are broadly socialized.

Pillar 2: Wellness and Fertility

p. 88 *Study after study shows that fear-based education:* See, for example, Gigi Engle, "Comprehensive Sex Education Could Curb Everyone's Trauma Around Sex," TheBody, April 2, 2021, thebody.com/article/comprehensive-sex-education-reduces-trauma; Guttmacher Institute, "Federally Funded Abstinence-Only Programs: Harmful and Ineffective," fact sheet, May 2021, guttmacher.org/sites/default/files/factsheet/abstinence-only-programs-fact-sheet.pdf; Christopher Bergland, "The Neuroscience of Fear-Based Learning vs. Fear Extinction," *Psychology Today*, September 19, 2017, psychologytoday.com/us/blog/the-athletes-way/201709/the-neuroscience-fear-based-learning-vs-fear-extinction.

p. 93 *More children now in elementary school:* See "Is IVF on the Rise?" Reproductive Fertility, March 6, 2023, reproductivefertility.com/blog/is-ivf-on-the-rise.

p. 106 *Studies show that cisgender women:* Carolyn J. Gibson, Yixia Li, Guneet K. Jasuja, Kyle J. Self, Karen H. Seal, and Amy L. Byers, "Menopausal Hormone Therapy and Suicide in a National Sample of Midlife and Older Women Veterans," *Medical Care* 59 (February 2021): S70–S76, doi.org/10.1097/MLR.0000000000001433; "Suicide Rates in Women of Menopausal Age Rise," ITV News, November 17, 2021, itv.com/news/2021-11-16/suicide-rates-in-women-of-menopausal-age-rise.

p. 106 *Men experience the lowering of testosterone:* S. N. Seidman and B. T. Walsh, "Testosterone and Depression in Aging Men," *American Journal of Geriatric Psychiatry* 7, no. 1 (Winter 1999): 18–33, pubmed.ncbi.nlm.nih.gov/9919317/.

p. 107 *the research shows that* body compassion: Lessa Van Niekerk, Lucy Johnstone, and Mandy Matthewson, "Predictors of Self-Compassion in Endometriosis: The Role of Psychological Health and Endometriosis Symptom Burden," *Human Reproduction* 37, no. 2 (February 2022): 264–73, doi.org/10.1093/humrep/deab257; Lessa Van Niekerk, Holly Bromfield, and Mandy Matthewson, "Physical and Psychological Correlates of Self and Body Compassion in Women with Polycystic Ovary Syndrome," *Journal of Health Psychology* 27, no. 11 (September 2022): 2566–80, doi.org/10.1177/13591053211059390; Lessa Van Niekerk, B. Dell, Lucy Johnstone, Mandy Matthewson, and Michael Quinn, "Examining the Associations Between Self and Body Compassion and Health Related Quality of Life in People Diagnosed with Endometriosis," *Journal of Psychosomatic Research* 167 (April 2023): 111202, doi.org/10.1016/j.jpsychores.2023.111202.

Pillar 3: Pleasure

p. 126 *Self-pleasure can also be seen as a workout:* "Masturbation," Cleveland Clinic, October 25, 2022, my.clevelandclinic.org/health/articles/24332-masturbation; Karthik Kumar, "Is Masturbation Healthy?" MedicineNet, accessed May 14, 2025, medicinenet.com/masturbation/article.htm; Gabrielle Kassel, "17 Benefits of Masturbation That Show Masturbating Is Good for You," mindbodygreen, March 22, 2023, mindbodygreen.com/articles/benefits-of-masturbation; Cori Ritchey, Melissa Matthews, and Ro White, "11 Incredible Health Benefits to Masturbation," *Men's Health*, June 13, 2024, menshealth.com/sex-women/a19534050/5-reasons-you-should-masturbate-tonight/.

Pillar 6: Intersecting Identities

p. 167 *Core concepts of intersectionality:* Patricia Hill Collins and Sirma Bilge, eds., *Intersectionality*, 2nd ed. (Polity, 2020).

p. 182 *a sense of our gender between ages three and five:* Jason Rafferty, "Gender Identity Development in Children," HealthyChildren.org, American Academy of Pediatrics, updated May 7, 2024, healthychildren.org/English/ages-stages/gradeschool/Pages/Gender-Identity-and-Gender-Confusion-In-Children.aspx; "Understanding Sexual Orientation and Homosexuality," American Psychological Association, October 29, 2008, apa.org/topics/lgbtq/orientation.

Pillar 7: Power and Trauma

p. 187 *"we must confront the wounds of the past":* Isabel Wilkerson, speech given at the College of Willam & Mary, Women's Weekend, September 16–18, 2022.
p. 192 *According to the APA Task Force on the Sexualization of Girls: Report of the APA Task Force on the Sexualization of Girls* (American Psychological Association, 2007), apa.org/pi/women/programs/girls/report-full.pdf.

Pillar 8: Relationship

p. 235 *Ashley Manta, an expert on cannabis and sex:* "What is CannaSexual?" Ashley Manta, accessed May 13, 2025, ashleymanta.com/cannasexual.

Pillar 9: Connection

p. 243 *The CDC describes connectedness:* "Promote Social Connectedness and Support," Suicide Prevention Resource Center, sprc.org/effective-prevention/a-comprehensive-approach-to-suicide-prevention/promote-social-connectedness-and-support.
p. 243 *She lists them as to be seen, heard, and valued:* Brené Brown, "The Gifts of Imperfection | Connection Is the Energy…," Brené Brown, accessed May 13, 2025, brenebrown.com/art/tgoi-connection/.
p. 252 *Robert Sternberg's triangular theory of love:* "Duplex Theory of Love: Triangular Theory of Love and Theory of Love as a Story," Robert J. Sternberg, accessed May 13, 2025, robertjsternberg.com/love.
p. 256 *"The essence of true love":* bell hooks, *All About Love: New Visions* (Harper, 2000), 185.
p. 256 *"When we choose to love":* hooks, *All About Love*, 93.
p. 257 *"To truly love we must learn":* hooks, *All About Love*, 5.
p. 257 *"Of all the definitions of love":* hooks, *All About Love*, 4.
p. 260 *"When we can see ourselves":* hooks, *All About Love*, 53.

Your People Await You

p. 273 *As a man in Afghanistan told:* James Orbinski, *An Imperfect Offering: Humanitarian Action in the Twenty-First Century* (Doubleday Canada, 2008), 17.
p. 273 *"Contrary to what we may have been taught":* hooks, *All About Love*, 209.

RESOURCES

I RECOMMEND starting with these books:
Barbara Carrellas's *Urban Tantra*
Bernie Zilbergeld's *The New Male Sexuality*
Betty Dodson's *Sex for One*
Betty Martin's *The Art of Receiving and Giving*
Chidera Eggerue's *What a Time to Be Alone*
Emily Nagoski's *Come as You Are*
Esther Perel's *Mating in Captivity*
Ian Kerner's *So Tell Me About the Last Time You Had Sex*
Jaiya's *The Erotic Blueprint*
Dr. Jen Gunter's *The Vagina Bible*
Dr. Jennifer Gunsaullus's *From Madness to Mindfulness*
Juno Roche's *Queer Sex*
Justin Lehmiller's *The Psychology of Human Sexuality*
Dr. Kelly Casperson's *You Are Not Broken*
Dr. Laurie Mintz's *Becoming Cliterate*
Rae McDaniel's *Gender Magic*
Rebecca Chalker's *The Clitoral Truth*
Sarah Chadwick's *The Sweetness of Venus*
Stella Harris's *Tongue Tied*
Vanessa and Xander Marin's *Sex Talks*
Zoë Kors's *Radical Intimacy*

CHECK OUT these additional experts:

Ashley Manta
Aydian Dowling
Cam Fraser
Cyndi Darnell
Erica Smith
Ericka Hart
Dr. Fabiola Trejo
Hannah Witton

Dr. Kate Balestrieri
Lauren Rogers
Dr. Lori Brotto
Marquis Bey
Shan Boodram
Shelby Sells
Sonalee Rashatwar
Wendy Maltz

CHECK OUT these websites:

amaze.org
beducated.com
cora.life/blogs/blood-milk
omgyes.com
o.school

plannedparenthood.org
saltyworld.net
scarleteen.com
sexedcenter.org
siecus.org

CHECK OUT these podcasts:

Chris and Charlotte's *Speaking of Sex with the Pleasure Mechanics*
Dr. Emily Morse's *Sex with Emily*
Esther Perel's *Where Should We Begin?*
Ev'Yan Whitney's *The Sensual Self*
Juliet Allen's *Authentic Sex*
Justin Lehmiller's *The Sex and Psychology Podcast*
Kate Sloan and Bex Caputo's *The Dildorks*
Dr. Kelly Casperson's *You Are Not Broken*
Nikki Boyer and Molly Kochan's *Dying for Sex*
Poppy and Rubina's *Brown Girls Do It Too*
Raquel Savage's *The Savage Life*
Vanessa Geffrard's *VagEsteem*

DISCUSSION QUESTIONS

1. What was your sex education like? From whom did you first learn about sex, and what did you learn? Did you have a sexual guide later in life?

2. The concept of agency is threaded throughout holistic sexuality. How do you define agency? How have your ideas about agency shifted as a result of reading the book? Where do you have the most agency in your sexual life? Where might your agency need to be built up?

3. What does holistic sexuality mean to you now?

4. What was the most memorable, relatable, surprising, or impactful story, anecdote, or sexercise to you? Why did it stand out to you?

5. In reviewing the Reveal Yourself to Yourself sections at the end of each chapter, what journal prompt would feel the most challenging for you to answer in front of a group?

6. What is an experience within your sexual journey that would be fun, ease-filled, and/or meaningful to share with a group?

7. What passages did you underline or find particularly affected you?

8   How did the book change your opinion or perspective on sexuality? Did it confirm or contradict any of your assumptions or expectations?

9   What was the most surprising or shocking thing you learned from the book?

10 Where do you see yourself going next with your sexual journey? How has this book influenced your view on your own sexual journey?

11 Who else do you want to read this book? Who do you think needs this book the most?

12 How do you think the cultural background or experiences of the author influenced her thinking about holistic sexuality?

13 If you could ask Dr. Juliana one question, what would it be? How do you think she would answer?

TO DIVE EVEN DEEPER into holistic sexuality for yourself or with a group, there are resources and a comprehensive book club package available to you at therevealedlife.com/bookresources.

Need some extra support? Bring Dr. Juliana to you! Either in person or virtually, Dr. Juliana will guide you through your book club session and provide expert guidance and teaching on sometimes challenging topics. Get a taste of Revealed and experience what it's like to bring holistic sexuality and sexual agency to life. Write Dr. Juliana directly to inquire: drjuliana@therevealedlife.com.

Dr. Juliana loves hearing about experiences with her work. She welcomes anecdotes, questions, photos of you with the book, and feedback about the book.

PHOTO: JOELI BOATRIGHT

ABOUT THE AUTHOR

DR. JULIANA HAUSER is a licensed couples and family therapist, licensed professional counselor, academic, theorist, thought leader, and bona fide (s)expert. Through decades of counseling, teaching, and supporting thousands of individuals and couples on their own paths to discover and thrive within their sexual agency, Dr. Juliana has become an expert in guiding couples and individuals through common topics like libido, orgasms, infertility, perimenopause and menopause, sexuality and identity, body compassion, and evolved sex ed for adults. Dr. Juliana's flagship course, Revealed, is currently taught in eight countries, and her Revealed facilitator course equips people all over the world to share her work with others.

After graduating from Centre College, she pursued her master's degree in counseling at Auburn University, then earned her PhD from the College of William & Mary in 2005.

Dr. Juliana's career involves speaking internationally; running retreats and workshops; teaching at the collegiate and doctoral levels; filming a documentary and docuseries; and working with a variety of groups and clients like football teams, fraternities, federal prisons, politicians, CEOs, and medical schools. Dr. Juliana's work is global.

She has appeared on *The Doctors* and the Discovery Channel's *The Sex Files*, was a regular panelist on ShareCare, and is featured in numerous international publications such as *O (The Oprah Magazine)*, *Women's Health*, *Forbes*, *The Sun*, *Wall Street Journal*, *Martha Stewart*, *Cosmopolitan*, *Conde Nast*, and *The Standard*. She has been a guest on countless podcasts such as *You Are Not Broken*, *A Certain Age*, *Hotter Than Ever*, and *Dating Brazen*. She has consulted with organizations such as Tempur Sealy, FemmePharma, Kindra, Momotaro Apotheca, Beducated, Sharecare, Huha, Hårklinikken, the Broadway Collective, Campowerment, and many more.

Beyond the Book

Revealed Course Community Movement®

This book is based on my course Revealed, which is more than just a course: It's a community and movement too. The Revealed course has traveled to eight countries, has been translated into five languages, and isn't stopping there. Here's how you can connect with my work and Revealed beyond the book.

Write to The Revealed Life with your stories, questions, and reactions to the book at support@therevealedlife.com. We love adding to our large collection of Revealed stories!

Additional Resources

Go to therevealedlife.com/bookresources for exclusive exercises, along with multimedia representations of people's stories, tips, resources, and more!

Course

Take Revealed! The DIY course dives further into the pillars of holistic sexuality and guides you through your own process of self-discovery, supporting you to write your own stories on your terms. I also offer one-on-one Revealed support, as do some of our facilitators. Learn more at therevealedlife.com.

Community

Take Revealed in a group anywhere in the world with a trained facilitator. This is a highly recommended, powerful experience. Looking to be a facilitator? Write to support@therevealedlife.com for the application.

Revealed has been shared with prisons, churches, book clubs, community and friend groups, and more.

Movement

If you have connections, ideas, or questions, please reach out! If you'd like to book me for a speaking opportunity, workshop, or other event, contact me below. Let's keep the momentum going!

- @drjulianahauser
- drjuliana@therevealedlife.com

www.ingramcontent.com/pod-product-compliance
Lightning Source LLC
Chambersburg PA
CBHW020518080526
44583CB00013B/645